THE CLASSIC ARABIAN HORSE

The Classic
Arabian Horse

by

JUDITH FORBIS

LIVERIGHT / *NEW YORK*

Grateful acknowledgment is made to the following:
Oxford University Press, for the selection from *The Mufaddaliyat*, edited by Charles James Lyall. By permission of the Oxford University Press, Oxford.
William Morrow & Co., Inc., for maps "Kingdom of the Hyksos, 1750–1580 B.C." and "The Three Empires After 1400 B.C.—Egypt, Hittites, Mitanni." From Werner Keller, *The Bible as History*, copyright © 1964 by Thames & Hudson, Ltd. Reprinted by permission of William Morrow & Co., Inc.

FIRST EDITION

The text of this book is typeset in Linotype Janson. Composition, printing, and binding are by the Vail-Ballou Press.

TITLE PAGE ILLUSTRATION FROM A PAINTING BY HARRINGTON BIRD
COURTESY OF MUSGRAVE CLARK

Library of Congress Cataloging in Publication Data
Forbis, Judith.
    The classic Arabian horse.
    Bibliography: p.
    Includes index.
    1. Arabian horse. I. Title.
SF293.A8F68   1976   636.1′1   75–38979

ISBN 0 87140 612 8

1 2 3 4 5 6 7 8 9 0

To Moniet and Dr. Marsafi—for the inspiration they provided in our early quest for the classic Arabian horse.

CONTENTS

ACKNOWLEDGMENTS

DURING THE PAST eighteen years, while I have been traveling throughout the world compiling data for this book, many people have given me counsel and assistance. It would be impossible to acknowledge all of them here. However, I would expressly like to thank

the late Carl Raswan, whose educational letters and encouragement directed us to Egypt in our quest for the classic Arabian horse;

Ahmed, Hoda, and Gulsun Sherif, for their translation of Arabic records and the Abbas Pasha manuscript into English, and for their warm hospitality and friendship which will remain treasured memories of our life in Egypt;

the late Professor Walter Emery, for taking time out to discuss the ancient Egyptian horse while he was engaged at a dig in Saqqara;

Mr. John Dorman of the American Research Center in Egypt, who provided helpful information and allowed me the use of the Center's library;

El Sayed Sayed Marei, former Minister of Agriculture of Egypt, and Dr. Abdel Magid Youssef, Director General of the Egyptian Agricultural Organization, for opening doors that otherwise might have remained closed;

Dr. Mohamed El Marsafi, for his patience in the early years during our enthusiastic question periods at El Zahraa;

Dr. Khalil Soliman Khalil, for assistance with photos and records of early Egyptian horses bred by the E.A.O.;

Sheikh Isa bin-Sulman al-Khalifa, ruler of Bahreyn, for allowing me to see his horses, and his stud manager, Hasan bin-Saleh al-Ruway'i, for recounting stories about the horses of Bahreyn and their relation to Egypt;

Mrs. Danah al-Khalifa, for her interest in my work and her assistance in making my visit to Bahreyn possible.

Miss J. Backhouse of the British Museum manuscript department, for her guidance in connection with the Wentworth Bequest;

the Lady Anne Lytton, granddaughter of Lady Anne Blunt, for her many kindnesses and for allowing me to stay with her at New-buildings, where I copied many of her grandmother's records and photos;

Jerry Sparagowski, who reproduced many of the photographs in this book and supplied many of his own;

my uncle, George Whitwell, for educating me in my formative years about the wonders of Egypt, and for assisting me in research on ancient Egyptian horses;

my mother, Audrey L'Hommedieu, my father, William Freni, and my aunt, Evelyn Whitwell, for patient guidance during my life;

my husband, Don, who has posed many a horse for me to photograph, and has put up with my years of writer's cramps.

THE CLASSIC ARABIAN HORSE

Arab Tent

BY EDWIN LANDSEER—THE WALLACE COLLECTION, LONDON

1

THE HORSE OF THE EAST

THE ORIGIN of the Arabian horse is a great zoological mystery. When we first encounter him, he is somewhat smaller than his counterpart today. Otherwise he has remained unchanged through all the centuries. "As old as time itself and as fleet as its flying moments" perfectly describes him. Throughout early civilization we find the Arabian firmly established as a definite breed and as firmly entrenched in the affections and daily life of his master.

Neither sacred nor profane history tells us the country where the horse was first domesticated, or whether he was first used for draft or riding. He probably was used for both purposes in very early times and in various parts of the world. We know that by 1500 B.C. the peoples of the East had obtained great mastery over their Arabian horses. In fact, the principles underlying modern horsemanship do not vary greatly from those practiced by ancient masters of the horse 2500 years ago.

The horse appears in Egyptian hieroglyphics about the sixteenth century B.C. and Old Testament writings are filled with references to Egyptian horses. The prophets often used them as allegorical figures to teach psychological and spiritual truth, and as symbols of vanity and strength. Even King Solomon compared his love to Pharaoh's horses in comeliness and grace.

As a result of his graceful symmetry, speed, vigor, docility, and endurance, the Arabian horse has played an important part in the history of our race. Because of him we are far advanced from our barbarian forefathers. Without his aid we probably would not have fulfilled our destiny to "multiply and replenish the earth, and subdue it, and have domin-

"After God we owe it to the horses."

"ARAB SCOUTS" BY ADOLF SCHREYER

ion over the fish of the sea, and the fowl of the air, and over every living thing that moveth upon the earth."

About 3500 years ago the Arabian horse assumed the role of king-maker in the valley of the Nile and beyond, changing human history and the face of the East. Through him the Egyptians were made aware of the vast world beyond their own borders. The pharaohs were able to extend the Egyptian empire by harnessing the Arabian horse to their chariots and relying on his power and courage. With his help, societies of such distant lands as the Indus Valley civilizations were united with Meso-potamian cultures. The empires of the Hurrians, Hittites, Kassites, Assyrians, Babylonians, Persians, and others rose and fell under his thundering hooves.

His strength made possible the initial concepts of a cooperative uni-versal society, such as the Medo-Persian, Hellenistic, and Roman empires. The Arabian "pony express" shrank space and accelerated communica-tions during pharaonic as well as mameluke dynasties and linked empires together throughout the Eastern world.

Genghis Khan, Tamerlane, Alexander, Napoleon, George Washing-ton, and many brilliant generals shaped the world on Arabian horseback. The Spanish conquistadors mounted on Arab horses conquered the great Indian races of the Americas. From these Spanish imports were de-rived the mustangs, and when the Indians learned to utilize them, the history of the American West was changed. "After God we owe it to the horses," wrote a great conquistador, an appraisal certainly in accord with the teachings of the Prophet Mohammed, whose Arabian chargers bore the warriors of Islam throughout the Middle East and Mediter-ranean countries as far east as China and as far west as Spain. Until the pushbutton era of destruction evolved, the strategic and tactical concep-tions of warfare were based upon the use of the horse.

Today in Egypt one still finds descendants of those famous Arabian horses of antiquity. So avidly did Egyptian pashas, beys, sultans, kings, and princes collect them that a man's wealth was often measured in Arabian steeds. These noble horses of the desert are a living link between the ancient East and the modern West, for we have become the en-thusiastic preserver of the horses which can now be afforded only as a luxury.

Everyone is familiar with the term "classic," a word which immediately brings to mind the idea of something singularly pure and perfect that for centuries has been accepted as a model by which everything else of the kind is measured. The most frequent association of the word is with ancient Greek culture. When the ancient Greeks obtained the Arabian horse, they became conscious of his immortal and celestial derivation. In his honor they fashioned a god called Pegasus—a winged Arabian horse who occasionally descended to earth, but otherwise lived in heaven with the rest of the Olympians—a symbol of perfection, poetry raised to the heights, one of God's most beautiful and spiritual ideas.

Pegasus, Bellerophon, and the Medusa as depicted by E. Picault.

While some chroniclers of the Arabian horse prefer to ignore or dismiss the mythological and poetical allusions to the breed's creation, most breeders will agree that the Ishmaelite traditions and the Biblical version of the Book of Genesis are inspiring. These traditions have stimulated literature and provided many thought-provoking ideas, enabling us to gain insight into the spiritual properties of the breed. There is no dedicated Arabian owner who will not agree that there is a spiritual bond and kinship between the Arabian horse and his master such as exists with no other breed.

IN THE BEGINNING

In traditional writings, the genesis of the Arab peoples is traced to Seth, son of Adam and Eve. Seth ruled in harmony with the Universal Principle, and the Sethites became renowned for their wisdom in astronomy. Eventually, the children of Seth fell out of harmony with the Law, and only the Three Patriarchs—Methuselah, Lamech, and Noah—failed to join the encampment of Cain.

Noah came to live in Babylonia after the Great Flood, in about the third millennim B.C. He had a son, Shem, from whom the Semites are descended. Shem had five sons, including the grandfather of Eber. Eber had two sons, Peleg and Joktan or Qahtan. The "first Arabs," or southern half of the great Arab race, claim descent from Qahtan. They were the older branch of Abraham's ancestors and called themselves 'Arab al-'Ariba, or "those who were Arabs from the first," to distinguish themselves from 'Arab al-Musta 'Ariba, or "Arabs who became Arabs." Arab historians believe that Yarab, the son of Qahtan, was the father of the ancient Arab peoples and gave his name to Arabia.

The Semites originally worshipped the sun, Venus, and the moon, all astral deities. Monuments and inscriptions in South Arabia dating from about the ninth century B.C. symbolically represented the sun and moon by a disk and crescent. The name for the South Arabian deity, Illah or Il, the common Semitic word for god, corresponds to the Hebrew-Aramaic name El or Elohim and is but one of the many names of the moon god. Likewise, the North Arabic Al-ilah or Allah, who became the supreme and only god of the Mohammedan religion, is the ancient and prehistoric moon god.

The Arab bedouins led pastoral lives, grazing their flocks in the moonlight and observing the moon condensing dew on the pastures. They believed their lives to be regulated by the moon and became moon worshipers. Later agricultural societies, whose lives were regulated by the sun, became sun worshipers. The bedouins, however, believed the sun to be destructive. As in most primitive societies, the religion of the bedouins was basically animistic.

In early civilizations, the horse was particularly sacred to the many-titled mother goddess who was worshiped throughout the East. The renowned mythographer Robert Graves symbolizes her as the white goddess because white was her principal color, the color of the first member of her moon trinity, the new moon, goddess of birth and growth. The

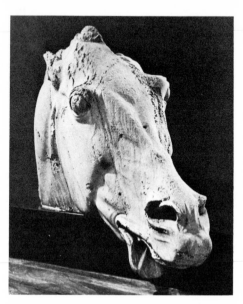

The horse of Selene, Greek goddess of the moon.
FROM THE EASTERN PEDIMENT OF THE PARTHENON

full moon was the red goddess of love and battle, while the old moon represented the black goddess of death and divination. The crescent shape of the moon was a common symbol, an object of worship throughout the old and new worlds, and by it the Egyptian goddess Isis was recognized as the reigning goddess of heaven and earth. The crescent was symbolic of time and the lunar calendar, and was appropriated by the Romans to Diana, the goddess to whom horses at certain times were sacrificed. In classic mythology, the moon was known as Astarte when crescent, and it is quite logical that the symbol of the horseshoe as a sign of good luck owes its origin to the crescent. Significantly, the star and crescent are the symbol of Islam, and the most agriculturally productive area of the Arab world has always been known as the Fertile Crescent.

With the advent of the great Babylonian lawgiver Hammurabi, a religious conflict arose. Hammurabi established the worship of Shamash, the sun god. To protect their religion, the bedouins were driven to make a pilgrimage from their cult's southern center at Ur to the northern sanctuary at Haran. Among them was Abraham, five generations removed from his ancestor Peleg.

Abraham had a son, Ishmael, of whom it was said: "He will be a wild ass of a man [or among men]; his hand shall be against every man, and every man's hand against him; and he shall dwell in the presence of his brethren" (Gen. 16:12).

The wild ass to which Ishmael is compared eloquently personifies the character of the bedouin, their nature being typical of that haughty, graceful, and independent wild desert animal. It is also an apt description of the Arab horse, were the word "horse" transliterated instead of "ass," as the late Lady Wentworth (owner of Crabbet Stud) maintains it should have been. Aside from Arab tradition, the primitive inhabitants of Babylonia, the Sumerians, knew of the horse and named it "the ass from the East" or "from the mountains," the first positive record being inscribed on a Babylonian tablet of about 2100 B.C. Remains of horses found in the mounds of Turkestan indicate the Hittites, who may have been among the first groups to migrate out of South Arabia, employed the horse dating from at least the beginning of the second millennium B.C., and Hittite cuneiform inscriptions (circa 1355 B.C.) used the Babylonian word *anshu.kur.ra*, the "beast from the East," in describing the horse. Some philologists also translated the ancient writings to mean "beast of the desert," *pas.kur.ra*, or "foreign beast," and contend the word "mountain" is also synonymous with "desert," just as the early Egyptians depicted it hieroglyphically. Unquestionably, however, both Hebrew and Arab annals prove that the Arabian horse flourished under the Semitic "people of the East" and primarily under the Ishmaelites.

The likening of Ishmael to the ass is also worthy of study in mythological terms, for there is a striking resemblance between characteristics attributed to him and properties of the Egyptian desert god, Set, whose cult remained the rallying point for the dispersed people of pre-dynastic Egypt and apparently later times, and to whom the ass was a sacred animal. Eventually Set became the patron of Arabian horses under the warrior pharaohs of Egypt. The breath of Set was the searing south wind, from which the Arabian horse allegedly sprung forth, the power which swept the children of the desert like a sandstorm over the fertile land. Traditionally a harbinger of violence, like the outcast Ishmael, Set was a representative of physical, but not of moral, evil; a strong and powerful personage, worthy of reverence, but less an object of love than fear. It is noteworthy that Set's ass-eared reed scepter was the sign of royalty which all the dynastic gods of Egypt carried. And the cult of ass-eared Set in southern Judea was also an established one, the ass occurring symbolically in early historical books of the Bible.

El Naseri records that originally the Arabian horse was wild and untamed by humans, and that Ishmael, the son of Abraham, was the first to mount and master the horse. Ishmael was the recipient of this divine gift because he discerned the universal presence of God in nature.

The traditional story goes on to say that further, when God permitted Abraham and Ishmael to lay the foundations of the sanctuary at Mecca, because of their faith in the One God, he gave them this special treasure. He told Ishmael to go to the summit of the mountain and call this treasure. God inspired Ishmael with the words he should speak. There was not one horse from all of Arabia that did not answer to the

The Set animal, typical of the Arab saluki hunting dog.

words of Ishmael. They ran toward him and put their manes beneath his hand and yielded themselves with docility to his will.

Although this is impossible from a historical standpoint, the horse having been domesticated prior to Ishmael's time, it is certainly probable that Ishmael and his tribesmen became masters at the art of horsemanship and horsebreeding, particularly hunting and raiding. The son of a bedouin and an Egyptian bondswoman, Ishmael personified the Arab bedouins as well as the Egyptian lunar god, Set, and the horse made him Prince of the Desert.

Ishmael married an Egyptian woman and twelve sons were born of this union. Their tribes migrated from Havilah, by Shur in Egypt, all the way to Asshur (Assyria). An Arabian nation, these Ishmaelites lived by robbing and plundering their kinsmen.

An Arab raiding party.

Ishmael was half-Egyptian by birth, and as his wife was also Egyptian, his children were of predominantly Egyptian blood. Therefore, the relationship and cultural ties to that country cannot possibly be denied.

Hagar would certainly have taught Ishmael the religion of the Egyptians, and the Ishmaelites would have been thoroughly familiar with its practice—and with the worship of Seth.

As the Egyptian historian Breasted pointed out, the Egyptians were the first to attain monotheism.[1] Palestine, the land across which Egyptian armies had marched even before 2500 B.C., had lain for centuries under the eaves of the Egyptian civilization's great structure, and people such as the Ishmaelites and Israelites who settled in the region found themselves in the midst of an already old and largely Egyptianized civilization of the area itself.

The course of Eastern history was witness to a change in direction, however, when shortly before 2000 B.C. warrior tribes speaking related Indo-European languages descended from Oxus-land (roughly, present-day Uzbekistan) into Media and made their domineering presence felt

1. James H. Breasted, *The Dawn of Conscience* (New York, 1968), pp. 346–47.

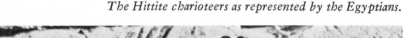

The Hittite charioteers as represented by the Egyptians.

on the eastern mountain border of the Semitic kingdom of Babylon. These foreign tribes brought horses with them from central Asia. Up to this point, the Babylonians apparently did not employ the horse militarily, but rather went to war in chariots drawn by asses. According to legend, the kings of Babylon had been in touch with the horse-breeding Hittites in the third millennium B.C. Some historians suggest the Hittites may have been emigrants from the desert of Arabia; however, most contend they were among the Indo-European movement from central Asia.

Babylon was taken and sacked by the Hittites (circa. 1926 B.C.), who retired to distant Anatolia after their raid, and the derelict kingdom was subsequently pounced upon by the Aryan Kassites, who established dominion for six centuries. The Kassites are credited by some historians with bringing the horse into Babylonia and using it only for drawing wheeled vehicles like those Aryans who were taking it at about the same time into northern India. The decline of Babylonia and the establishment of the Kassite Dynasty were also contemporary with sweeping movements in the West. The Hyksos came to power and the horse came to the fore in Egypt with Indo-European (Aryan) and Hittite influences being subsequently found as far south as the borders of Egypt.

HORSES AND THE HYKSOS: THE HORSE COMES INTO PROMINENCE IN EGYPT

Egyptian scribes maintained meticulous chronicles of annual events, but from the period 1730 B.C. to 1580 B.C. archaeologists have found a complete void. During this period Egypt was victimized by the Hyksos, whose warriors, mounted upon horses or driving in chariots, eventually extended their empire from the river Euphrates to the first cataract of the Nile. Initially these intruders used the horse and chariot to uphold their power. They also became skilled in the use of superior weapons, daggers, swords, bronze implements, the strong compound Asiatic bow, and scaled armor.

Many Egyptologists believe that the Hyksos brought the horse into Egypt. However, international trade was well developed. Egyptians frequently traveled throughout Asiatic countries and Asiatic visitors were numerous in Egypt. It seems obvious that the Egyptians were familiar with the horse and that it did exist within their boundaries. Up to that point in their civilization, however, they had been a peaceable people and found no real need to use the horse.

The Greek historian Manetho considered these Hyksos to be Arabians or Phoenicians. The reduction of Egypt by the Hyksos was, according to Manetho, effected with great ease. That the Egyptians were so easily defeated suggests a familiarity with the desert-dwelling Amu, whom they did not expect to be capable of totally overpowering them. Some of these Amu are depicted on a Twelfth-Dynasty tomb, about 1900 B.C., their chief's title and name being given as Absha, "prince of the desert," a title afterward used by the Hyksos and one which the Ishmaelites could well have claimed. The Bible refers to the sons of Ishmael as "twelve princes according to their nations." The Amu settled within the territory naturally belonging to Egypt and held all the northeastern portion of the delta where the Ishmaelites and Israelites subsequently lived.

Arabs encamped in the Wady Sabooah.

Although Palestine was ruled by the Hyksos after the mid-eighteenth century B.C., Hyksos culture seems to have existed there about the twentieth century. The tale of Sinuhe, an Egyptian noble of high rank who fled to Palestine during the reign of Sesotris I, gives the oldest account of pre-Israelite Palestine from any source. The account appears to be essentially true to the facts, and shows how superior was the Egyptian of this time to the bedouin of Palestine.

> . . . I beheld the bedouin.
> That chief among them, who had been in Egypt,
>   recognized me.

"I beheld the bedouin, that chief among them who had been
in Egypt. . . ."

He gave me water, he cooked for me milk.
I went with him to his tribe,
Good was that which they did (for me).
One land sent me on to another,
I loosed for Suan,
I arrived at Kedem
I spent a year and a half there.

It is of interest to note that Kedem no doubt refers to the land of Bene Kedem, the land of the Ishmaelites, the region east of Jordan and the Dead Sea. It was Sinuhe who advised the tribe he lived with on military tactics to be followed "when they became so bold as to oppose the rulers of foreign countries." These Egyptian words may have been the origin of the word *Hyksos*, which is said to derive from the Egyptian *Hequ Shaasu*, that is, "princes of the Shasu" or "princes of foreign countries," apparently nomadic Arab tribes even within Egypt proper and to the east and northeast of her boundaries. It must be remembered that the nearby red desert was still considered "foreign and hostile" to the black-land–dwelling Egyptian. According to Josephus, the Hebrew historian, Manetho says these Hyksos were called "shepherd kings," the term king often being applied in the East to the chief of a tribe or the ruler of a small town.

Of particular relevance mythologically is the fact that the deity Sut, or Sutekh (Set), was worshipped in many places in northern Syria and by the Hittites as well as by the Hyksos, who initially made war against the entire Egyptian pantheon. Eventually they acknowledged the likeness between their ancestral god and the Set of the Egyptians. Set also became identified with gods of war and the chase, and was known to have a warlike disposition. He was considered a harbinger of battles along with Montu, Lord of Thebes. Both loved horses and under the Twelfth to Seventeenth Dynasties, Set appears to have been the national god of the delta. Under the Nineteenth Dynasty he became "Great God, Lord of Heaven" and the kings delighted in calling themselves "Beloved of Set." The period of Hyksos rule was one of great confusion and internal despair for the Egyptians, and Seth (Set) was an apt god indeed for the Hyksos "princes," or "shepherds." So indelibly did they stamp their mark of oppression on Egypt that shepherds were considered an abomination to Egyptians ever after.

In further support of the conclusion that the Hyksos were Semitic, archaeological evidence points out that the Hyksos royal names were predominantly Canaanite or Amorite and that most of the Hyksos names were pure Semitic. With reference to the horse, the names associated with it are likewise Semitic. The word for chariot, *markabata*, is the same as the Hebrew, *merkabbah* (Akkadian *narkabti*). The name of the female horse was *ses-mut*, the last word probably expressing "mother,"

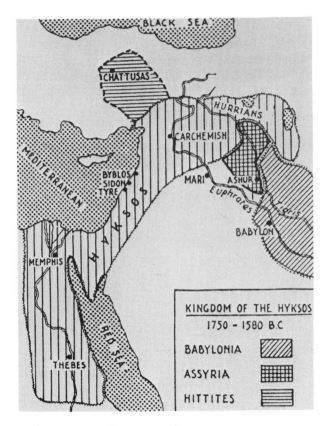

The empire of the Hyksos, 1730–1580 B.C.

as in the English "mare," or the plural. *Ses-mut* was also Semitic, being the same as the Hebrew *sus-im*, *sus* meaning horse (in Syrian, *susya*; Assyrian, *sisu*; Elam, *susa*). Two general titles pertaining to the chariotry were: officer of the horses, *mr ssmwt*, and scribe of the horses, *ss ssmwt*. In Arabic *sais* means groom—thus all are indicative of a common original, *susu*, which is probably Semitic.

As in Arab annals, we find the horse in Hebrew chronicles first associated with a Semite, in this case Joseph. In the Bible it is related that Joseph (son of Jacob, son of Isaac, Ishmael's brother) had been sold by his Hebrew brothers to passing Ishmaelites who in turn sold him into Egypt. Here he found favor with Pharaoh, who put him in charge of all the land of Egypt and "had him ride in the chariot of his second-in-command." This is the first indirect Biblical reference to horses (Gen. 41:43) aside from the Creation, and one which implies the time of the Hyksos, for they were the first to use the horse-drawn ceremonial chariot on public occasions in Egypt as a sign of prestige. The first chariot belonged to Pharaoh, the second to his chief minister. When the chariot superseded the palanquin as the ordinary mode of conveyance, much attention was paid to the equippage and the stud.

In further support of the theory that the Hyksos were Semites, and probably Ishmaelites, is the ancient tradition claiming that the pharaoh of this time was Apepi. It is probable that the Biblical Joseph's arrival did not fall, like Abraham's, into the period of the Old Empire. Under Joseph, chariots and horses were in use, as well as carts or wagons, all of which are unmentioned until the latter period of the Hyksos rule. It would more logically follow that Joseph, a foreigner, should have been advanced by a "foreign" king than a native one. The favor shown to his brethren, who were shepherds (Gen. 46:32), is consonant at any rate with the tradition that it was a shepherd king who held the throne at the time of their arrival. Specific references to horses in Egypt thereafter abound.

As to the Arabs, particularly the bedouins, ethnic purity has been their reward for geographical isolation. In almost every respect they are the ideal representatives of the Semitic race, just as the Arabian horse is the purest and oldest breed of horses.

George Rathbone, whose article "The Ancient Egyptian Ancestor of the Thoroughbred Horse" appeared in that classic magazine *The British Racehorse*, concluded that "the Arab, Turk, and Barb, although themselves probably incapable of quite matching the specialized racing 'galloway' for sheer pace, nevertheless inherited a longer stride, endurance and 'Class' from an original ancestor common to all three, namely the little Ancient Egyptian blood-pony—the world's first true racehorse and the source of all Oriental pace and quality. It must be em-

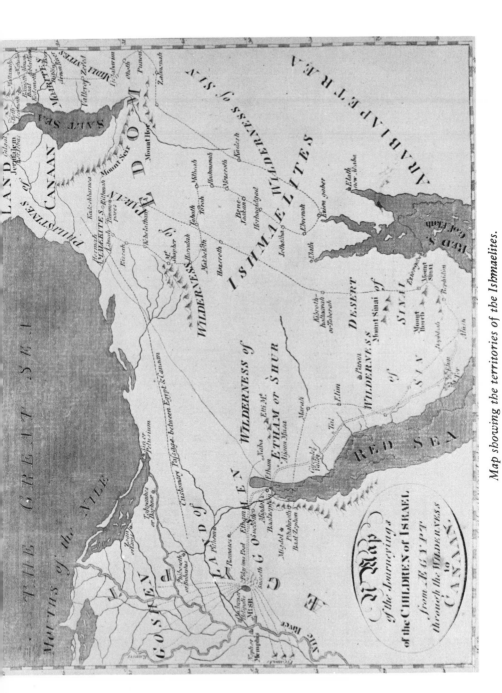

Map showing the territories of the Ishmaelites.

phasized here at the outset, that the Ancient Egyptians are the only civilized nation with an entirely sedentary culture to have ever maintained an all conquering military arm dependent upon the horse *for over four consecutive centuries.*"[2]

All evidence considered, the Arabian breed was native to the southern desert of Arabia, Yemen, and lived within Egyptian boundaries during preceding centuries. It is likely that the Indo-European groups improved their stock with Arabian blood. The close cultural ties between

2. George Rathbone, in collaboration with John Paget, "The Ancient Egyptian Ancestor of the Thoroughbred Horse," *The British Racehorse* (Oct. 1965).

The black tents of Arabia—unchanged since the time of Abraham.

the Arabs and Egyptians, notably their common animal worship, are indisputable, and there seems no question as to the Arabian horse being known in Egypt prior to its domestication.

It it obvious that the wild horses of central Arabia were closely akin to those of Egypt, Syria, North Arabia, and Chaldea, which formed a continuous country until volcanic disturbances and progressive aridity cut them off somewhat from each other. But until there are more digs for evidence in Arabia, as archaeologists have carried out in Egypt, Palestine, and Mesopotamia, the early centuries of Arabia and even Egypt will remain obscure.

2

THE HORSE AND CHARIOT IN ART, ARCHAEOLOGY, AND MYTHOLOGY

IN THE PERIOD after the Hyksos were driven out of Egypt, the Egyptian artists delighted in portraying horses on monuments and in tomb paintings. Having achieved prominence as a protector in war, the horse now became an integral part of Egyptian life. The proper gods were assigned to protect him, and the scribes duly noted his exploits and courage in the annual chronicles. Yet to archaeologists he remains an enigma.

How and when the Egyptians obtained the horse—whether the Hyksos brought it, or whether it existed in Egypt prior to their rule—is still open to debate. The late Professor Walter B. Emery thought that the nomadic inhabitants of Nubia perhaps had acquired the horse from Arabia before the Egyptians and probably used it for riding. The horse skeleton he unearthed in 1959 at Buhen in the Sudan he believed dated from the end of the Middle Kingdom (approximately 1700 B.C.), when Egypt held power over Buhen, and would appear thus to have predated the Hyksos. The horse skeleton was small; the color of the coat was brown, and the animal was nineteen years old. The early dating of this find was so startling that the British Museum cabled the famed archaeologist to reverify that they weren't the bones of an ass instead.

Another early find is the skeleton unearthed by the Metropolitan Museum's expedition of Lansing and Hayes at Deir el-Bahri in 1936. Various Egyptologists believe that the Emery find could not be older than, if as old as, this horse, which was buried in an enormous coffin in about 1500 B.C. with all the honor usually accorded a human member of

Top, *the mummy of a horse*, Egypt, Eighteenth Dynasty (circa
1500 B.C.), *unearthed by Lansing and Hayes*. Bottom, *the mummy
of a horse, with wrapping removed*.

the family. As with human mummies, it had been entirely eviscerated to arrest decay. It stood about 12.5 hands or 127 cm high and was rather light-boned. Its hooves were unshod, its short mane was tied up in tufts, and it appeared to be a yellowish brown color. A large protective blanket with a leather top lay over its back.

Additional early representations are found on monuments and scarabs and in tomb paintings. What is without doubt the earliest quotation in-

HTR means "horse" in hieroglyphics.

Scarab dating from the reign of Thutmose I (1557–1501 B.C.).
#301750, SCARAB 475, COURTESY OF THE BRITISH MUSEUM

volving chariotry, and thus indirectly horses, is found on the stela of King Kamose, late Seventeenth Dynasty (circa 1575 B.C.), line 13: *nhm. j htrjw,* "I (shall) seize the chariotry." A scarab dating from the reign of Thutmose I (1557–1501 B.C.) provides the first pictorial representation of horses. Thutmose is depicted in a battle scene pursuing the enemy from his chariot, his horses in a rearing position. Rearing horses are also found in hunting scenes, the earliest examples occurring in the chapel of Djehuty-hetep at Debeira in Nubia and in the chapel of User at Thebes.

Representations of man on horseback are rare, and perhaps the earliest known example is found on a plaque of glazed steatite in the Metropolitan Museum of Art, showing an Egyptian horseman brandishing a mace and bow.

Bronze ax head with man riding bareback on a horse; early Eighteenth Dynasty (circa 1500 B.C.).
#36766, COURTESY OF THE BRITISH MUSEUM

The Egyptian artists provide us with an excellent idea of the kinds and types of horses existing more than 3000 years ago. They did not involve figures in a spatial context as we know it and did not use perspective; every figure existed primarily as an isolated phenomenon. The Egyptians' use of geometry in art requires us to look for a ritualistic rather than an aesthetic meaning in most renderings. The created work was for them a unity, in which every detail and all measurements were determined in relation to the whole, based on sacred geometry. Royal personages were drawn on a larger scale than others, and animal forms were all too often disproportionately small. The good draftsman captured in his work the turmoil of the battle or the hunt, bringing the animal world to life with great sensitivity and understanding. The Egyptians believed that something translated into art would become a reality in the spirit world and they strived to achieve contact with the absolute through sympathetic renderings. Some of the liveliest and most spontaneous works are those done on faiences or ostraca, known as the poor man's papyrus.[1] Artists who were bound to strict rules when decorating the royal tombs gave free rein to their imagination in these drawings.

The horses of the New Kingdom (ca. 1580–1085 B.C.) were undoubtedly Arabian. They appear on monuments as small, elegant, very high spirited animals, with proudly arched necks and "dished" faces. They are fine-boned, but many have a peculiarly long back, which appears weak, and although the tail carriage is high, the tail is set on somewhat low; perhaps these faults are due to artistic license, for the freer sketches on ostraca and faiences are usually more correct in conformation. The colors range from various shades of bay and chestnut to black

1. Faiences were made of a friable kernel of pure quartz, covered with a thin glaze of very silicous glass. Ostraca were a cheap material for writing or drawing. Artists gathered flakes of limestone from the foot of the rocks or collected shards of baked pottery from refuse dumps.

and grey, and piebalds are also in evidence. Strange stripings on various representations of horses have raised the question as to whether these markings indicate piebalds or are, in fact, the result of artistic license.

Egyptian artists were careful to distinguish the dress and physical characteristics of the various nations of Asia and Africa. They depicted no difference between the horses of the Egyptians and those of their Asiatic enemies, which makes it unlikely that "African" and "Asiatic" breeds were distinctly recognized. Nor were there any obvious physical

In Egyptian art, every figure existed primarily as an isolated phenomenon. A wooden casket from the tomb of Tutankhamen depicts the pharaoh vanquishing his enemies.

CAIRO MUSEUM

differences shown between chariot and riding horses. In describing their horses and chariots, the Egyptians called the animal "the Beautiful" and the vehicle "the Equipment."

The renderings of horses by Egyptian artists provide an interesting study in style, spirit, and force. Liebowitz, writing about horses in New Kingdom art, notes that horses are depicted in a variety of poses.[2] An examination of representations of horses trotting and at rest, which are preserved from Dynasties Eighteen to Twenty (1580–1090 B.C.), suggests that three distinct phases in the treatment of horses' legs may be

2. Harold A. Liebowitz, "Horses in New Kingdom Art and the Date of an Ivory from Megiddo," *Journal of the American Research Center in Egypt* 6 (1967):129–34.

Blue faience tile, Eighteenth Dynasty. Note the airiness and freedom of the drawing.

THE METROPOLITAN MUSEUM OF ART, GIFT OF J. PIERPONT MORGAN, 1917

distinguished during this period.

In works from the Eighteenth Dynasty prior to the Amarna Period (the Pre-Amarna Phase, 1580–1375 B.C.), horses are depicted with all four legs on the ground. The forelegs are spread apart, forming a narrow-based isosceles triangle, while the hindlegs are similarly treated (figure 1). Liebowitz notes the rarity of examples of horses in Egyptian art which antedate the Amarna Period, but states that they are consistent enough to establish a distinct style. (There are, however, several exceptions—see figure 2.)

Figure 1. The Pre-Amarna Phase.   *Figure 2. An exception to the Pre-Amarna Phase.*

In the Amarna Phase (1375–1315 B.C.), horses are depicted as if about to rear, with the forelegs placed close together and thrust slightly forward and the hindlegs similarly placed (figure 3). In some examples a foreleg is raised. In addition, more examples of horses are found in the Amarna Period than in the Pre-Amarna Period.

Figure 3. The Amarna Phase.

Another change in style is noted during the Ramesside Phase (1315–1090 B.C.), as Liebowitz explains. Although the hindleg treatment is similar to the Pre-Amarna Phase, the forelegs are depicted in a new way: one is straight, touching the ground and almost perpendicular to it, while the other comes forward and lifted (figure 4). Secondly, the near leg is brought forward in most instances (figure 5); prior to the Rames-

Figure 4. The Ramesside Phase.

Figure 5. The Ramesside Phase.

side Phase, the far legs of horses were usually brought forward.

Although horses and chariots were a favorite with Egyptian artists, there are few representations of Egyptian cavalry, an important branch of the military. The prevailing opinion is that the horse was never ridden, and was used only to pull the chariot. Many scholars have dismissed numerous representations of scouts as being just grooms or mounted orderlies. The arguments that the breed of horse was too weak to carry riders has been subsequently disproved by Schulman. For example, it was noted that skeletons unearthed from a New Kingdom horse burial at Sakkara compared favorably with the skeleton of Eclipse when photos of both were examined. The mummy was of relatively powerful build and displayed a moderately deep chest and strongly developed body frame and large head. No significant differences were detected between that skeleton and those of modern horses. Further, it is unlikely it could have pulled a chariot together with occupants and weapons if it was unable to support a single rider on its back. In the Twelfth Dynasty, during the reign of Amenemhet III (1849–1801 B.C.), riding was known and practiced by Asiatics in the vicinity of Serabit el-Khadim in Sinai; furthermore, that this was known to the Egyptians is evidenced by the above-cited representations [four pictorial graffiti at Serabit el-Khadim] in an Egyptian temple. From this we might infer that the knowledge of riding might have been transmitted by them (the Egyptians) to Egypt proper.

The armies employed by the kings of the Eighteenth and Nineteenth Dynasties during their conquests of Syria and Palestine were made up of infantry and chariotry. The chariot could be utilized to great advantage on level ground, but not in the broken terrain of the Syrian and Palestinian highlands. Horsemen of course were at no such disadvantage.

Chariotry could be considered as a form of cavalry, though not in a strict sense of the word: there is no evidence that mounted combat troops were formally organized into units. Evidence shows that mounted riders were used as scouts in tactical situations where chariots were restricted because of the terrain.

Schulman further notes that individual soldiers serving in the chariotry consisted of two categories, according to the duties assigned them. The tactical (fighting) element was comprised of the chariot warrior, the charioteer, the shield-bearer, the tkm-bearer, the runner, and their officers, the first charioteer, the commander of chariot warriors, the standard-bearer of the chariot warriors, the marshaller of a host of chariotry, and the commander of a host of chariotry.

There is some question, however, as to whether all personnel of the second category of the chariotry were actually members of the military. Those in question were the adjutant of the chariotry, the stablemaster, the scribe of the stable, the scribe of horses (ss ssmwt) and the scribe of chariotry. Servants (probably grooms and craftsmen), who actually cared for the horses and equipment, are sometimes mentioned. The operational and administrative element of a chariotry unit was known as the stable. Here the chariots were maintained and stored, the horses were stabled and probably trained, and the men learned the techniques of chariotry.

Two of the general titles pertaining to the chariotry were officer of the horses (mr ssmwt) and officer of the chariotry (mr ti-nt-ḥtry), the former being the most frequently used.[3]

Eventually horsemen were used as formal cavalry. Shishak (Sheshonq —945–924 B.C.), who ruled at the time of King Solomon, is recorded to have had with him 1200 chariots and 60,000 horsemen when he went up to fight against Jerusalem. The Egyptian cavalry is mentioned in other historical records. The hieroglyphics state that the "command of the cavalry" was a very honorable and important post and generally held by the most distinguished of the king's sons.

It is to the great credit of the Egyptians as craftsmen that they quickly organized a strong force of light chariots and manifested a decided improvement in skill in their construction over their originators. The chariot was also an instrumental means of carrying the mail. An inscription records the existence in the New Kingdom of a relay system of postal service. A love letter provides the evidence:

"O, if you could come quickly to your beloved—like the royal courier—whose master waits impatiently for the message—his heart longing to hear it. Whole stables are harnessed for him—the horses wait for him at the stages—the harnessed chariot is in its place—the courier has no rest on his journey. When he arrives at the house of the beloved his heart leaps for joy."

Although people have long valued their domestic animals, they have reserved their greatest pride for their horses. The Arabian charger and chariot were part of the magnificence of Egyptian life, and the pharaohs

3. Alan Richard Schulman, "Egyptian Representations of Horsemen and Riding in the New Kingdom," *JNES* 16 (4):263–71 (Oct. 1957), and "The Egyptian Chariotry: A Reexamination," *JARCE* Journal of Near Eastern Studies 11 (1963):75–98.

and military chiefs appear to have been first to think of (and to afford) showing off the splendor and nobility of their animals by lavishly decorating them from head to tail. Egyptian tomb paintings have provided us with the first pictorial proof of horse and chariot caparisons. These have been gradually embellished and amplified over the years by Turks, Persians, Assyrians, Crusaders, Arabs, and so forth—even down to the present-day Americans, in whose horse shows the "costume classes" are great crowd pleasers.

During special celebrations the Egyptian horses were bedecked with fancy trappings. A decorative striped or checkered housing, trimmed with an ornate border and large pendant tassels, covered the whole body, and two or more feathers (ostrich plumes) inserted in lions' heads or some other device of gold, formed a crest upon the summit of the headstall. This display of ceremonial magnificence was confined to the chariots of the head monarch, or the military chiefs, and it was apparently considered sufficient in the harness of the town carriages to adorn the bridles with rosettes (not unlike our modern horseshow prize ribbons, which are derived from the rosette shape). Plumes probably representative of *maat* feathers adorn the chariot horses of royalty only. Thus one can imagine the splendid sight as the king went forth, his horses richly caparisoned, his gold-encrusted state chariot blazing under the rays of the Egyptian sun: "His Majesty ascended a great chariot of electrum,[4] like Aten when he rises from his horizon and filling the land with his love. . . ."[5]

All primitive societies, and even modern societies today, have accepted the idea of the evil eye. This notion goes back to the roots of all civilizations, and to this theme we owe the many and varied charms which human beings have devised in order to avert catastrophe. The horse, which pulled the war chariot and mounted the cavalry, as well as his use in agriculture by other civilizations, was for thousands of years a very important source of power and needed all possible protection. Thus talismans, amulets, and decorations had a very symbolic or magical meaning for defensive purposes against the evil eye. English horse brasses, now valuable collectors' items, undoubtedly owe their origin to early Egypt, for many of the mythological symbols used then have prevailed throughout the ages.

4. An alloy of gold and silver.
5. Quote from a tablet of Akhnaton.

Amulets in the shape of an eye, or *utchat*, representing the eye of the sun god or moon god, were held to give the wearer the same qualities of strength and health as were enjoyed by the god. These designs were often used in decorating the blinkers of horses, and the Arabs of later times tied blue beads or glass eyes in the manes, tails, or forelocks of their horses, just as Ishmael is claimed to have done. Blue was considered especially desirable in warding off the evil eye. The blue lotus was a favorite motif and was the most sacred of water lilies, suggesting the perfume of divine life. It was the floral emblem of pharaonic Egypt, and the color was attributed to the God of Heaven. Yellow represented gold, the flesh of the gods; white brought luck and joy, while red represented unconquerable force.

The lion in the headdress was symbolic of the sun, whose journey brought him "from the jaws of the lion of the West to the jaws of the lion of the East," whence he was reborn in the morning. It was the symbol of resurrection and was known as the king of beasts; swift, devouring like a flame, burning like the eye of the sun, a defender, a protector. Ramses II was compared to "a powerful lion with claws extended and a terrible roar." The Ramesside kings seem to have domesticated the beast for they had lions as hunting and battle companions. Gold was also likened to the sun, and the idolatrous tribe of Judah, known astrologically as Leo, the sun, sacrificed horses to that golden orb, as did many of the ancients. Even Christ was known as "the lion of the tribe of Judah."

Ostrich plumes were indicative of *Maat*, representing the weight of truth and justice, universal order and ethics. It was the custom for a warrior to show he was at war in a ritual manner by affixing one or more ostrich plumes in his hair; the chargers of Pharaoh bore these *maat* feathers for similar reason.

Almost a thousand years later the trappings were still staggering in splendor and value. The discovery of the X group of kings at Ballana and Qustol in Nubia in 1931 by the late Professor Emery revealed a magnificent collection of horse trappings.[6] One tomb contained the skeletons of six horses which had been sacrificed along with their groom. They were adorned with jeweled silver bridles and trappings of most elaborate design. Lion-headed medallions of beaten silver had eyes inlaid with lapis lazuli and a protruding tongue of carved ivory. The bits were a most severe curb type and were attached to the headstall by hinged brackets

6. Walter Emery, *Egypt in Nubia*, Hutchinson & Co. (London, 1965), pp. 63, 67–70.

English horse trappings of the 19th and 20th centuries reflect the ancient symbolism of stars, crescents, and the sun.

JOHN VINCE

Fourth-century silver horse trappings found on the Esquiline Hill in Rome. Note the lunar crescents and lion heads.

NOS. 338–343, COURTESY OF THE BRITISH MUSEUM

in the form of seated lions. Reins were of silver rope chains and the workmanship was of such superb perfection that the excavator considered that it probably was done in ancient Meroe, once the capital of Nubia. All six horses had bronze bells attached to their necks with tasseled cords; some had necklaces of cowrie shells. A sensational find was a red leather horse collar, adorned by a series of silver medallions set with precious stones. Five were in the form of lion's heads, the eyes set with garnets; the rest were open fretwork of silver with large oval onyx set in the center. The largest of the medallions, which was placed in the center of the collar, had a frame set with garnets, beryls, and moonstones, which surrounded a large blue faience Egyptian scarab held in place by a claw setting. Today these magnificent pieces are on view in the Egyptian Museum, although the horses on which they are displayed are unfortunately not Arab.

Many of the horse trappings, such as the rosette and the lion, were sacred to the goddess Astarte (also called Ashteroth, Anat, etc.), the Semitic goddess of war and Magna Mater of Syria and Palestine. Examples of Astarte as "the mistress of mares" on horseback are common from the Eighteenth Dynasty on, when she came to be worshiped by the Egyptians. In the treaty made between the Hittites and the Egyptians, she appears as a national goddess of the Syrian Hittites, and this at a time when her worship had become so familiar to the dwellers of the Nile that Ramses II called his son *Mer-As-Trot.t* after her. Indeed, several proper names compounded with her name were then current. As "lady of the horse and chariot," she entered Egyptian mythology late.

Anta (Anat) is named along with Astarte in the Hittite treaty. She figures on Egyptian monuments as "lady of heaven and mistress of the gods," with helmet, shield, and lance, and swinging a battle-ax in her left hand; sometimes she is represented on horseback. Ramses II named his favorite daughter after her, *Bint Anta*, and one of the royal steeds was named *Anat-Herte*, "Anat is satisfied."

Asit was also an equestrian war goddess who bore a spear and shield. She appears to be a goddess of the Eastern Desert, according to a stele found near the temple at Redisieh.

While the Hyksos reimposed the cult of Seth on the Egyptians, when they were driven out, the Egyptians reverted to the worship of Amon. Set was still in great favor, particularly under the Ramessides, who worshiped him for some four hundred years. Ramses II even gave to Seth the goddesses Anat and Astarte as consorts, the most logical of all goddesses for him to enjoy.

The horse did not initially enjoy sacred honors in comparison to some other animals, nor was it the specific emblem of any great deity in Egypt. This is rather remarkable since horses were considered of the highest importance and very dear to the Egyptians after the Eighteenth Dynasty. The fact that the Egyptians were exposed to the horse through early contacts with the Amu and learned its use and employment from the Semitic "shepherds," whom they considered "an abomination," may have prevented them from according it godlike status. Perhaps it came into significance too late to acquire godlike elevation.

3

PHARAOH'S HORSES

HISTORY has not bestowed the title of kingmaker upon the horse without good reason. Pharaohs, kings, and warriors could not have wielded power and built empires without the aid of swift and courageous war steeds. The resourceful pharaohs of Egypt wasted no time in acquiring the choicest Arabian horses available in the East, and they established such carefully planned breeding programs that the Egyptian horses quickly surpassed all competitors. The pharaohs were excellent horsemen themselves, and because their lives depended on their chargers in battle, they naturally took great personal interest in the royal stables.

Once the Hyksos were driven out of Egypt by the warrior princes of Thebes, the succeeding pharaohs Ahmosis, Amenophis I, Amenophis II, and the various Thutmoses determined to secure their country against foreign invaders. From this time forward the pharaoh became head of the army, commanding and leading the troops to battle in his gleaming horse-drawn chariot.

During this period, horse-training, the art of riding, and a special form of two-wheeled chariot were perfected. The light battle chariot revolutionized the waging of war. It is tribute to the cleverness of Egyptian craftsmen that they quickly mastered the art of chariot making and developed a light vehicle which was suitable for swift driving over the desert.

We find the large-scale military use of horses by Egypt began under the reign of Thutmose (1504–1450 B.C.). During his era the powerful and highly civilized kingdom of Mitanni became a serious threat in the East and as a consequence of war, Egyptian horsemen became influenced by them. These Mitanni, an aristocracy of warlike charioteers, were completely devoted to their horses. They held the first derbys along the banks of the Tigris and Euphrates and were well advanced in the care of stud animals. They were masters in breeding and management, and all phases of training cavalry horses.

Archaeologists were astounded when they turned up a text of some

Pharaoh's Horses.

BY J. HERRING, SR. ENGRAVED BY J. GILBERT, 1849

thousand lines containing instructions on the breeding and training of war steeds. It is without a doubt the oldest handbook of equestrianism extant, dating back some 3400 years. The language of the text is Hittite, and the remains of the library were found in a place once the capital of the Hittite kingdom. However, the author of the book identified himself as "Kikkuli of the land of Mitanni"—a Hurrian who obviously was working within an ancient tradition. Kikkuli's treatise stipulated a seven-month period for training a horse properly, and emphasized exact adherence to the specific and carefully formulated rules set down. The Hittite king had wisely hired this Hurrian horse master from the land of Mitanni to manage his royal stables on the most modern principles, and the Hittite Empire became a formidable one, based on the maneuverability of its war horses and exceptional weaponry.

Thutmose might well have been called the Napoleon of Ancient Egypt. Leading his troops in a "golden chariot," he penetrated Palestine and Syria, defeating the Mitanni and extending the empire of Egypt as far as the Euphrates. Chariots and horses were among the most valuable booty. A constant stream of horses were led south to Egypt along with captives who knew how to care for them. Among them were Hurrians, students of Kikkuli's methods.

The Egyptians preferred to use stallions for drawing chariots and an interesting situation arose during the great battle against Kadesh. The king of Kadesh, knowing all was lost unless he could defeat Thutmose's army, made a desperate last resort. While engaging the Egyptians in battle before the city, he sent a mare against the Egyptian chariotry, hoping she would excite the stallions and produce enough confusion to cause a break in the battle line, of which he could take advantage. But seeing the ruse, Amenemhab, an Egyptian, leaped from his chariot, sword in hand, and pursued the mare on foot until he caught and killed her. He then cut off her tail, which he triumphantly presented to his king. Thutmose swiftly closed in on the city and Kadesh was doomed. Never again as long as Thutmose lived did the Asiatic princes make any attempt to shake off his yoke. During a period of nineteen years and the course of seventeen campaigns, he had beaten them into submission, thus beginning the era of Egypt's warrior kings. With the fall of Kadesh disappeared the last vestige of the Hyksos power which once held Egypt in subjection and transformed it under the kings of the Eighteenth Dynasty into a vengeful conqueror of Asia.

Thutmose made sure that his son Amenophis II (1450–1415 B.C.) would be trained and capable of holding on to the empire he had courageously established. Amenophis was an apt pupil and it is recorded that "at eighteen he was completely mature. He had learned to master every craft of Montu [the god of war]. On the battlefield he had no equal. He learned to ride and train horses. There was none like him in this great army. There was not a single man who could draw his bow. He could not be overtaken in the races."

Thutmose was justly proud of his son's accomplishments and ordered: "Let him be given the very best horses of the stable of My Majesty which is within the Wall, and tell him to take charge of them, to make them obedient, to train them, to look after them." Thereafter,

*A gold fan showing Tutankhamen in his chariot, accompanied
by his saluki hound, hunting ostrich for plumes for the fan.*

*Map showing the three empires (Egyptian, Hittite, Mitanni)
after 1400 B.C.*

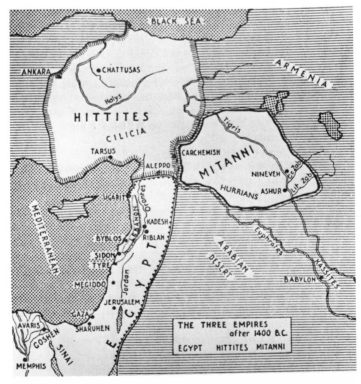

Amenophis II took charge of the horses of the royal stable, hoping to please the gods Reshpu and Astarte, and the horses he trained were superior to all others. Despite long gallops, when he held the reins they were never tired or lathered with sweat. Later Amenophis II had to resubjugate Syria, and he too sequestered steeds and chariots. By now Egypt was becoming the leading horse center of the East, and the stables of the pharaoh and his army contained thousands of the best Arabian horses of the millennium.

The pharaohs were also avid hunters and possessed exceptional prowess. Thutmose IV (1420–1411 B.C.) "did a thing that gave him pleasure upon the highlands of the Memphite nome, upon its southern and northern road, shooting at a target with copper bolts, hunting lions and wild goats, coursing in his chariot, his horses being swifter than the wind." The comparison of horses to the wind is noteworthy, for this became a common simile about the Arab horse.

The reliefs at Karnak depicting the campaign of Seti I (1318–1298 B.C.) in Palestine historically illustrate the use of horses and chariots in the campaign, and among the chargers of Seti we find some of the finest Arabians represented. Seti, too, supervised the upbringing of his son, Ramses II, in the traditional warrior-king manner; a pharaoh worthy of the crown worn by the Seth-worshiping rulers of Egypt. Even as a child Ramses reported as "Lord of Infantry and Chariotry" and was an accomplished horseman. At maturity he was known to be "stout hearted in the array, firm on the steed, beautiful in the chariot."

By the time Ramses II (1292–1225 B.C.) ascended the throne, he faced a dangerous situation in Syria with the Hittites. As a general rule the Egyptians proposed a fixed day for battle, and postponed it if their opponents were not ready. Surprise attacks were forbidden. However, the Hittites did not adopt such noble practices. They deliberately attempted to trick Ramses II by making a surprise attack on the king's camp when the four divisions of his army were still a considerable distance away. Advancing upon the Hittites, Ramses fell into a trap cleverly laid for him by Metalla, the Hittite king. During the heat of battle, Ramses became surrounded by a number of the enemy's chariots, but he fought on, his courageous chariot chargers carrying him through the conflict without harm. Eventually the tide of battle turned in favor of Egypt and the Hittites retreated, even though it had cost both sides

Above, *the campaign of Seti I in Palestine. Note the classic Arabian horse drawing his chariot. Temple of Ammon at Karnak.* Left, *a horse depicted in the battle of Seti in Palestine. Note the dished face and slightly convex nose—the "camel bump," yet the head is not coarse.*

PHOTOGRAPHS BY HELEN STAUBLI

Left, *one of Seti's teams of horses.*
Again, note the sharp contrast in types
of heads. Here the shorter, broader,
and squarer type is portrayed. Below,
the most elegant of Seti's teams, show-
ing extreme refinement of head and
perfect proportions.

PHOTOGRAPHS BY HELEN STAUBLI

dearly. When Ramses alighted from his chariot, his first thought was for his horses who so gallantly carried him through the battle. The horses were unwounded, but their caparison was sullied with blood and dust, the feathers that decorated their heads were in shreds, and their collar harnesses half broken. To be sure that future generations were aware of his noble steeds' valor, as well as his own, he recorded for

The battle of Ramses II against the Hittites. The head on the near horse differs greatly from that of the horse on the off side. The former is coarser, convex, and shows the ears back (a relatively rare rendering), while the far horse shows refinement of the head, with ears forward.

PHOTOGRAPH BY HELEN STAUBLI

posterity: " I have fought, I have repulsed millions of nations with mine own hand. Force-in-Thebes and Maut-is-satisfied were my great horses; they were under my hand when I was alone in the midst of the trembling enemy. Henceforth their food shall be given them before me each day when I am in my palace." A place of honor in the royal stables was reserved for these favored steeds, and they received unlimited rations of forage and splendid decorations for the remainder of their lives.

In descriptions of the Hittites under combat with Ramses II, it is recorded that some fought on horses, which they guided by a bridle, without saddles, but the far greater part in chariots. These references to the use of the horse appear to have been introduced to show a peculiarity of Asiatic warriors, for the custom of employing large bodies of cavalry, as already mentioned, seems not to have been so commonplace or important militarily in Egypt as in some Eastern countries, and is rarely represented in Egyptian art. Reliefs at the battle of Kadesh do provide some pictorial examples of Egyptian "scouts" at the time. The harnesses worn by their horses are simple compared to those of the chariot horses, and the four horsemen are dressed similarly in kilts and headcloths, carrying with them quivers and bows as well as whips. One of them is shown riding sidesaddle.

With the Asiatic campaigns of Ramses II, the military aggressiveness of Egypt which had awakened under Ahmose I with the expulsion of the Hyksos was completely exhausted. Nor did it ever revive, although horsebreeding continued to flourish in the land of the Nile and Egypt became the East's prime supplier of Arabian horses. Notwithstanding Ramses' conquest of various northern Hittite strongholds, he did not succeed in breaking their power; however, it was just cause for congratulation that he stopped the southern advance of so formidable a group of people.

Peace was short-lived. Within a few years, the Philistines descended on the Holy Land and Egypt. Mighty fortresses fell before their onslaught, the magnificent stud horses of Cilicia were seized as plunder, and even the Hittite empire was obliterated. As the Philistines moved toward Egypt, Ramses III (1198–1166 B.C.), in the tradition of the Ramessides before him, prepared to do battle. He decreed general mobilization of his country: "The chariot detachments consisted of the swiftest runners, and every first class charioteer available. The horses flew like the wind, ready to crush foreign lands under their feet. . . . His troops were like bulls ready for battle; his horses were like falcons amid a flock of tiny birds."

Ramses III warded off the deadly threat to Egypt in two decisive battles with a victory such as had never been witnessed in the history of the Nile.

By the time of the famed King Solomon (ca. 900 B.C.), the hot-blooded Arabian horses were in great abundance throughout Mesopotamia, Asia Minor, and Palestine, yet the Egyptians had developed such superior strains of Arabian horses that Solomon looked to Egypt, as did the kings of Syria and of the Hittites, as their source.

The earliest account of the horses of Solomon, son of David, is related by Ibn el-Kalbi (A.D. 786–828) in his book: "The Prophet David was known to love horses and it was said that no sooner did he hear of a mare famous for its pedigree, purity, beauty or speed, than he sent for it, until eventually he had collected 1000 of the choicest horses. When David died he was succeeded by his son, Solomon, who declared: 'Of all the wealth I inherited from David, nothing is dearer to my heart than these horses.' "

Solomon established a relationship with Pharaoh, the king of Egypt, by taking Pharaoh's daughter in marriage and bringing her to the city of David. And as a wedding present, "Pharaoh king of Egypt had gone up, and taken Gaza, and burnt it with fire, and slain the Canaanites that dwelt in the city, and given it for a present unto his daughter, Solomon's wife" (1 Kings 9:16).

Unfortunately, like his Egyptian contemporaries, Solomon fell prey to the charms of Ashteroth, the Eastern goddess to whom the horse was sacred, and he erected places of worship to her. Arab tradition relates that one day Solomon said: "Bring these [David's] horses to me in order that I may get acquainted with their breed and origin." And he spent time studying these horses from noon until sunset, forgetting his midday and afternoon prayers. His subjects, seeing that their king was not praying, followed suit. When Solomon came to his senses and remembered his shameful neglect of the One God, he asked the Lord for forgiveness, saying: "Take these horses back as no wealth is worth forgetting the Lord and prayers to him." He then destroyed nine hundred of his horses, keeping only one hundred. These latter steeds he said "are most precious to me, more so than the 900 which made me forget my prayers." Solomon loved these horses and kept them until he died. Another tradition handed down by the Arabs was that God gave

Solomon one hundred winged horses out of the sea which were said to be of especially good luck, and that Solomon used to race them and wager on the races.

Of Solomon's special love for his Egyptian horses, there can be no shred of doubt—for as long as we read the Bible, the immortal Song of Songs will forever remind us of Egypt's desert steeds.

Reconstruction of the stables of Solomon at Megiddo.
PENNSYLVANIA MUSEUM

The Hebrew chronicler Josephus records of Solomon that "accordingly there went a great fame all round the neighboring countries, which proclaimed the virtue and wisdom of Solomon . . . kings demonstrated the regard they had for him, by the presents they made him; for they sent him vessels of gold, and silver, and purple garments, and many sorts of spices, and horses, and chariots. . . . These horses also were much exercised in order to their making a fine appearance, and running swiftly, that no other could upon the comparison appear either finer or swifter, but they are at once the most beautiful of all others, and their swiftness was incomparable also."

Solomon was king over all of Israel, and he built forty thousand stalls of horses for his chariots and kept twelve thousand horsemen. He built great warehouses to store his supplies, and cities for his horsemen. He looked after the welfare of his officers so that they lacked nothing, and had dromedaries bring choice barley and straw for the horses.

Loud and Guy unearthed one of Solomon's strongholds and found a remarkable series of stables grouped around a courtyard laid with

beaten limestone mortar. A ten-foot-wide passageway, purposely rough-
ened to prevent the horses from slipping, divided each stable through the
center, and the roomy stalls some ten by ten feet square still had remains
of feeding troughs and watering arrangements. Even by pharaonic or
modern standards, these were luxurious structures. The entire Megiddo
stable held stalls for 450 horses and sheds for 150 chariots; therefore considering it, together with what was unearthed at other similar sites such
as Tell el-Hesi at Hazor, at Taanach, and also at Jerusalem, the Biblical
references in all likelihood fell short in their estimate. These buildings
were so well constructed that some two thousand years after Solomon,
the crusaders tethered their horses in one of the ancient stable buildings
cut deep into the rock under the walls of Jerusalem.

The Queen of Sheba, impressed with Solomon's wisdom and faith in
God, and knowing of his great love for horses, presented him with a
mare named Safanad. A choice strain of Arabians descended from this
lovely creature. The Sheba (Ar. Saba') were associated with the Tema,
a tribe of Ishmael (Job 6:19), and in consequence must have been superb
horse breeders.

Arab annals relate that many of the animals trained and employed by
Ishmael lost something of their purity, and that one pure stock, Zad El-
Rakeb, was preserved by Solomon. This is the stock whose high renown spread at a later period throughout the world and was distinguished by a respiratory duct whose size enabled it to accomplish
fabulous journeys. Zad El-Rakeb, which means "the support of the
horseman," was given by Solomon to his relatives from the Azd tribe in
Yemen when they came to congratulate him on his marriage to the
Queen of Sheba.[1] This horse enabled its rider to pursue and catch even
the swiftest of game, providing food for his owner as well as many
others. We do not know whether this was one of the famed Egyptian
steeds, but the possibility exists.

The next two hundred years found Egypt in an imperial decline, but
references to her horses are still numerous. The Piankhi record is one
of the most moving of all inscriptions found to date about the Egyptian
pharaohs and their horses.

Pharaoh Piankhi (751–716 B.C.) was especially devoted to his horses,

1. King Solomon was a favorite subject in Islamic tales and while Zad El-Rakeb's pedigree has credence, the story of his being connected with Solomon is open to conjecture.

perhaps even more so than the pharaohs who had preceded him, and the Piankhi Stele records his poignant reaction upon finding Namlot's stable in total disorder: "His majesty proceeded to the stable of the horses and the quarters of the foals. When he saw that they had suffered hunger, he said: 'I swear, as Ra loves me, and my nostrils are rejuvenated with life, it is more grievous in my heart that my horses have suffered hunger, than any evil deed that thou has done, in the prosecution of thy desire.' " Previously Namlot had brought gifts to the king, for the stele records that: "he filled the treasury with his tribute; he brought a horse in the right hand and a sistrum in the left hand of gold and lapis lazuli." Evidently horses were still high on the list of gifts, if the symbolic holding in the right hand means anything. It is also obvious that horses were graded according to quality, for mention is made on the stele of "many horses of the best of the stable, and the first of the stall." Horses are always rated along with gold and costly stones in tribute value.

When Piankhi died, the four horses which made up the standard number for him were sacrificed so that their spirits might go with their royal master into the other world, for his service there. The highly favored horses were all buried standing, and all with their heads looking to the south. They were equipped with full trappings, mostly of gilded silver.

Thus did the golden era of Egypt's horse-loving pharaohs come to an end. Struggling against the Ethiopians and Assyrians, Egypt settled down to a gradual decline.

4

THE AGE OF POETRY

꧁꧂꧁꧂꧁꧂꧁꧂꧁꧂꧁꧂꧁꧂꧁꧂꧁꧂꧁꧂꧁꧂꧁꧂꧁꧂꧁꧂꧁꧂꧁꧂

IN THE Days of Ignorance, before Mohammed rose to preach Islam, the Arab was a free man, a poet and a warrior. Poetry was the Public Register of the people; genealogies were recorded and glorious deeds handed down to posterity. In ancient Arabia, the poet (*sha'ir*) was held to be endowed with supernatural knowledge—he was the oracle of the tribe, their guide in peace and their champion in war. Ibn Rashiq of Kairouan (d. A.D. 1064), a great poet of his era, once said: "The Arabs congratulated each other on three things: the birth of a boy, the emergence of a poet in their midst, or the foaling of a mare."

The oldest form of poetical speech in Arabia was rhyme without meter (*saj'*) or "rhymed prose." Out of this evolved the most ancient of the Arabian meters known as Rajaz ("a tremor"). The later ode (*qasidah*) of the Classical Age suggests a poem with an artistic purpose and has a strictly prescribed sequence of ideas and subjects. From the main theme of women, love affairs, or the comeliness of his mistress, and the shifting habitations and pasturing places of his tribe, the poet turns to the main object of his poem, the description of his horse or camel, displaying his close acquaintance with their habits and an intuitive communion with their souls. He never talks down to them; they are rational, living creatures of God. The tie that bound the Arab to his horse was not material, but spiritual, for the bedouin, like the American Indian, possessed an understanding of nature and realized his kinship with all life.

It is impossible to fix the date when the Arabs first began to practice the art of poetry. Generally speaking the oldest poets of whom we have any records (except for Job) would place them about 130 years before the Hegira. The first Arabian ode was composed, according to tradition, by Muhalhil ibn Rabiah, the Taghlebite.

One of the greatest poets before the rise of Islam was Imru-al-Qeis, who was descended from the ancient kings of Yemen. While he was wandering in search of help in procuring vengeance for the murder of his father, he spent some time with the Tayi (Tai, Tayyi) tribe, and there married Umm Jundub. During this time he made acquaintance with the celebrated poet Alqamah, and the two poets challenged each

A modern Arab poet—Hasan bin-Salah al-Ruwayi, stud manager and poet to the ruler of Bahreyn, Sheik Isa bin-Sulman al-Khalifa.

other to produce the finest poem describing a camel and a horse, the decision as to the merits of each being committed to Umm Jundub. Both thereupon composed and submitted their poems, and she decided that the horse described by Alqamah was the nobler animal of the two. Imru-al-Qeis in a fit of rage divorced her, and Alqamah is said to have married her, thus acquiring his name, Al Fahl ("the stallion"). Two of his poems are among the most celebrated ancient literature of Arabia.

One of the most lauded poets and warriors of the pre-Islamic age was Antara. The name of Antara ibn-Shaddad al-Absi had lived through the ages as the paragon of bedouin heroism and chivalry. Knight, poet, warrior, and lover, Antara exemplified in his life those traits most highly

Antara and Abla.

esteemed by the bedouins. His deeds of valor as well as his love for his cousin, Abla, became a part of the literary heritage of the Arabic-speaking world. He was born about the mid-sixth century, a slave, and the son of a black maid. He was eventually freed by his father after an encounter with an enemy tribe, in which he refused to take active part. Few passages in the whole of ancient Arabian literature equal the dramatic poignancy of his tender description of his horse in battle during those years of raiding and tribal wars:

Mu'allaqa of Antara

When I beheld the people advancing in solid mass
urging each other on, I wheeled on them blamelessly;
"Antara!" they were calling, and the lances were like

well-ropes sinking into the breast of my black steed.
Continuously I charged them with his white-blazed face
and his breast, until his body was caparisoned in blood,
and he twisted round to the spears' impact upon his breast
and complained to me, sobbing and whimpering;
had he known the art of conversation, he would have protested
and had he been acquainted with speech, he would have spoken to me.
The horses frowning terribly plunged into the crumbling soil,
long-bodied mare along with short-haired, long-bodied stallion
and oh, my soul was cured, and its faint sickness was
healed by the horsemans' cry, "Ha, Antara, on with you!"

(Trans. by A. J. Arberry)[1]

Among the greatest Arabian poems were the Seven Odes, written in gold ink during the Golden Age of Poetry and said to have been suspended in the temple at Mecca about the beginning of the sixth century A.D. A particularly descriptive poem among the seven was "The Golden Ode," by Labid (ca. A.D. 570–662), wherein he tenderly describes his war mare:

THE GOLDEN ODE OF LABID

Well have I my tribe served, brought them aid and armament,
Slept, my mare's reins round me, night-long their sentinel;
Ridden forth at day-dawn, climbed the high-heaped sand ridges
Hard by the foes' marches, dun-red the slopes of them;
Watched till the red sun dipped hand-like in obscurity
    Til the night lay curtained, shrouding our weaknesses;
And I came down riding, my mare's neck held loftily
    as a palm fruit-laden: woe to the gatherer!
Swift was she, an ostrich;[2] galloped she how wrathfully,
    from her side the sweat streamed, lightening the ribs of her;
Strained on her her saddle; dripped with wet the neck of her;
    the white foam-flakes wreathing, edging the girth of her;
Thrusteth her neck forward, shaketh her reins galloping;
    flieth as the doves fly bound for the water-springs.

(Trans. by Wilfrid Scawen Blunt after Lady Anne Blunt)

---

1. A. J. Arberry, *The Seven Odes* (London, 1957). By permission of George Allen and Unwin, Ltd.
2. This powerful bird that looks like a camel can cover twenty-five feet at a single stride and is capable of running considerable distances at a speed of about 30 mph. Only the very swiftest of horses could catch her.

"Well have I my tribe served, brought them aid and armament."

PAINTING BY ADOLF SCHREYER

A contemporary of Amr ibn-Kulthum, the author of the famed Mu'allaqa, was Salamah ibn-Jandal of the Tamim tribe, a branch of the Mudar. He was one of the most celebrated warriors of his clan, and in a masterpiece of his work, the description of the horse is particularly beautiful and admired by the Arabs:

The day we pushed on our steeds homewards the way they had gone,
    with hoofs chipped, jaded and worn by onset again and again;
And the galloping steeds came home with streaks of blood on their breasts,
    as though their necks were the stones where victims in Rajab[3] are slain.
Yea, each one fleet, when the sweat soaks through the saddle-pad, clear
    of skin, smooth-cheeked, bright of hair, a galloper tireless of pace.

"Not thin his forelock, nor humped his nose." Ghazal, by
Nazeer out of Bukra, in Germany.

PHOTOGRAPH BY ERIKA SCHIELE

Not thin his forelock, nor humped his nose, no weakling of limb;
    preferred is he in the dealing of milk, well nurtured at home.
Each leg apart in its gallop seems to stream with a rush
    of speed as though from a bucket of water poured o'er the field.
Up starts he briskly, as starts a shepherd who in his sleep
    has left his flock to a wolf to harry, and wakes in alarm.
His withers rise to a neck far reaching upwards, below
    a breast blood-stained, like a stone on which saffron is ground.

3. Rajab: one of the sacred months in which victims were offered at holy places.

The folds of fat on his breast are set close, fold upon fold:
    all kinds of movement are easy to him, gallop and trot;
He races down the wild asses, brown, green-lipped with the grass:
    a thousand drop off behind him, easily wins he unspurred.
To how many wretches have they by God's will brought wealth and ease!
    how many rich have they spoiled and stripped of all luxury!
With such as these do men enter battle with confident heart
    in spite of spear-play: with such, hard pressed, secure is their flight.[4]

"With led mares, all pressing on, frisky, prancing. . . ."
PAINTING BY HARRINGTON BIRD, COURTESY OF MUSGRAVE CLARK

Bishr ibn-Abu Khazim was the most renowned poet of the Asad tribe during the century before the appearance of the Prophet. In a poem of Bishr some verses vividly describe the war mares of Asad:

With led mares, all pressing on, frisky, prancing out of the road in wanton-ness, made lean and spare by constant duty in places of danger and in distant raids,

4. Syed Muhammad Badruddin Alavi, *Arabian Poetry and Poets* (Cairo, 1924).

Striving against the reins unquiet as though in each of them there were a
locust in a cloud of dust, yellow in color,

Thrusting back with their elbows the girth, with the space between their
teats stopped up with dust;

Thou mayest see them grey from the sweat dried upon them—here a plenti-
ful flow, there only a little;

In every place of soft soil, wheresoever they wheeled about, is a well-like
footprint of the hoof with the side crumbling in.[5]

The opening century of Islam was not favorable to literature, and
the poets of this century were those of the pagan age who embraced
Islam. It was natural that there was no change in their style. Those who
were born under Islam for a time followed slavishly in the footsteps of
the ancients as though Islam had never been. However, the advent of
Mohammed proved detrimental to the old poetry and in a century or
so it was dead, although its traditional forms remained. The Arab turned
his mind toward conquest in the name of Islam. Character changed; the
luxurious life of the courts of the caliphs of Cairo, Baghdad, and Aleppo,
the refining influence of Persia, the classic influence of Greece became
known. Indeed the great poets of later day did not come from Arabia
itself, but from other parts of the Arab empire.

With the advent of Islam and the change in poetical style, a poem
by Yazid called Muzzarid written in the seventh century A.D. is remi-
niscent of the bygone era:

In Praise of His Mare

And I have for use, what time war
stirred up again and again, becomes
pregnant with mischief, and desperate
affairs manifest their beginnings.

* * * *

. . . A mare long of body, short of hair, whose spirit is unfailing,
compactly and firmly built, slender as a staff, that has borne no foal,

A bay, with her back strongly knit: as-Sarih and Jafil, her sires, have lifted
her line to the best of strains.

She is one of those steeds of race that stretch themselves fully in their gallop,
springing and light of foot, pressing on in her eagerness: her longing is
the far-extended desert, plain giving unto plain.

5. Ibid.

"*A mare kept always close to the tent . . .*"

COLLECTION OF PRINCE MOHAMMED ALI, EGYPT

She turns her cheeks briskly to right and left, though her gallop has lasted long, as an adversary vehement in his contention casts his hands this way and that.

Her noble endurance, and her impetuosity in which is no flagging carry her to the front of the dash of the galloping steeds;

And if that which was withheld of the reins is restored to her, she lets herself go at full speed like the darting flight of a sand-grouse which hawks pursue.

A mare kept always close to the tent, never has she been bestridden except for a foray, nor have foals ever tugged at her teats.

When she has been fined down by training, she is like a young gazelle fed on hullab, with her muscles and upper parts firmly knit, and her lower limbs made nimble and light.

And in truth she has ever been to me a precious possession, born and brought up in our tents: of all possessions that which has been born and bred with one's people is the most precious.

And I will keep her as my own so long as there is a presser for the olive, and so long as a man, barefoot or shod, wanders on the face of the earth.

(Trans. by Sir Charles Lyall)

In the post-Islamic period learned Moslems have written numerous books about horses in which they discourse at length about their qualities, colors, maladies, treatments, and so forth. However, the poet was equally well versed in horse lore. An interesting situation arose between an author and a poet, and the Emir Abd el-Kader made special note of its humor as well as the moral behind it. It seems the famous author Abou Obeida, a contemporary of the son of Harun al-Rashid, the noted caliph of Baghdad, composed some fifty volumes about the horse.[6] "This Abou Obeida met with a little misadventure, which shows that it is not the author of the most ponderous and numerous volumes who imparts the soundest information," said the emir, "and that not the worst plan is to consult men themselves."

"How many books has thou written upon the horse?" the vizir of Mamoun, son of Harun al-Rashid, asked a celebrated Arab poet.

"Only one," was the reply.

6. The earliest recorded works on the horse are attributed to Abou Obeida, who was born 106 years after the Hegira, and of El Asmai (Abd el-Malik ibn-Qoreyb), a few years his junior.

The Lion Hunt.

Then turning to Abou Obeida, he asked him the same question.

"Fifty," replied the author.

"Rise then," said the vizir, "go up to that horse and repeat the name of every part of his frame, taking care to point out the position of each."

"I am not a veterinary surgeon," answered Abou Obeida.

"And thou?" said the vizir to the poet.

Upon that [the poet relates], I rose from my seat, and taking the animal by the forelock, I began to name one part after the other, placing my hand upon each to indicate its position, and at the same time recited all the poetic allusions, all the sayings and proverbs of the Arabs referring to it. When I had finished, the vizir said to me: "Take the horse." I took it, and if I ever wished to annoy Abou Obeida, I rode this animal on my way to visit him.

During the ninth century A.D., poems by the celebrated Al Mutannabbi had earned their place and were quoted near and far by the Arab poets as they recited at the pretentious courts of caliphs and kings. This panegyric to Kafur, the black eunuch ruler of Egypt whose court Al Mutannabbi joined for a time, is of note, particularly the last four lines:

And many a day like the night of lovers I have ridden through, watching the sun when it should set,
my eyes fixed on the ears of a bright-blazed horse which was as if a star of the night remained between its eyes,
having a superfluity of skin on its body which came and went over a broad breast;
I cleaved with it in the darkness, drawing close to its reins so that it rebelled, and at times slackening them so it played,
felling with it any wild beast I followed, and dismounting from it and it the same as when I mounted.
Fine steeds, like true friends, are few, even if to the eye of the inexperienced they are many;
if you have seen nothing but the beauty of their markings and limbs, their true beauty is hidden from you.

(Trans. by A. J. Arberry)[7]

7. A. J. Arberry, *Poems of Al Mutannabi* (London, 1967). By permission of Cambridge University Press.

5

DAUGHTERS OF THE WIND

⟨⟨⟨⟨⟨⟨⟨⟨⟨⟨⟨⟨⟨⟨⟨⟨⟨⟨⟨⟨⟨⟨⟨⟨⟨⟨⟨⟨⟨⟨⟨⟨⟨⟨⟨⟨⟩

THE SOURCE of the allure of the Arabian over all other breeds of horse is to be found in the Arab tradition about its spiritual creation, yet little explanation has been forthcoming as to why and how the legend evolved. Whence came these "drinkers of the wind"? From a handful of the south wind! Why not the north, east, or west wind? Why was the color of the horse *kumait*, red mingled with black, and for what reason was it blessed with a white star on its forehead and a white mark on its leg? Why did the angel Gabriel assist in the creation instead of another angel, such as Michael? Let us further attempt to penetrate the mystical haze of pre-Islamic Arabia, Egypt, and the East, bearing in mind that a true science of myth begins with a study of archaeology, history, and comparative religion as well as the political systems then in existence.

Although the Arab horse had been celebrated long before Mohammed's time, as we have seen, it was under the banner of Islam that it reached its peak of glory as "Arab." It was primarily by means of the horse that the Moslem hosts succeeded in thrusting home the sword of Islam upon the unbelievers, and it was indispensable therefore that the steed of the desert should be revered as a sacred animal, a providential instrument of war, created by God for a special purpose and of a nobler essence than that which He created in other beasts. But before Mohammed could inculcate such religious zeal among his previously idolatrous followers, it was necessary that he incorporate into his own thought the wisdom handed down by sages of the ancient East: Noah, Job, Jeremiah, Zachariah, David, and Solomon, among others, and of particular consequence, the wisdom of Amenemope, an ancient Egyptian wise man who provided the fabric upon which most of the prophets wove their patterns.

In studying the following legends, we must remember that the history of religion is but a long attempt to reconcile old custom with new reason, and that the Eastern writer incorporates extracts from his sources verbatim (without credit), only amending them on occasion to conform to his particular viewpoint, or, as in the Old Testament and Koran, in accordance with the religious principle he wishes to inculcate. He then adds such original writing as is necessary to knit the sources together into a relatively coherent narrative.

Biblical researchers have often observed that the book of Job shows familiarity with Egypt; for instance, it describes the Nile, with its canals and strange animals such as the crocodile and the hippopotamus, both sacred to Set, and contains as well an affectionate observation of the desert and its creatures. The chargers of Egyptian pharaohs were favored subjects of the Old Testament prophets, and Job's inspiring and immortal tribute to the Arabian horse is the classic appraisal of the desert steed's character:

> Hast thou given the horse
> strength? hast thou clothed his
> neck with thunder?
> Canst thou make him afraid
> as a grasshopper? the glory of his
> nostrils is terrible.
> He paweth in the valley, and
> rejoiceth in his strength: he goeth
> on to meet the armed men.
> He mocketh at fear, and is
> not affrighted; neither turneth
> he back from the sword.
> The quiver rattleth against
> him, the glittering spear and the
> shield.
> He swalloweth the ground
> with fierceness and rage; neither
> believeth he that it is the sound
> of the trumpet.
> He saith among the trumpets,
> Ha, ha; and he smelleth the

battle afar off, the thunder of the
captains and the shouting.

(Job 39:19–25)

In his vivid description of the Arabia of Mohammed in *Heroes and Hero-Worship*, Thomas Carlyle wrote of the Book of Job: "They had many prophets, these Arabs; teachers each to his tribe, according to the light he had . . . such a noble universality, different from noble patriotism or sectarianism, reigns in it. A noble book; all men's book! . . . the never-ending problem—man's destiny, and God's ways with him here in this earth. And all in such free flowing outlines; grand in its sincerity, in its simplicity; . . . material things no less than spiritual; the horse—'hast thou clothed his neck with thunder?'— he 'laughs at the shaking of the spear!' Such living likenesses were never since drawn. . . . There is nothing written, I think, in the Bible or out of it, of equal literary merit."

From what source more eloquent than Job could Mohammed have frequently borrowed in metaphor and spirit, for the people which he intended to convert were bound to some degree by the teachings of the ancients.

AL ADIYAT
(The Chargers)

In the name of God, Most Gracious, Most Merciful

By the snorting chargers
Running swiftly to the battle
By the strikers of fire
Dashing their hoofs against the stones
By the dawn raiders
Making sudden incursion on the enemy
Blazing a trail of dust
And cleaving forthwith the adverse host
Verily, man is ungrateful
Unto his Lord;
And he bears witness thereof by his deeds;
For violent is he
In his love of wealth

(Sura 100)

The most moving tribute of all, and traditionally some of the earliest words ascribed to the Prophet about the horse, was occasioned by the arrival of several tribes from Yemen who had come to see him and accept his doctrines, and to present to him, in token of their submission, five magnificent mares belonging to the five different races of which Arabia was then said to boast.[1] When Mohammed went forth from his black haircloth tent to receive the noble animals, he caressed them with his hand and expressed his delight in these words: "Blessed be ye, O Daughters of the Wind." Which in the light of his teachings may be interpreted, "Blessed be ye, O partakers of the Spirit." For he often reminded his followers: "Never utter coarse remarks on the subject of the camel or of the wind: the former is a boon to men, the latter an emanation from the soul of Allah." Thus did "daughters of the wind" or "drinkers of the wind" become also a poetic tribute of the Arab to his horse.

The inspiring legend of how the Arab horse was created is also attributed to the Prophet Mohammed, and has been repeated over the centuries by his various disciples and followers. In the *hadithes* (conversations of the Prophet as handed down by tradition) related by Wahb ibn-Munbeh, it is recorded:

I have heard that when God, praise be unto Him, desired to create the horse he summoned forth the South Wind, which the people of Egypt call El Marees[2] saying: "I shall create from thy substance a new being which shall be good fortune unto my followers and humiliation to my enemies. Condense thyself!"

And the wind condensed itself. And the angel Gabriel caught a handful of it and said to God: "Here is the handful of wind."

And God created therefrom an Arab horse of bay [*kumait*] color and addressed him saying: "I have created thee and named thee *faras* [horse]. I have bestowed my blessings upon thee above all other beasts of burden and made thee their master. Success and happiness are bound to thy forelock; bounty reposes on your back and riches are with you wherever you may be. And I have endowed thee to fly without wings; you are for pursuit and for flight. And thou shalt carry men who will glorify me, and thou shalt glorify me with them thereby."

And when the horse neighed, He said to it: "I have blessed thee and will affright the pagans with your neighing and I will fill their ears with it and fill their hearts with great fear from it, and humiliate their necks with the sound of it!"

1. The five, "Al Khamsa," more probably means "related to," as in Banat al-Khams, "daughters of the five" or "related by blood to the five."
2. The searing hot south wind of the desert.

"I have bestowed my blessings upon thee . . . success and happiness are bound to thy forelock." *Ansata Bint Mabrouka, by Nazeer out of Mabrouka.*

PHOTOGRAPH BY SPARAGOWSKI

And God imprinted on the horse's forehead a white star, and on its foot a white marking.

Tradition also relates that a contemporary of the Prophet said:

I have seen the divine Apostle [Mohammed] twist between his fingers the flowing forelock of his horse saying: "In the forelocks of horses are entwined success, rewards and bounty until the last hour of the world." And he went on to say: "On the great day of the final judgment my people will appear with a white star on their foreheads as a sign of their religious prosternations, their feet as marked by the water of their numerous ablutions. These signs will not be seen on any other people in the world."

The angel Gabriel figures prominently in a tale handed down from the time of Ishmael: "And the angel Gabriel said unto Ishmael: 'This noble creature of the dark skin and painted eyes is a gift of the Living God to serve you as a companion in the wilderness and reward you, be-

"My blessed companion and friend of my Creator, thou wilt never fail me."

DRAWING BY HOMER DAVENPORT. COURTESY OF MARGUERITE PIERS

cause you have not defiled yourself with pagan gods, but remained in the faith of your father, Abraham.' " This wild mare which Ishmael received was in foal, and she produced a son from which many celebrated Arabian horses are said to have descended. Ishmael is said to have taken a blue bead, for good fortune (an ancient Arab custom to ward off the evil eye), and attached it to the forelock that fell between her luminous black eyes and over the white star in the center of her forehead, saying: "My blessed companion and friend of my Creator, thou wilt never fail me." Ishmael's understanding of nature and the spiritual spark within all God's creation enabled him to know that this wild creature of the

*"If you hear that a bay horse fell from the highest mountain and was safe, then believe it." *Tuhotmos, by El Sareei out of Moniet El Nefous; a Saklawi Jedran.*

desert was not just a physical being created to serve him, but a rational being as well, capable of love, of spiritual affection and intelligent reasoning like himself.

"The horse's coat must be an index to his character," said the Arabs. "It is beyond all question that the *kumait*, i.e., red mingled with black appearing as a deep chestnut, is preferred by the Arabs to all others." The bay was praised for his vigor, endurance, and strength and it is said in the common proverbs: "If you hear that a bay horse fell from the highest mountain and was safe, then believe it." Moussah, the celebrated Arab warrior who conquered Africa and Spain, reportedly said: "Of all the horses in my armies, the one that has best borne the fatigues and privations of war is the true bay [*al ahmar al assam*]."

It is also related that a companion of the Prophet who was fond of horses asked if there were any in Paradise. "If Allah causes thee to enter Paradise," replied the Prophet, "thou wilt have a horse of rubies, furnished with two wings, with which he will fly whithersoever thou willest." The ancients considered the ruby to be an antidote to poison, to preserve persons from the plague, to banish grief, to repress the ill effects of luxuries, and to divert the mind from evil thoughts. It was the alchemist's term for the elixir, or philosopher's stone:

> He that once has the flower of the sun
> The perfect ruby, which we call elixir,
> Can confer honour, love, respect, long life,
> Give safety, valour, yea, and victory,
> To whom he will.
> *(Ben Jonson:* The Alchemist, *II:i)*

The Eastern and bedouin superstitions about colors stem from the most ancient times. In the Bible the prophets refer to them symbolically, as in Zechariah 6: 1–7 and Revelations 6: 2–8, where we find that the four horses of the Apocalypse correspond to the colors attributed to the moon in its various phases, and to the properties accorded the four seasons:

". . . Behold a white horse: and he that sat on him had a bow; and a crown was given unto him; and he went forth conquering, and to conquer." White was the principal color of the new moon, goddess of birth and growth, representing the spring. White was symbolic of victory and success, and the Arabs said: "This is the mount of kings, because it brings good fortune and luck, and with it you are able to obtain what is necessary." White horses were symbolically sacrificed throughout history and have long been ceremonial favorites.

"Behold a white horse. . . . this is the mount of kings. . . ."
*Sakr, by Sultan out of Enayet; a Kuhaylan Rodan.

PHOTOGRAPH BY SPARAGOWSKI

"And there went out another horse that was red; and the power was given to him that sat thereon to take peace from the earth, and that they should kill one another; and there was given unto him a great sword." The red horses are said to be symbolic of war and bloodshed. As the Prophet said: "If thou hast a dark chestnut, conduct him to the combat, and if thou hast only a sorry chestnut, conduct him all the same to combat." Likewise did he believe that: "The good fortune of horses is in their chestnut coloring, and the best [swiftest?] of all horses is the chestnut horse." And the common proverbs remark that if it is said to you that "an *ashqar* [chestnut] horse was seen flying, then believe so." Red was the color attributed to the full moon, goddess of love and battle. Symbolically it represented summer.

"And I beheld, and lo a black horse: and he that sat on him had a pair of balances in his hand." Black was the color of the old moon, the goddess of death and divination. It represented harvest and fall, and was symbolic of deep calamity and distress, judgment and resurrection, as well as eternal life. And it was related by Abu Habib that the Prophet said: "Good fortune is in *al adham al akhrah* [the pure clear black], with three leg markings and the right fore free; and he is the most precious of the blacks."

"If thou hast a dark chestnut, conduct him to the combat. . . ."
Alaa El Din, by Nazeer out of Kateefa; a Kuhaylan Rodan.

"And I looked and behold a pale horse: and his name that sat on him was Death, and Hell followed with him. And power was given unto them over the fourth part of the earth, to kill with sword, and with hunger, and with death, and with the beasts of the earth." The pale horse (lit. "green") was a symbol of the terror of death and typified winter and barrenness. Some interpreters render the translation "piebald grey," emblematic of a dispensation mixed in characters. Of this color the Arabs said: "Fly from him like the plague, he is the brother of the cow." "Never purchase a bald-faced horse with four white feet, for he carries his shroud with him." Legendary traditions and experience agree in according a decided superiority to coats of a deep and decided hue; coats of a washy or pale color have never been esteemed, and they judged long and broad white markings on the head, body, and legs to indicate a degeneration of the species and be signs of unsoundness.

It is obvious that the ancient Arabs had discovered certain scientific and Mendelian truths in their rigid selection and testing under nature's watchful eye, for in the early days vigor and stamina were necessary simply for survival. The subject of coat colors interested Sheik Fatouh el-Badjirmi so much that he wrote a treatise on descriptions of praised horses, etc., dedicating it to Abbas Pasha "as a service to His Highness, his grace, the glorious leader and magnificent ruler" of Egypt from 1848–1854. Modern hippologists have named about sixty different coats, while Badjirmi fell short of this mark by only eight. These are not true basic coats, but rather individual peculiarities attributed to each of the basic coats. A century and a decade later, Federico Tesio made a study of color inheritance as related in his book *Breeding Thoroughbred Horses*, and it is of particular relevance here.[3] He concluded that there are three basic coats. "The bay coat consists of various shades of reddish brown hair, the legs, mane and tail being black. With an increase in the number of black hairs, the bay becomes darker and darker until he appears black. So far as the Mendelian laws are concerned, the black horse comes under the same heading as the bay." The Prophet placed them in similar order; bay was preferred most, then black. Badjirmi's treatise divides the bay color (*el kumait el ahmar*) into ten sections or subtypes, i.e., pure bay with different shades of gold, rust, and black. Black (*al adham*) has five subtypes, while chestnut (*al ashqar*) has seven.

Tesio continues:

The chestnut coat consists of yellowish brown hair, with legs, mane and tail of the same colour. It too, although basically a variation of yellow, appears in various shades which go from golden to a dark chestnut.

The hair of these two basic coats always grows from a skin which is almost black. Both coats may, in certain cases in which the pigmentation is affected, turn to grey.

But there is also in nature a horse with an entirely white coat. This horse is born white and his skin is pink instead of black.

Tesio notes that "in Arabia the pink-skinned white horse certainly existed."

3. Federico Tesio, "Breeding the Race-Horse" (London, 1958), pp. 18, 19, 26–29, 39, 43–45.

He goes on to state that: "Judging by the physical characteristics of horses as they are today, we must conclude that the original pure breeds of wild horses could be identified not only by the three basic coats, but also by differences in the muscular and bone structures, and particularly by different degrees of nervous energy." Statistics prove that on the whole bay dominates over chestnut. Tesio wondered why, and concluded that the color of the coat is determined by the hair itself, rather than the skin. Colors are determined by different pigments which are products of chemical combinations, and it therefore follows that the color of the hair originates from chemical combinations. Scientific experiments have proved that the chemical composition of hairs varies according to their color so that the following is to be considered:

That each colour strikes the eye with a different wave-length.
That the bay coat belongs to the family of red colours.
That the chestnut coat belongs to the family of yellow colours.
That the wave-length of the colour red is greater than the wave-length of the colour yellow.
That the wave-length of the bay is therefore greater than the wave-length of the chestnut.

"It therefore seems plausible," Tesio continues, "that the greater wave-length is the element responsible for the dominant character of the bay over the recessive character of the chestnut, for in nature the small gives way to the large." Were the alchemists of Egypt and Arabia not aware of this?

Considering the Arab traditions and leaving room for further scientific revelations, it is quite possible that there is or was a relation of bay to stamina, chestnut to speed in ancient times. But it is also likely that there were more bays than any other color.

As to the color grey, Tesio remarks that "grey is not itself a coat, but a pathological discoloration of the only two basic coats which are the bay and the chestnut." Grey horses lose the pigment in their coats at an early age, either partially or completely. As we know, all grey foals are born either bay or chestnut (with the occasional rare exception); thus grey are of two distinct varieties, having white hairs on a bay background, or white hairs on a chestnut background. According to Badjirmi, the Arabs divided the grey, *al ashab*, into seven subtypes. The most favored was *al ashab al marshoush*, "and he resembles the bird and is the strongest and tallest, and he is called *al thobabi* [fleabitten, also *debbani*]." He also mentions in this section about *al ashab al qortasi:* "He is the one whose white is so intense so it is not mixed with any other colour. And he resembles the white of *al ghora* [the star on a horse's forehead], because it is the most intense and clearest white. And his skin is white [pale pink]. And he may have blue eyes or one blue eye. And if his eyes are black he is called *ashab akhal*. Other divisions of grey are *al asfar*, having seven sections, and *al akhdar*, having five: a total of 19 for grey. All these greys have dark skin, except the one mentioned above, who apparently belongs to the true white coat."

The "fleabitten" color. Maisa (by Shahoul out of Zareefa), a Dahmah Shahwaniyah.

Tesio's comments are relevant here: "By crossing the original bay and chestnut breeds, primitive man created hybrids which to this day have strictly conformed to the law of Mendel. Now, however, observing the white markings, we find that a third character has to be considered: the white hair on the pink skin." As he points out, here "we are not dealing with a colour, but with a lack of colour, that is to say with a lack of pigment which, through chemical changes would result in a colour. Therefore dominance cannot take place, because what does not exist cannot either dominate or be dominated. One variety of pigment may dominate another variety of pigment, but it cannot dominate a lack of pigment." It is found in crossing bays or chestnuts with the true whites that the color of the bay or chestnut parent was partially but not completely dominant. "Therefore in a hybrid mating between two animals of pure breed, one rich in skin pigment and the other totally lacking, the offspring will be born with half of his skin surface occupied by pigment and the other half without pigment, and in the confusion typical of hybridism he will appear irregularly patched." The spotted horses are divided by Al Badjirmi into *al ablaq*, ten subtypes, and *al abrash*, three subtypes—thirteen in all.

The sisters Ansata Nile Queen and Ansata Nile Mist, by Ansata Ibn Sudan out of Falima.

White markings have been cropping up in the Arabian breed from ancient times to the present day and are the subject of much discussion among Arabian breeders, yet little has been written about this in Arabian books of reference and various aspersions as to the purity of horses having high white have been frequently hurled by those who do not like these markings. However, we must not forget that purity should not be confused with selection. As Tesio mentions: "We can only say with certainty that horses with large white markings are less energetic than others, and more susceptible to afflictions of the skin on their white legs. This would explain why they have been less in demand and have been given a poor press." White markings occurring in wild animals that are not hybrids are symmetrical, that is, similar on both sides of the body of each individual of the same breed, as with penguins or zebras and so forth. Horses do not have symmetrical markings and the "disorder" is contrary to nature, a consequence of hybridism.

"Now it is generally recognized among horsemen that piebalds are usually of a lymphatic disposition and less energetic than other horses. . . . This lack of energy must have been apparent to our primitive ancestor who was the first to experiment with cross-breeding. . . . Having eliminated by selective breeding the horses with large patches of white because they were not sufficiently energetic, he observed that certain individuals with white only on their legs and on their faces were animals of considerable power and could be used as stallions for the improvement of the breeds."

Almost as pervasive as the symbolism of color is the tradition of a connection of horses with the sea or sacred wells. The well in the desert with its cleansing, healing and life-giving water became an object of worship: the well of Zamzam, according to Arabian authors, was pre-Islamic and derived its holiness from the time it supplied water to Hagar and Ishmael. Horses were sacred to the moon, which controlled the tides, their hooves making a moon-shaped mark and the moon being regarded as the source of all water: hence the association of the winged Greek Arabian, Pegasus, with springs of water, and the notion of horses as sacred to Poseidon, god of the sea. On Helicon rose the spring named Hippocrene, "the horse well," which was horseshoe-shaped. According to legend, it had been struck by the hoof of Pegasus, whose name means "of the springs of water." Poets were said to drink from the Hippocrene for inspiration. Again, it is relevant that the age of poetry, for which the Arabs were noted, began in the matriarchal age and derives its magic from the moon, not from the sun. The ancient Semites, as Robertson Smith was the first to point out, were originally matrilineal people, whose matriarchate endured in Israel down into the historical period and among the Arabs till the advent of Mohammed. The Moslem calendar is also a lunar one, and even the ancient Egyptians reckoned learning and wisdom to the lunar deity, Thoth. He was god of the divine word, the great scribbler, patron of magicians, incarnate as the ibis, the sacred phoenix of

Arabia and the peoples of the East.

Constantly did the Prophet admonish his followers to honor and cherish the ancient traditions handed down from the wise men of the East: "Keep horses as they are the will of your father, Ishmael: they were [wild] beasts and he besought God who bestowed him this gift." Mohammed thoroughly understood the mentality of the bedouins, knowing that in the days of paganism they loved the horse through motives of selfish interest, that is, what it could do for them in terms of gain. He was patient and clever with the incentives he used to accomplish their conversion and wisely set a standard that two spears should be given to every warrior who captured as plunder the noble horse, that is, the Arabian horse, as he called the true breed, while only one spear was given to the captor of a lesser animal.

In order to allay their superstitious fears of the evil spirits and *jinn*, which had plagued the bedouin mind from time immemorial, Mohammed assured them they had no further cause to worry if they kept Arabian horses. Sheik Fatouh el-Badjirmi relates from tradition that the Prophet said: "The especially noble and steadfast Arab horse is most precious because the Jinn do not enter a house in which there is one of them. So if many or one are tied in a house, the Jinn will be ejected from it."

Mohammed further admonished his followers: "Whoso keeps a horse for the holy war in the way of the Most High, increases the number of his good works. The hunger and thirst of such a steed, the water he drinks, the food he eats, every one of his hairs, each step he takes, and every function of nature, shall all weigh in the balance at the day of the last judgment." And he reminded them: "The horse prays thrice a day. In the morning he says: 'O Allah! Make me beloved of my master.' At noon: 'Do well by my master, that he may do well by me!' In the evening: 'Grant that he may enter into paradise upon my back!'" Should man not say his daily prayers if his noble beast does as much!

Gradually, by constant repetition and speaking of it in terms of the highest praise, the instinctive love of the Arab for his horse was transfigured into a religious duty. On the eve of the Moslem invasions the Arabs had improved their horses and made them superior to anything in the world. The teachings of the Prophet that "Every man shall love his horse" had borne fruit: a new era was about to dawn in the East.

6

THE AGE OF SPLENDOR

AFTER THE DEATH of Mohammed in A.D. 632, the eruption of Islam shook the whole civilized world and every able bedouin warrior followed Amr ibn el-As forward to the conquest. Volunteers thronged to the fighting fronts, where the faith was being spread by the sword among the heathen. These warriors were nicknamed El Murabatin, which meant "pickets," from the *ribat* (literally, "horselines") in which they lived. Mounted on their noble Arab coursers, and armed with lances, swords, and bows, but above all their new Islamic creed, the Arab warriors seemingly became invincible. Indeed Amr's anxiety to take Egypt was so great that he set off with only four thousand horsemen, eventually to be reinforced by another twelve thousand under the leadership of El Zubeir ibn-el-Awwam. Egypt went down like a pack of cards before them, and Amr founded his capital at Fustat, "the tent," just outside the modern city of Cairo. Unhappy at this turn of events, the Romans dispatched a fleet to Alexandria in A.D. 645 in an attempt to defeat him, but despite the fact that the imperial archers shot Amr's horse out from under him, the Moslems were victorious.

For the next two centuries Egypt was but one of the provinces of the Moslem caliphate which ruled the land of the Nile through the successive caliphs of Medina, Damascus, and Baghdad, among them the famed Caliph Harun al-Rashid and his son, Maamun, under whom a great period of Arab civilization flourished. Turkish influence at that time was also being felt in the Arab world. Various elements of a Turkish realm, which had been disintegrating over a period of some centuries, had found a new home in the Middle East. Most of them arrived as mercenaries or as slave holders, but some also appeared as conquerors, such as Ahmed ibn-Tulun, founder of the Tulunid Dynasty of Egypt. The son of a Turkish slave, Ibn-Tulun was a trained and professional soldier who had been dispatched from Baghdad as governor of Egypt in September A.D. 868. Ibn-Tulun epitomized the mounted warrior ruling class. An intelligent and cultivated man, he had been a student of Moslem theology at the University of Tarsus in Anatolia and was well

The Stallion of Abd El Kader.

PAINTING BY ALFRED DEDREUX, COURTESY OF SCHWEITZER GALLERY

versed in the traditions of Islam. A discovery of treasure, perhaps from ancient Egyptian tombs, provided him with means to become an independent ruler, and he was regarded as a rebel against the caliph of Baghdad.

Mameluke weapons.

This takeover of Egyptian sovereignty by Turks of Central Asian origin, who now embraced the faith, kept the Arab horse occupied at many and varied eastern battle fronts. Ibn-Tulun held kingly sway over Egypt, and wherever he went, his retinue was sure to follow. His personal escort, mounted on Arab steeds, was comprised of a hundred powerful young slaves, "beautiful to behold dressed in their elaborate finery," Persian cloaks, and brandishing silver-mounted whips. In A.D. 870 Ibn-Tulun ordered construction of a magnificent palace on the site of Yeshkur between Fustat and the Mukkatam hills. Adjoining the palatial residence was a huge garden and a spacious enclosed *meydan*,[1] or hippodrome, where his horses were exercised daily. Bedouin steeds provided one of his greatest pleasures, and when he died in May A.D. 884 at the age of fifty, he left behind more than seven thousand mounted Mamelukes and a stud of three hundred horses.[2] The word *mameluke*

1. *Meydan* means a square, in this case a hippodrome.
2. Stanley Lane-Poole, *History of Egypt in the Middle Ages* (London, 1968), vol. 2, p. 59.

(past participle of the verb *malak*, to possess) means "slave" and is from the same root as *malik*, an owner or king. Mamelukes were the white slaves of Russian, Greek, Armenian, or Turkish origin who served as the personal army of bodyguards to caliphs and sultans. Slavery in Islamic society was such that the relation of personal slaves to their master approached kinship rather than servility. The mamelukes were known by their master's title, received the same education as his sons, and frequently the foremost mameluke succeeded his master as head of the family, rather than his master's own son. Although faithfully attached to their masters, as a body they occupied such a powerful position that they often forced the sultan to bend to their will.

After the fall of the Tulunids (868–905), Egypt remained in an unsettled state until the advent of the fourth caliph, Al Moizz, who sent his mameluke general, Jawahar, to invade Egypt in 969. As conqueror of Egypt he brought about a new phase of progress under the Fatimids, founding Al Kahira, "the victorious" city known today as Cairo and laying the foundation of the Al Azhar mosque. When Al Moizz triumphantly entered his new palace city, he received splendid gifts from near and far to celebrate the occasion, including Jawahar's present of five hundred horses with saddles and bridles encrusted with gold, amber, and precious stones. Of the size and splendor of his great palace the Arab historians still speak with bated breath, and there is no doubt that under the Fatimids great artistic activity prevailed. Their rule subsisted for two centuries, but the caliphs became absorbed in their own pleasures and the empire soon shrank in territorial size.[3]

The Ayyubid Dynasty (1193–1250) which was to follow was also Turkish in origin. The most illustrious sultan of its era was Salah el-Din Yusuf ibn-Ayyub, known as Saladin, the son of a Kurdish chief, Ayyub, from whence the dynasty took its name. Saladin's rule, though brief, is considered by many to have been the most glorious in the history of Moslem domination in Egypt, and one in which the Arabian horse played a historic role during the Crusades. Saladin had caused many improvements to be made in Cairo, and following the custom of having a Saracen castle built to dominate the town, he created the great Citadel against the Mukattam Hills overlooking all the city. Of his twenty-four-year reign he passed only eight years in Cairo, spending the rest in Syria,

3. Ibid., p. 108.

The mamelukes were born archers and riders.

ENGRAVING BY V. ADAM

Mesopotamia, and Palestine, where he prevented the crusaders under Richard I, "the lion heart," from capturing Jerusalem; he also kept them out of Egypt. His valor and high principles were immortalized in Sir Walter Scott's *The Talisman*, which, although a work of fiction, is based on historical evidence and was written through understanding of the Saracens, who were civilized by general comparison to the barbaric northern interlopers. Scott stresses the superior attributes of the desert steeds over the war horses of the Frankish knights, and his sensitive description of the Arab mounts used by Saladin and his Saracens remains a living tribute to the horses of that era:

They spurned the sand from behind them—they seemed to devour the desert before them—miles flew away with minutes, yet their strength seemed unabated, and their respiration as free as when they first started upon the wonderful race. The motion, too, as easy as it was swift, seemed more like flying through the air than riding on the earth, and was attended with no unpleasant sensation, save the awe naturally felt by one who is moving at such astonishing speed, and the difficulty of breathing occasioned by their passing through the air so rapidly. . . .

These horses . . . are of the breed called the Winged, equal in speed to aught excepting the Borak of the prophet. They are fed on the golden barley of Yemen, mixed with spices, and with a small portion of dried sheep's flesh. Kings have given provinces to possess them, and their age is active as their youth. . . . Time lays his touch so lightly on these generous steeds, that the mare on which thou sittest has seen five times five years pass over her, yet retains her pristine speed and vigour, only that in the career the support of a bridle, managed by a hand more experienced than thine, hath now become necessary. May the prophet be blessed, who hath bestowed on the true believers the means of advance and retreat, which causeth their iron-clothed enemies to be worn out with their own ponderous weight! How the horses of yonder dog Templars must have snorted and blown, when they had toiled fetlock-deep in the desert for one-twentieth part of the space which these brave steeds have left behind them, without one thick pant, or a drop of moisture upon their sleek and velvet coats!

With the passing of Saladin, Cairo still remained the seat of the Arab caliphate, the center of the Islamic empire. A change in political direction came about, however, when the caliph's praetorian guard instituted a palace revolution in 1250, deposing the last of the Ayyubid caliphs, Tur-in-Shah, and taking power itself. This corps of mameluke guards was comprised of Kuman Turks, natives of the Qipchaq territory of the

Caucasus, who had been taken prisoner by the Mongols and later sold to the Sultan El-Malik el-Saleh. He had specifically selected the Kumans because they were born archers and riders, and absolutely fearless, ruthless warriors. To house these bodyguards and personal army, he built a large fort on the island of Roda, in the Nile, where they also received vigorous training. These troops got the name "Bahri" from their river barracks, the word *bahr* meaning a sea or river.

The most famous and enterprising of all the Bahri sultans was Baybars (El-Malik el-Zahir Rukn el-Din), reigning from 1250 to 1277. One of the greatest soldiers in history, he is credited as the real founder of the Mameluke empire. Born in 1228, he was sold into slavery at the age of fourteen, but because of a cataract in one of his eyes, he was at first rejected by slave buyers. This humiliation heightened his determination to succeed, despite his "defect," and eventually his leadership ability, superb horsemanship, and brilliance in archery came to be noticed by the caliph, El-Malik, who drafted him into his Bahri regiment. Within a year he was promoted to the rank of colonel, a great honor for a young man of twenty, and when he eventually succeeded in capturing the sultan's throne, he remained a man of action throughout his rule. More at home in a tent than the palace, he spent much of his life in the saddle and in the battlefield, and when possible he devoted two days a week to archery and polo, his favorite sports.

One of Baybars's chroniclers recorded that people were in agreement during his time that nobody was a better or more skillful horseman than Baybars, and nobody was more expert in conducting wars. Thus when he went forth among his subjects, it was in keeping that he should present a regal and awe-inspiring spectacle. Riding in the center of his mounted escort, he managed with ease the spirited white stallion beneath him. Garbed in the traditional sultanic black silk garments and silk turban gilded and woven with gold, Baybars was hailed "like the full moon rising on a dark night." A gleaming and expensive bedawi sword hung by his side, while other weapons were carried behind him. In front a great lord bore the royal saddle cloth, emblem of sovereignty, encrusted with gold and precious stones which glinted and sparkled in the sunlight. The housing of the royal stallion's neck was yellow silk embroidered with gold, contrasting with a cloth of red atlas satin which covered the crupper. Aloft before him fluttered the royal standard, woven of the finest silk and gold thread, while the troops marched smartly in their regimental colors of heavily embroidered yellow Cairene silk. Just ahead of the sultan a pair of richly caparisoned white horses bore two pages, their robes of yellow silk bordered in gold brocade with

Mameluke stallion saddled and bridled with golden trappings.
ENGRAVING BY V. ADAM

a matching headdress, known as a *khufiyah*. It was their duty to see that the road was sound and clear. These horses were identical to those the sultan rode and appeared to be harnessed and prepared for him perhaps in case of emergency. Music was provided by a musician on horseback playing the flute, but the tone was somber and grave in keeping with the austerity and auspiciousness of the occasion. Following the sultan were the led horses,[4] as usual. They provided a retinue of luxury and

4. The led horses were the most prized of all, being used as personal mounts of the sultan, caliphs, and emirs, and as royal relay horses.

on a voyage or journey were always ready to serve as relays. Behind
the sultan came the high officials of state and the ax bearers, a troup of
Kurdish guards who presented a formidable protectorate for their royal
master.

Such were the surroundings of the Arabian horses of Baybars, who
often trod on Oriental silks and satins which had been laid in the road
to provide a luxurious pathway for their sultanic master. So spectacular
in splendor were some of the celebrations that the chroniclers found it
"impossible to describe."

In order to maintain his empire, both efficiency in government and
vast sums of money were necessary to obtain, for the royal household's
expenditures were high. The horses belonging to Baybars and his mamelukes alone consumed 120,000 ardabs[5] of grain in a year and the expenditure for boats, including transport vessels used especially for horses
amounted to 100,000 dinars per annum. No sum was too great to lavish
on the steeds of Islam's warriors, however, and when conversion to the
faith by Mongols, Franks, and Nubians reached a peak, Baybars was
known on one such occasion to give away as many as "one hundred and
eighty horses in one hour" as gifts to the converts for the holy cause.
Baybars's chronicler, Al-Qadi, mentions in the year A.H. 662 that the
fodder (lucerne, hay) eaten by the royal horses and camels of the stables
was valued, and found to amount to fifty thousand dinars.[6] As if to jus-
tify the expense, he exclaims:

I say: "God has urged us to have many horses and indicated in his Sacred
Book that their number should be increased. God the Exalted has said:
"Against them make ready your strength to the utmost of your power, including steeds of war."[7] The Prophet (may God bless him and grant him
peace) said: "Good things will be attained by means of horses till the Day
of Judgment." For three [types of] men who keep a horse, it is a reward for
the first, a shelter for the second, and a burden for the third. As regards the
person for whom it is a reward, he keeps it for the cause of God; then whatever it eats means a reward for him; if he has grazed it in the field, then
everything it has eaten means a reward for him; if it ascends to one or two

5. One ardab equals from 5 to 8 bushels, depending on the region of the country (Cairo,
5; Rosetta, 8).
6. Al-Qadi Muhi al-Din (b. Abd al-Zahir), who wrote "Sira al-Malik al-Zahir," translated by Dr. Syedah-Fatima Sadeque, London, 1956. Quoted by permission of Dr.
Sadeque.
7. "Sura Al Anfal," verse 60.

high places, then every step will bring a reward for him; if he has passed by a river and has watered it from there, then for every drop it drank, there will be a reward; so much so that a reward will be counted for him even in its dung and urine. As regards the man for whom it is a shelter, he keeps it for self-restraint, generosity and adornment, and he does not forget the rights of its back and stomach during poverty and prosperity. As regards the man for whom it is a burden, he uses it for pride and vanity, and hypocrisy before the people, and to show superiority over them. Everyone knows that this sultan only keeps it for the cause of God, for fighters in the Holy War to ride on. So he has many rewards which God has stored for him as the greatest treasure.

A born horseman, Baybars was naturally a connoisseur of his Arab steeds, and their supremely high quality is affirmed by a passage referring to his review of the army:

One day during the first decade of the month of Dhul Qada the sultan sat at sunrise on the platform placed beside the House of Justice, . . . the army filled the whole place, so that the eye saw nothing but shining helmet, great illumination, neighing horses, advancing troops, riding parties and armies overtaking armies. Each Emir came forward at the head of his group dressed in his breastplate of war. They drew the led-horses, which were like wind charging and mountains in appearance, having upon them war equipment which reassured the hearts of the riders by its strength.

The sultan came down while his led-horses were drawn before him, at the beauty of which eyes were dazzled, as also at the beauty of the crescents, metal plates and banners upon them.

Al-Qadi further relates that an associate had told him about a year before this time that the banners of yellow satin which had been used in (mounting) the metal plates amounted to a value of ten thousand dinars, and afterwards how many were made was beyond calculation.

The sultan made his way to the field of the festival, preceded by his led-horses, regarding which it had never been heard that any king gathered together horses like these and paid such high prices as these. He had sent to the ruler of Medina (best of blessings and peace be upon its inhabitants) asking for one of these horses. The son of the ruler of Medina came with a number of horses, among which was that horse. He said that he had been sent to Najd, where he came to an understanding with its owners and gave them some camels, slave girls, and cloth, in order to obtain it from them. The sultan bestowed on the ruler of Medina two thousand dinars, in addition to robes of honour, and special attention, and gave his son a large sum, most of these horses being obtained in this manner. And they were as had been said:

These horses bearing men in armour, are like winds that blow, carrying abundance of water with the clouds.
With their lances they are so familiar [a sight], that if the lances are taken away from their ears we cannot recognize them.
These horses are under the control of a man of great determination, who retains them in Egypt under the auspices of God and good fortune.

Baybars greatly enjoyed "the sport of kings" and it is related that during one of his outings: "He alighted at Tarujah, and ordered the Bedouin there to compete at horse racing. Two thousand bedouin horsemen gathered, and they were joined by some of the horsemen from the army. The course was from the towerpost to the hill near Tarujah. The sultan stood on the hill and had stakes fixed in the ground surmounted by a piece of satin and striped silk, which contained the sum intended for the prizes. Within an hour the horses suddenly approached as if they were eagles. Then each rider seized the wager of the race, but the sultan showed no desire to have any of the horses."

Having built an efficient government and successfully fired his people with religious zeal, Baybars also became a patron of learning and architecture, and had many mosques, foundations, hospitals, and schools to his credit. In order to keep in contact with his vast domains, he utilized his royal relay horses in such a manner that news came from Damascus to Cairo in four days and returned equally as fast. News from the provinces reached him twice a week and without leaving the Citadel he was able to make necessary far-ranging decisions. Few documentations of "pony express" can match that handed down by the mamelukes.

Because of his daring exploits on the battlefield, and perhaps because of the story behind his rise to power, tales which grew up around Baybars's name after his death lingered in the memory of the people of Egypt so that in some ways he has made an even deeper impression on them than the famed Saladin.

The House of Kalaoun (Kala'un, Qalaoun, etc.) followed, reigning from 1279 to 1382. El-Malik el-Mansour Kalaoun founded a princely house which lasted a hundred years and was patterned along the lines Baybars had established. However, he had a predilection for the Barcean horses, which the Greeks bred in Cyrenaica, Libya, and bought them in preference to Arabian horses. Unlike his horse-minded son, El Nacer, he did not pay extravagant sums and never acquired a horse for a price exceeding five thousand drachmas. It was his opinion that "the Barcean horse is the horse of utility; the Arabian horse is for parades."

When El Nacer Mohammed ibn-Kalaoun succeeded to the throne, he did not share his father's enthusiasm for the Barcean horses and when he acquired any they were reserved to be offered as gifts to foreign emirs and notables. El Nacer was enamored of the horses of the Arabs, and consequently created one of the most remarkable Arabian stud farms that ever existed in the Orient. He became an expert on the desert steeds he so avidly collected, knowing their genealogies as well as understanding the physical and mental qualities of the breed. He had a phenomenal memory when it came to his favorite subject, and recalled the names of all the persons who had provided him with horses, as well as the prices he paid.

Magnificent studfarms were erected at his command and he established equestrian exercises and horse races which he encouraged by his own personal largesse, often taking part in the competitions himself. The rival Meydan el-Zahiri, a magnificent hippodrome which Baybars had constructed near Bab el-Louk, was demolished in 1314 and turned into a tremendous garden and orchard. In the same year construction of El Nacer's hippodrome was begun in the former garden of El Kashab, situated between old Cairo and the later city. When the building of his fabulous new hippodrome, the Meydan el-Naceri, was completed in 1318, the Sultan joyfully prepared to attend the opening ceremony with all the pomp and circumstance befitting such a momentous occasion, and one so dear to his heart. His elaborate entourage bedazzled the onlookers. After the sultan had ceremoniously officiated at the events, he presented the most select Arabian horses as gifts to his emirs as a ceremonial gesture and token of his esteem. El Nacer took pleasure in honoring those emirs who protected him, and twice a year at designated periods he distributed gifts to them. When he visited the place where his horses were pastured at the close of the green pasture season, it was his custom to give to his centurion emirs—the chiefs of a hundred mamelukes—horses completely saddled and bridled and covered with golden horsecloths. To the emirs of the Tabl-Khanah he gave horses unadorned. The second distribution took place at a special celebration when he attended the carousels at his hippodrome and played *jeu de paume*, an ancient sport similar to tennis on horseback. Then he gave to his emirs horses already bridled and wearing horsecloths adorned with silver. Thus by the close of the year his favorite and most intimate courtiers often received as presents as many as a hundred superb mounts.

El Nacer's passion for only the choicest Arabian steeds became known quickly to all the Arabs, as well as the fact that he was willing to pay enormous sums for them. The majority of his horses were soon being provided by the tribe of the Beni Mouhanna Arabs, the Beni Fadl, Al Murrah, and others, all Syrian tribes who traversed the vast lands of modern Syria, Iraq, and Palestine, regions inhabited or migrated through in recent times by the once numerous Anazeh Arabs.

From early times the Beni Mouhanna ruled over the tribes of the Syrian bedouins. The Beni Mouhanna and the Beni Fadl were of the same family, the same Tayiid origins, and consequently came from Nejd. Some centuries ago all these tribes had emigrated to Syria. Mouhanna, who gave his name to the tribe, was the son of Fadl, who was the father of the Beni Fadl tribe. The two tribes were thus brethren.

And from Bahreyn, Koteif, Hedjaz, and Iraq the *crème de la crème* of Arab horses were brought to him. For the least celebrated horses he gave sums from ten to thirty thousand drachmas (equal to 1500 dinars of gold), not counting the gifts of costly clothing, sugar, and other items for the seller and his wives. Such was his consuming desire to own the finest of bedouin horses, however, that many times he had Kerim el-Din, the purser of his private estates, pay out one million drachmas for horses in one day alone. He bought Mouhanna horses for the price of sixty to seventy thousand drachmas a head; for broodmares he gave eighty to ninety thousand drachmas each, and for the daughter of El Karta, a celebrated mare, he paid the sum of one hundred thousand drachmas which he paid with five thousand mitkals[8] of gold, adding a property of land in Syria as a special consideration to the seller. Consequently, the Mouhanna Arabs and other celebrated tribes searched zealously to obtain only the purest horses of the race, for which they too had to pay considerable sums, but knowing, of course, they would be more than adequately recompensed. There was no Arab tribe which did not send to

8. One mitkal or dinar was 24 carats or 96 grains of gold. One drachma was 16 carats or 64 grains of gold.

this sultan *"min keraim khoyoul-hom"* (Arabic, "of the most elect of their horses").

El Nacer did not leave his courtiers to administer the stables for him, as some rulers were wont to do. He took genuine interest in the studs and followed with care the horses of greatest value and those closest to his heart. When some accident or disease befell them, or when one animal began to age noticeably, he would have it placed in special stables to recover, or to finish out its days. Mares were serviced in his presence by the stallions of whose nobility he was perfectly sure. In a herdbook or stable register the servicing days were noted as well as the names of the stallion and the mare and pertinent information. Thus a large number of foals were produced and there was no need to import many horses from foreign countries. The stables of the sultan soon contained more than three thousand of the choicest Arabians. It was El Nacer's personal pleasure to make the annual inspection himself and have the foals of the year marked in his presence. He entrusted the young horses that were to be trained only to the most skillful horsemen and was most emphatic in his orders to his emirs about the training of each individual horse.

When it came time to prepare for the celebrated annual horse race, the grand master of the horses began training the sultan's horses well in advance of those belonging to the competing emirs, although this was a well-kept secret. The rumor was then spread about the land that the grand master had not, in fact, preceded the others in the training preparations, and all precautions were duly taken and executed so that the sultan's horses would have the complete advantage and that an emir's horse would not beat one of the royal steeds in the race. El Nacer did not know how to resign himself to defeat; he was a man to whom the slightest incident which appeared to affect, however slightly, his position as king was intolerable. Nor did the emir's or the sultan's retinue desire to incur the sultanic wrath.

Each year the great race was held in the Hippodrome of Kabak. The sultan was in attendance, and the emirs likewise presented themselves with their beautifully readied coursers. More than a hundred and fifty horses were usually engaged in the arena, the races succeeding one another with the sultan remaining on horseback until they were over. One of the most famous horses of the time was a dark bay stallion which, for three years in a row, had beaten all the finest racehorses in Egypt.

One year, however, the Emir Mouhanna, who held no fear of the sultan, sent one of his most notable horses to compete, a white stallion of great stamina and speed. Confident his horse would win, the emir announced: "If this horse defeats all the race horses of Egypt, he belongs to the Sultan; but if he is beaten, let him be sent back to me. However, for the race in the arena, no one will ride him but the bedouin who leads him."

When El Nacer arrived at the hippodrome in ceremonial splendour attended by his emirs, he was accompanied by Moussa and Suleyman, both sons of Mouhanna. The great race was announced and the signal was given for the horses to be led to the starting post at Birket el-Uadjdj, as was the custom. Among them pranced Mouhanna's horse whose bedouin jockey sat lightly astride him, bareback. And then the race was on! Mouhanna's celebrated white stallion sprang to the front, showing the pack his heels from the outset and leading the race from start to finish, an easy winner. The bedouin then pulled up his sweating steed into an easy canter and gleefully passed in front of the sultan, crying, "To you goes the palm today, O Mouhanna, it is full of success." This annoyed El Nacer, despite the fact that he was recipient of the horse as a gift, and from that time on he stopped racing preparations, although the emirs kept and continued the practice. In 1341 at the age of 58 El Nacer died, leaving some 7800 horses in his stables and over 5000 racing camels.

Horse races were abandoned after his demise, only to be resumed under the reign of Sultan Barquq, who, like Baybars, took the name of El Malik el-Zaher, meaning "the triumphant." He was the first prince of the Circassian or Burjite mameluke sultans in Egypt, seizing it in A.D. 1382 and becoming the twenty-fifth Turkish monarch to rule Egypt. Like his predecessors he too became an avid horse breeder and enthusiast and devoted considerable time to the equestrian arts, though he never apparently approached El Nacer's fanaticism toward the breed itself.

One of Barquq's great pleasures was hosting splendid fetes in the racecourse below the Citadel. On one occasion when he defeated the Grand Emir Aitamish al-Bajasi at a game of polo, the emir as loser was obliged to pay for the festivities at a cost of some 200,000 dirhams of silver. However, the sultan grandly took it upon himself to pay the costs of the celebration; tents were erected on the racecourse and a sumptuous feast provided in which were consumed 20,000 pounds of meat, 200 pairs of geese, 1000 chickens, 20 horses, 30 hundredweight of sugar, etc. This is a rare instance where the chronicles mention that horses were eaten along with other beasts at that time.[9]

Considering the magnificence of the gifts bestowed upon, as well as bestowed by, the sultans, a considerable number of horses were constantly changing hands. For example when the viceroy of Aleppo came to Egypt to see Sultan Barquq, he was presented with seven led-horses from the royal stables with saddles of gold and gold brocaded under-saddle cloths as a token of the sultan's esteem. When Emir Baidamur, viceroy of Damascus, arrived, the sultan presented to him eight horses with gold cloth coverings. The emir reciprocated by presenting the sultan with 20 slaves; 33 camels with coverings of silk, wool, and fur; 23 saluki hunting dogs, 18 horses with silk horse cloths, 50 stallions, 32 mares, and 100 horses of mixed breed (chroniclers listed separately the horses that were not Arab), together with numerous choice camels, many richly caparisoned.[10]

When the viceroy of Damascus, Tanam al-Hasani, arrived in Cairo in 1396, he went to the sultan and presented him with ten kuhiya falcons, slaves and precious gems, silver and gold, a jeweled sword, and 150 horses together with a horse's housing of gold which contained 400 mitkals of that precious metal and for which the goldsmith had received for his work alone the sum of 30,000 dirhams in silver. Later the emir and the sultan went hunting together and upon their return the sultan bestowed upon Tanam eight led-horses from the royal stables with horse cloths and saddles of gold. Such was the splendor of the mameluke courts.

Tanam was known as a very excellent warrior and a story about him gives us some insight into the superstitions of the mamelukes, not unlike those of the Arabs. When Tanam drew up his five thousand cavalry and six thousand infantry in battle order during a conflict, the sultan's emirs followed suit. But at the very beginning of the battle Tanam was thrown from his horse and it was because of this fall and his capture that the lines broke. The mamelukes who had been with him in the battle said that "the horse which he rode had some ill-omened characteristic" (ei-

9. *History of Egypt*, translated from the Arabic annals of Abu L-Mahasin ibn-Taghri Birdi by William Popper (California, 1954), vol. 13, p. 159.
10. Ibid., vol. 13, p. 7.

ther long hair or whiteness on the legs, the informant assumed), and although Tanam had been warned by his constituents against riding it, he proceeded and was consequently defeated.

That Sultan Barquq loved horses was evidenced by the keenness he displayed toward equine sports, and when he died there were some 7000 horses left in his stable, all said to be mares. But unfortunately he was the last of the great horse-loving mameluke sultans.

After the Osmali conquest Egypt sank into the position of a mere province of the Turkish empire and was separated from her neighboring provinces of Syria and Arabia. Yet the power of the mamelukes was not extinguished and as time went on the authority of the Turkish pasha shrank before their reviving strength. They became as insolent, turbulent, prodigal, and rapacious as any soldiery that ever existed. Living in luxury upon the wealth wrung from those they oppressed, they forbade anyone who was not a mameluke to go on horseback. Exceptionally brave and superbly skilled in the use of weapons as well as at horse breeding and horsemanship, they rode only entire horses (stallions) or mares, and their custom was to gallop or walk. The French noted that they never trotted their horses, and exercised them at a gallop to rush one against the other, to rear when approaching each other, to pass each other by and return. The riders scrimmaged with sabers and their blades were so keen and they handled them so dextrously that many of them could cut a clew of wet cotton like a piece of butter. One of their favorite movements was to stop their horse suddenly, on the spot, in the midst of a full-out gallop. Such exhibitions exposed the horse to unnatural maneuvers and often strained the tendons, the French noted.

A favorite sport of these daring cavaliers was throwing the *djerid,* a staff made of palm branches four feet long and weighing five or six pounds. So armed, they would enter the arena and riding at full speed throw these staffs at each other from considerable distance. After heaving his staff the assailant would wheel his horse about, and his antagonist would pursue and throw in turn. The horses were accustomed and trained for the exercises and seconded their masters so well that they seemed to share in the fun of the sport. The pleasure was, nevertheless, attended by considerable danger, for the *djerid* if thrown with great force could easily wound and sometimes kill. "Ill-fated was the man who could not escape the djerid of Ali Bey" was a common saying. This brave warrior supported by a large force of valiant mamelukes expelled the Turkish pasha, proclaimed the independence of Egypt in 1768, subdued part of Arabia, and attempted to annex Syria. He was killed, however, and then Napoleon entered the scene, defeating the remaining mamelukes at Embaba when the Battle of the Pyramids in 1798 converted Egypt into a province of France.

Mameluke carrying the djerid, *a staff made of palm branches.*
ENGRAVING BY V. ADAM

As a result of this battle the notorious mameluke Murad Bey was defeated. His stud, reputedly an excellent one, apparently was disbanded, for it is recorded that the seven-year-old Arab stallion Selim, foaled 1794, by Achmet, a favorite horse of the mameluke chief, out of an Abyssinian mare, was procured and presented to the late General Sir

"Every mameluke was an arsenal on horseback."

WATER COLOR BY H. VERNET

Ralph Abercromby (1734–1801) by the Turkish grand vizier on Abercromby's arrival in Egypt. The horse was later imported to America by Capt. James Barron, U.S.N.

Another celebrated stallion was Tajar, meaning "the swift or flying one." Tajar was taken as booty by the mercenaries hired by Mohammed Ali to kill the mamelukes at the famous Citadel banquet, and later Baron von Fechtig saw the horse when he was offered for public sale. It was then learned Tajar had been in the stud of Murad Bey. The Baron bought him and shipped him to Europe.

Napoleon himself immediately fancied the horses and horse trappings of these mameluke cavaliers, and in the famous painting of him by Gros at the Battle of the Pyramids, his charger is equipped in the mameluke fashion. Vertray, in his book *Napoleon in Egypt*, provides a colorful description of that historic scene:

In the background, the desert under the blue sky; before us, the beautiful Arabian horses, richly harnessed, snorting, neighing, prancing gracefully and lightly under their martial riders, who are covered with dazzling arms, inlaid with gold and precious stones. Their costumes are brilliantly colorful; their turbans are surmounted with aigret feathers, and some wear gilded helmets. They are armed with sabres, lances, maces, spears, rifles, battle axes, and daggers, and each has three pairs of pistols. This spectacle produced a vivid impression on our soldiers by its novelty and richness. From that moment on their thoughts were set on booty.

The Mamluke army, even with its reinforcements on foot, was numerically far inferior to the French. But every Mamluke was an arsenal on horseback. Riding Cossack style, he would first discharge his carbine, slide it under his thigh, then fire his several pairs of pistols and throw them over his shoulder to be picked up by his footservants later, then throw his lethal djerids . . . and finally charge the foe with scimitar in hand. Sometimes he carried two scimitars, swinging both while gripping the reins with his teeth. Years of practice enabled him to sever a head with a reverse blow. Torn from his parents while still a child, a warrior from the age of twelve, usually without progeny, he knew no fear, no attachment. A Mameluke was almost never captured: he was either victorious, or he was killed, or he fled with the same lightning speed with which he attacked. As a consequence he carried with him, in jewels, clothes, and coins, a veritable fortune. Over a muslin shirt, he wore layers of bright and brilliant silken vests and caftans, the whole encased in gigantic silken trousers, a single leg of which a large man could have wrapped himself. The Mamelukes' stature was usually gigantic—they were picked as boys by experts—and their features handsome.

Such were the colorful and spectacularly rich pages of mameluke history in Egypt; a span of 1000 years and truly the age of splendor. Nevertheless, despite their courage and maneuverability, the mameluke army had little chance against the discipline and drill of the French army, who defeated them and placed Egypt under French rule. The French occupation was short-lived, however, and in 1798 the British forced them out at the battle of Abou Kir, restoring authority to the Sublime Porte and paving the way for the rise of Mohammed Ali, the Great Albanian, who brought about the renaissance of Egypt and established the beginning of the finest Arabian stud the world has ever known.

7

THE RENAISSANCE OF HORSE
BREEDING UNDER MOHAMMED ALI
THE GREAT

THERE ARE few names in modern history so generally known or remembered as that of Mohammed Ali. He occupied a short space in the history of the world, yet caused a great commotion in both Europe and Turkey. As viceroy of Egypt, in spite of his want of education and the cruel covetousness which seems to have been a trait of the Turks and their mamelukes, he was an able ruler. In craft and cunning he was more than a match for most diplomats, and was not deceived by the subtlety of Turkish intrigue. Vainglorious and self-gratifying, he nevertheless brought Egypt into its renaissance, earning the title of Mohammed Ali the Great.

Born in 1769 at Cavalla, a small seaport town in Macedonia, Mohammed Ali lost his father while still a young boy. The town governor took him under his protection. He arranged for the boy to receive the proper instruction in horsemanship and the use of arms, a necessary education for anyone desirous of rising to power in those tumultuous times. Although he did not learn to read until he was about forty years old, his natural abilities compensated for his lack of formal education.

For many centuries Egypt had been ruled locally by the mameluke military caste under the remote suzerainty of the Ottoman sultan. Mohammed Ali acquired rank as an Albanian officer in the army sent by the sultan to resist the French occupation of Egypt. When the

Mohammed Ali Pasha.

ENGRAVING BY V. ADAM

One of the mameluke military caste.

DRAWING BY H. ALKEN

French finally evacuated Egypt it was he who emerged as ruler. In 1805 Constantinople conferred upon him the pashalik of Cairo, at which time he felt secure enough to send for his sons, Tousson and Ibrahim, who were still in Cavalla. For the next forty years Mohammed Ali and his son, Ibrahim Pasha, dominated the Middle Eastern scene.

In order to maintain himself on the throne and hold the mamelukes in check, Mohammed Ali continued to make use of the western bedouins, particularly the Hanadi tribe, as regular cavalry. At that time there were no troops in Egypt except a small remnant of Turkish soldiers. These bedouins were of great service in his Syrian and Arabian expeditions. He transformed a considerable number of them into agriculturalists, thinking they might form a defense against the well-mounted and less amenable tribes who continued to be marauders.

He also sided with the mamelukes early in his rule and commanded some of their military groups. However, he realized that there could be no real security for him while the powerful and also traditional authority of the mamelukes continued to exist. Having gained control over their affairs, he decided it was time to completely eliminate the rebellious mamelukes and their twenty-four "accursed emirs" who were scheming against him.

Mohammed Ali called a meeting to announce that he would hold a fantasia in honor of his son, Tousson. This was always a favorite festival among horsemen, providing competitions for their skills at various equestrian events. The mamelukes fell headlong into his trap. With their leader, Chahyn Bey, they repaired to the reception hall where Mohammed Ali received them with apparent kindness and lavish hospitality. The parade took place and the troops marched to the Citadel, the pasha's men first, the well-mounted mamelukes following. The way in was through a passage cut out of the rock, and no sooner had the mamelukes entered it than the gate behind them was rammed shut. Cut off from escape, the cavaliers were shot down from the rocks and battlements above. There is a story that only one, Amim Bey, escaped the massacre. At the first attack he spurred his horse up the steep rampart and urged him to leap over the parapet. The fall was about forty feet and the horse was killed. The rider escaped, but the rest of the mamelukes were slaughtered. By further orders the mamelukes throughout the land were pursued, slain, or chased abroad. Thus ended the

Amin Bey escaping from the ambush.

mameluke race which had for generations ruled Egypt and provided some of its most fabulous horses.

Mohammed Ali's early education in horsemanship in his native land gave him a practiced eye for a horse. It wasn't long before he too became consumed with passion for the Arabian steeds. As with everything else, having the most and the best became an obsession with him. He used his position to obtain Arab horses from friends, allies, and foes alike. He sometimes invited tribal chiefs and their children to fantasias, and then held them prisoner until the horses he wanted but had been unable to acquire were delivered to him. He built ornate stables which were reputedly even more expensive and elaborate than his own palace, and was claimed to have spent some four and a half million gold pounds on his Arabian horses, their trappings and equipment. Special fantasias were held to show off his priceless steeds. At these celebrations he often invited ambassadors of Europe and allowed them to choose stallions as gifts to their sovereigns or government heads.

Mohammed Ali's decision to invade Arabia resulted from the rise in power of a fanatical religious sect, the Wahabbis.[1] Under the leadership of Saud, these Wahabbi bedouins attacked Medina and despoiled the Prophet's temple of its jewels and treasures. Then they pressed forward and captured the holy city of Mecca. Mounted on some of the choicest Arabians of Nejd, Saud and his warriors terrorized Arabia in the name of their new austere sect.

Infuriated at the sacrilege and affront to the faith, the government at Constantinople requested Mohammed Ali to suppress these fanatics and punish their audacious leader. The way was now open for Mohammed Ali to obtain the treasure of the Arabs—their Arabian horses—as spoils of war. He had already tried to buy them and failed.

Mohammed Ali first dispatched his youngest son, Tousson Pasha, father of Abbas Pasha, to Arabia. Although Tousson Pasha eventually occupied Mecca and Medina along with three other cities of the Hedjaz in about 1812, his expedition as a whole failed. The following year Mohammed Ali personally took command and went to Arabia himself. He too was unable to penetrate the heartland. The problem of supplies

1. Founded by Mohammed ibn-Abd el-Wahab, a pious and learned sheik of Nejd. He converted to his creed the powerful chief of Dereyeh, Mohammed ibn-Saud, who became the sovereign of the new sect. Under Saud and his successors the Wahabbi doctrines were spread throughout the greater part of Arabia.

and provisions was critical. Most were sent from Cairo by Nile barge to Kenneh, and thence by camel across the desert to Casseia. Mohammed Ali, fearing a defeat would damage his reputation, returned to Egypt, where he plotted further to subjugate Arabia to his will and also gain the horses he coveted. Tousson, who was left in charge, suffered a disastrous defeat near Taif, one of the horse-breeding centers of the bedouins, and would have lost had not Saud, the Wahabbi leader, conveniently died. Saud's son, Abdullah, negotiated a truce, which he had every intention of breaking when convenient to do so. Mohammed Ali, knowing the Wahabbi leader was stalling for time, agreed to the truce, but required that Abdullah deliver to him more than two hundred specified Arabian horses as a peace offering. This was a terrible price to pay in what was then irreplaceable horseflesh and the lifeblood of the Arabs.

View of the Mohammed Ali mosque in the Citadel.

Nevertheless, Abdullah accepted the terms, and on the day of surrender the horses were handed over to Tousson, who supervised their departure to Egypt.

Tousson died unexpectedly, leaving a void in army leadership. Mohammed Ali needed a commander in chief capable of attacking and defeating the Wahabbis at their capital in the heart of central Arabia. He summoned all his generals, ministers, officers, and statesmen to a meeting in Cairo, explaining to them the situation and his plans. According to the story, he then placed an apple in the center of a large carpet spread in the hall before them, and said that whoever could, with his hand, reach and hand the apple to him without placing a foot on the carpet would be the commander of the expedition against Nejd. Many tried and failed. At last, Ibrahim, Mohammed Ali's eldest son, rose and respectfully requested that he be allowed to try his hand. All laughed while he awaited the paternal authorization, but their scorn turned into admiration as they watched him quietly set to work rolling up the carpet from its rim inwards, until the apple was within his grasp. He then picked it up and handed it to his father, who promptly promoted him to commander in chief of the Egyptian army.

Ibrahim Pasha.

Ibrahim Pasha proved to be an able and courageous general. In the short space of two years, he defeated Abdullah ibn-Saud and broke the political power of the Wahabbis, causing Abdullah to surrender in 1818.

The Wahabbi leader was then sent to Constantinople where he was beheaded by the Turks, despite their promise that his life would be spared. Mohammed Ali was now in position to have Ibrahim acquire Abdullah's stud, and he did not hesitate to do so.

Ibrahim had also become an enthusiastic collector of the bedouin horses, and acquired as outright gifts from the tribal leaders, or by liberal payments of gold, choice specimens for his own stable. When Ibrahim captured the last stronghold of the Wahabbis in Nejd, the finest and largest group of bedouin horses ever said to exist in Arabia fell into his possession. Ibrahim's chronicler, Gouin, recorded in 1815 that two hundred choice mares and stallions were captured from Riad and other oasis towns (some of them later became the property of Abbas Pasha, as will be seen in later chapters).

The stud of Abdullah was now to be moved from the heart of the desert to the shores of the Red Sea. However, many of the horses died of exposure, hunger, thirst, and disease, and very few ever reached Egypt. Ibrahim attributed the severe losses to nature's displeasure. He later confided to friends that he had indeed transgressed against nature when he took from the bedouins their Arabian steeds, their rightful inheritance from their father, Ishmael. Ibrahim had become genuinely fond of the Arab race. He found the Arabic intellect more flexible than the Turk, and enjoyed mingling and talking with his Arab troopers, always praising the race from which they sprang. When asked, he said that he had come as a child to Egypt and the sun had changed his blood and made it wholly Arab. In losing so many horses, he had perhaps been forced to reflect, like some of his illustrious predecessors, that "there is no profit in covetousness; one cannot seize his own time and the time of another."

After Abdullah's capture and execution, his son Turki ibn-Abdullah came to power in Arabia. For some time he struggled against the Egyptian army which Ibrahim Pasha had left behind to rule, but eventually he somewhat reconciled himself to them. To appease Mohammed Ali, he sent several shipments of bedouin horses to Egypt. When Turki was murdered by his cousin, Mushari, Faisal ibn-Turki succeeded his father as prince of Arabia and set about to revenge the plunder of his father's precious stud by Feysul ibn-Dauwish, who had joined Ibrahim Pasha. Later, in 1836, Faisal ibn-Turki was ambushed by an Egyptian force and brought to Cairo where he was imprisoned in the Citadel to await the hand of fate. And it proved a providential one for the future Arabian horse world of the West. It was here he met Abbas Pasha, Mohammed Ali's grandson, an absolute fanatic about Arabian horses.

Despite having lost most of Abdullah's stud, Mohammed Ali succeeded in eventually obtaining magnificent Arabians from Nejd. These were stabled at Shoubra, his luxurious country estate. European artists marveled at this unrivaled collection of classic Arabian horses, and immortalized them on canvas.

A typical Nejd stallion.

ENGRAVING BY V. ADAM

James St. John, who visited Mohammed Ali's gardens in 1832, described the viceroy's stud as follows:

There were a great many horses in open places ranged round a yard, like bullock sheds in England. Several of them were milk-white. The grooms pretended they were all Nejdis; but this was not true, as some few were from Dongola. There were, however, many genuine Nejdis. Amongst others I remarked a small dark chestnut horse, of the true blood, as his points would testify. He had a fine snake head, with an expanding and projecting nostril; but, contrary to English ideas of perfection, a remarkably small pointed ear. His forehead was wide, with an eye expressive of boldness, generosity and alacrity. His shoulder was thick through, and finely laid back; his ribs and loins were round and deep; his legs short and very powerful, the hoof being rather donkey formed, with an open heel, and, from his muscular thighs and longish drooping pasterns, there is no doubt he would be elastic, speedy, and lasting. The groom said he was worth some hundred thousand *paras*.

. . . There were several other Nejdis, partaking more or less of the same formation as the one above described. They carried no flesh, had very rough coats, and reminded me much of the Hungarian cavalry horse; but the latter I saw in good condition. The Nejdi, however, is higher than the Hungarian, but looks small only from his fine proportions. The tallest horse I have seen of this breed was fifteen hands one inch; but they are generally two or three inches under this. In walking through the caravan encampment, about to leave Cairo for Mekka, we were admiring a finely formed horse, when his owner pointed out another, which he valued more highly. He was feeding out of a bag, so that the lower part of his head was not visible; but he was smaller than the other, and remarkably short and thick in all his proportions. He had what dog amateurs call a 'coarse stern,' his tail being entirely out of place, and his hind quarters cut off short like those of a camel. The Arab spoke much of his great speed, and said he was a Nejdi of the famous Hassan breed. He was surprised at our preferring the other. They were both chestnut.[2]

St. John also noted the harsh method in use among the Egyptian Arabs for securing their horses, whether in the stable, the field, or the camp, and thought it highly injurious.

How cruel to the horses!

Each fore leg is fastened to the corresponding one behind by a rope, so short, that the former are drawn considerably under the body, both when the horse is feeding and when at rest. In the field, two other ropes passing from his forelegs at right angles with his body, are pegged down at some

2. James Augustus St. John, *Egypt and Mohammed Ali* (London, 1834), vol. I, pp. 162–65.

distance on either side, and thus he is left to feed as far as he can before him. In the stable, besides the short ropes fettering his legs, the horse's head is tied by two ropes to the ceiling, and by two others to the earth, two ropes at right angles from his fore legs being fastened either to posts or to the wall, while his hind legs are tied either to the back wall, or to a strong rope, which passes along the ground behind the horses for that purpose. There may appear to be reason for putting some of these restraints upon horses placed near together without any partition to prevent their maiming each other; but it will scarcely be believed that I have seen a single horse, in a loose box, confined in the same manner, and this, not because he was vicious, but because it was customary. The practice of fastening the fore legs, and thus continually forcing them back under the body, must confine the natural freedom of action which a horse ought to possess; and, as it is applied to colts when very young, it seems not impossible that it may even displace the shoulder from the natural position which it would otherwise take. This appears to me to be the most rational way of accounting for the fact that the greater number of horses in Egypt have broken knees.

Various Europeans who saw Mohammed Ali's stud recorded that it was badly run and the horses were kept abominably. The viceroy noted the dissipation of his horses and realized his stud was not operating at anywhere near full potential. Weary of incessant disappointments and court intrigues, he took counsel from the Abou Zabal Veterinary Foundation and employed the French veterinarian P. N. Hamont to take over the stud. For fourteen years Hamont struggled against the corrupt administration in an effort to improve the horses' lot. When he arrived at the breeding establishment he found that the methods employed were those adopted by the Turks. The stables were very low with little ventilation, ill-kept, and consequently harbored a host of flies and mosquitos. The mares were pressed against each other and held motionless by eight ropes, two for the head and six for the limbs, in such a way as to render any movement impossible. The foals were crawling with vermin and were often stricken with glanders and distemper. Stallions were also tied up in a court not far from the mares. A manual rubdown was given every day to each horse, but there was only one groom per ten horses. The grooms were poorly and infrequently paid, and consequently they were reduced to stealing feed, which they sold in order to survive. Out of one hundred mares, fifty or sixty conceived and many aborted. Two-thirds of the foals died before reaching yearling age.

Within a short period of time Hamont was able to convince the viceroy that more spacious and airy facilities were necessary for proper maintenance of the stud. Mohammed Ali agreed to his idea of establishing a large stud in the Shoubra plain a short distance from the summer residence. Hamont then drew up the plans, conceived the architecture, and oversaw the engineering and general construction. When finished, the new establishment covered an area of 910 feet by 595 feet. The walls were of cut stone and the stud was divided lengthwise into two equal parts with two large courtyards, in the center of which were large fountains for the horses to drink from. High iron gates closed off the court, and around the building, edged by bright hedges of thorny mimosa, parks were laid out for the horses to run in.

The horses now began receiving frequent long walks and two manual rubdowns daily. Stallions, mares, and foals were freed from their shackles and allowed to run loose in the pastures without shoes. Feed was varied: clover, lucerne, sainfoin, crushed barley, and a blue-flowered lucerne (*berseem Hejazi*) from Mecca which proved very suitable and provided eighteen cuttings per year. Within a very few years the results were apparent; the foals showed considerable growth and increase in height. The Shoubra stud became an experimental center or practical school where anyone interested could learn more modern methods of horse husbandry. Mohammed Ali often visited his new stud, and was pleased with the beauty and strength of the foals, as well as with the improved health of the animals overall. The stallions and mares showed much more vigor, and at the age of two years, the foals produced at Shoubra were bigger than the four-year-olds born in the old stud. Hamont was able to carry on a breeding program the year round, but noted that the spring foals were better than the winter ones, and that "fat mares do not conceive easily and are more prone to diseases than mares which are maintained in a state very close to thinness."[3] Weaning was effected at three months, but he noted that "the foal's size comes especially from the dam, from nature, and from the quality of food which is given. Succulent food, provided in abundance, supplements, to a certain degree, the lack of size of the dam."

With regard to the horses themselves, Hamont recorded that in

3. P. N. Hamont, *Egypte de puise la conquete des arabes sous la domination de Mehemet Aly* (Paris, 1877; translated from the French by Gulsun Sherif).

1842 the Shoubra stud contained thirty-two stallions: they were Nejdi, Syrian, Anazeh, Egyptian, and one English, and one Russian. The best and most beautiful foals of the stud were those produced by the Arab stallions of Nejd, whose progeny were rarely ill and who acquired most distinguished forms. There were 450 mares maintained at Shoubra, and those which were annually culled out were sent off to the provinces for public service. "The great Pasha chooses the most beautiful for the use of his house," Hamont noted.

With regard to selecting the breeding program, Hamont wrote: "I myself designate for each mare the stallion which I believe to be the most suitable, regarding the form, the breeds of each, and in order that there be no mistakes, I put a number on the hoof of each horse. This number is also inscribed on a matriculation register. A European surveys all the servings, having in hand a copy of the register. If the result does not live up to my expectations, I modify and change the matings." As a result of the improved feeding program and generally better conditions, he was gratified when he counted eighty, then ninety births out of a hundred mares.

Despite his success in reforming the stud, there were still problems with the incompetent or indifferent and greedy administrators who were in charge of dispensing grain and other supplies necessary to the stud. One can imagine Hamont's consternation when "one year, in April or May, I think, there remained not a single grain of barley nor a stalk of hay in the storerooms. I ask Abbas Pasha, the grandson of Mohammed Ali, for some provisions. The prince sends back my reclamation with a recommendory note to some administrators. My letter comes and goes. All these proceedings are in vain. What is to be done? A day goes by. On the following one, we are still as anxious as ever. At night, I distribute cudgels among 30 men who, under the leadership of a European, go in the fields to steal the barley belonging to a peasant. I thus feed the horses for 48 hours more." All efforts to organize an administrative system which would ensure the existence of the stud met with opposition at every turn. " 'The stallions and mares freed from their shackles will hurt and kill themselves' the Egyptian and Osmanli grooms shouted," and as soon as his back was turned, the grooms, following the Turks' advice, reshackled the horses' feet. Finally Hamont had all the ropes burned and punished those responsible for disobeying the rules. " 'Mares must not work.' I ruin the stallions' kidneys when I have them ridden.' And the accusations continue to shower upon me from everywhere. My reply is given by the number of births and deaths." Indeed, it seemed no joyous task to care for what was perhaps the most valuable stud in the world at that time.

"May it be permitted for me to declare so, the stud of Mohammed Ali would have fallen into a deplorable condition caused by the in-difference and the apathy of the Turks brought up in France, had I not been able to withstand the destructive movement led by those to whom the Viceroy had given complete power," Hamont wrote in his memoirs.

One does not have to take Hamont's word alone, because Colonel Vyse visited the stud and observed:

When I revisited the stud on the 12th of November 1836, the finest mares and stallions had been removed to the new establishment, which was situated in a fertile plain, abounding in luxuriant crops of corn, cotton, etc. Two large enclosures in front of the stables, fenced in with reeds about seven feet high, contained 110 yearlings; many of them were promising—the best were two colts got by the English horse. The produce of Mufti were strong but coarse, which is often the case with young Arab stock; those from the fine bay were small. These horses were in tolerable condition and had the great advantage of being at liberty. Seventeen later yearlings were turned loose in a large barn; one or two of these, particularly a small bay colt, were very handsome, but they were in bad condition.

The buildings were very extensive, and being new were perfectly clean: they surrounded large courts into which the broodmares ought to have been turned in lots of 20 or 30, with sheds to shelter them from the sun. There were 48 barren mares tied up in a stable, some of which were handsome and apparently well-bred. In another stable were 61 mares in foal—they shewed much blood, and five of them (two white Nedgid and three greys from Syria, Nubia and Thebes) were remarkably fine. I did not observe at these stables any mares that had foaled, they were probably in separate buildings. Twenty-two stallions were in another stable; the grey horse Mufti, the fine bay, the chestnut already alluded to, and five other bay horses—one of which was a capital horse from the Hedjas, and two of inferior value which had been selected for the Army. Eight extremely handsome grey Nedgid and six white horses—of which five were Nedgid, and one an Egyptian stallion.

These horses and mares were in large boarded stalls and were not fast-ened by heel ropes, but by halters attached to posts let into the bottom of the stone mangers. The stalls were not paved; the mangers were high and by singular arrangement, the horses stood in two rows facing each other. A narrow path had been made along the walls behind, and a broad high walk extended in front of the stalls down the middle of the building. The horses had nothing before them but the manger, and were consequently kept in continual state of alarm and uneasiness, by people coming unexpectedly before them: many of them, indeed, which were easily excited, hung back, with the imminent risk of pulling the post to which they were fastened and the whole place to pieces, and it did not appear to be very substantially built. It is difficult to imagine why this absurd plan was adopted; which, beside other inconveniences, precluded the possibility of examining the horses without passing close behind them by the dirty path near the walls. The stalls, however, will not last long; and it is hoped these fine horses will eventually be kept in loose boxes and the mares in sheds which will not only save them much expense but contribute vastly to their health and enable them to make up by moving about in some degree for the neglect and the want of exercise to which they are exposed. The stud, however, is upon the whole much improved since it has been removed to this place and the French superintendent has been of service. Even the two year old colts sent to the stables in Cairo are in better condition: but nothing can compensate for want of air, liberty, proper exercise and good keep, particularly to young horses; and the colts at Shoubrah, it is to be observed, are principally fed with chopped straw, and have little or no exercise.[4]

THE STUD OF IBRAHIM PASHA

According to Hamont, the manner in which the stud was maintained was the same as in the old Shoubra stud and everywhere else in Egypt. The stables of the prince were at Kasserling near his castle, on the banks of the Nile, at a very short distance from Cairo. "The mares and the stallions are from Nejd. Ibrahim Pasha took them himself, in Central Arabia, when he conquered this country. There are still some Egyptian mares and horses, and many Anezis. In all, approximately 400 head. The locality is not suited to the purpose of rearing horses, because in the winter the humidity is very great. There is much less disease than in Shoubra, however. This difference comes from the fact that the horses of the Prince are of a superior race. No glanders or farcy is to be found among the Nejdis. Dysentery reigns annually during the cold season. Births are few: about 50 out of 100 mares."

4. Col. Howard Vyse, *Operations Carried on at the Pyramids of Gizeh* (London, 1840–42, vol. 3, pp. 130–35).

Hamont noted that the foals were shackled by the four legs as soon as they had reached the ages of six months to one year. The growth of the foals was poor, and the shackles deformed their legs. However, the results obtained in Mohammed Ali's new establishment found favor with the people of Ibrahim Pasha and Hamont was consulted as to whether he would assist the prince also. "I address to the Prince a report on the reforms to be introduced in his stud. The Prince gives the order to let me operate in all freedom." Assisted by Mr. Bonfort, another Frenchman who had long been in the service of Ibrahim Pasha, Hamont set out to improve the establishment as he had for Mohammed Ali. Again opposition to the new methods was encountered, but their advice prevailed for a time at least. "The Turks accuse the crushed barley of causing mange, and they say that lucerne gives indigestion. A report is made against me. My delegate is unable to withstand the current which drags him along. They revert to their first habits. The Turks have prejudices one cannot destroy. For instance, they assure that a mare must only be mated at a certain time of the full moon, or when a certain star is at a determined height, etc. I am unable to attain a complete reform. Ibrahim Pasha has the three year old colts sold at auction. The best horses are reserved for his house."

Vyse also saw Ibrahim Pasha's stud and found it in much worse condition than that at Shoubra, but reported that "several of the mares, of which there were between two and three hundred, appeared to be superior, shewed a great deal of blood, and although rather slight, had fine racing shape." He also made special note that "the horses which the Prince had taken at Acre had three round spots burnt in their hindquarters (which was not an unusual mark), although it did not appear to denote any particular breed." Ibrahim Pasha, however, "generally rode mules," even though he was passionately fond of his horses.

THE STUD OF KOURCHID PASHA

In studying the Abbas Pasha manuscript, one finds many references to Kourchid Pasha, for he was very active in the Arabian campaigns and also a lover of horses. He founded a notable stud in Egypt as a result of his expeditions. Hamont described it as follows:

It is situated in Embaba, facing Boulac, on the properties of the General. The mares and stallions have been brought from Nejd, the country of which Khourchid Pasha has been Governor for several consecutive years. The horses are very beautiful. There are some magnificent stallions and superb products, about 150 head. Khourchid Pasha is not prejudiced. He has a perfect knowledge of the horses which he loves very deeply. He has built on his domain a stud which is very well planned out. The horses' feed is rich and varied. A European is in charge of the establishment. If the occupations of Khourchid Pasha permit to give his full attention to the operation of his stud, he will obtain, maybe, the best horses in Egypt. It is to be feared that the natives should prevail upon the European and that they will oppose themselves to the full and entire execution of the best practices. Mohammed Ali has forbidden his old Mamluke to sell his mares or stallions, but leaves him free to sell his colts. If Khourchid Pasha should get rid of his mares or colts, it would be a great sorrow for Egypt.

THE STUD OF THE SHERIF OF MECCA, MOHAMMED IBN-AOUN

The name of Sherif Mohammed ibn-Aoun is frequently mentioned in the pedigrees of horses belonging to Abbas Pasha, Mohammed Ali, and Ibrahim Pasha. He was an exalted Muslim spiritual leader of that time, descending from the "noble" line of the Prophet. He maintained a residence in Cairo as well as a small select stud, and it is therefore valuable to have Colonel Vyse's description of the Egyptian branch of his stable. Colonel Vyse obtained a choice stallion from the sherif, which was exported to England and was perhaps the first horse of Abbas Pasha blood to reach there.

I requested permission to examine the stud belonging to the Shereef of Mecca, as the best horses came from that place; and, as I concluded that his would have been of the purest breed.

. . . The Shereef's stud did not appear to be numerous. The stables were, as is often the case, underground, and upon entering them, my attention was particularly directed to a grey mare in foal by a white horse then in the possession of Abbas Pacha; both the mare and the horse were of the purest breed, from Mecca, and were esteemed of great value, and the best, which the Shereef possessed. The mare shewed much blood, had a very handsome head, and good length, but was slight. The horse, which I afterwards saw at the stables of Abbas Pacha, was about 14 h. 3″ high, had good substance, and also shape, but not that of a race horse; I could not judge of his action, as he was led out in heel ropes, and with a heavy bit fastened into his mouth by a cord. There was also in the Shereef's stable a bay yearling got by the white horse out of the grey mare, which I subsequently brought to England on account of his blood. I procured this colt with great difficulty most probably because the Shereef perceived that I wished to have him. He said that he belonged to his son, and offered me any of his other horses, but I was determined to have the colt because I had previously heard that his sire was the highest bred horse in the stud, and because his dam had the appearance and also the reputation of being of the purest breed; and because a yearling was more easily conveyed by water than a larger horse.

. . . It was expressly stipulated by the Shereef that I was to send him in exchange for his horse, a golden watch and an English carriage with harness for four horses.

Eventually, after further correspondence, the arrangement was satisfactorily concluded and the pedigree of the horse provided. The translation of the pedigree was as follows:

All which is attributed herein is correct; the Shereef Muhammad Ben Aioon, Sherif of Mecca, the honoured, has written it. The pardon of God be for him.

This history is the truth of the bay colt which we presented to his Excellency the Col. Howard Vyse, the English Bey at Cairo, the protected. His name is Abeian, his breed is pure Nedgdi; he was born at Cairo, in our habitation, on the 21st of Giumal el Aker 1252 [Oct. 1, 1836], and his father and his mother are of the best Arab horses. His mother's name is El Abeieh, daughter of El Abeieh, her color is white, and the color of her mother was bay; and her father's name was Abeian the Hendees [Abeyan El-Honeydis], his color was white, and he pure Nedgdi.

The father of the before mentioned colt is Hadbaan, by name Gerboa; his color is white, and his mother is Hadba, the Nedgdi; her colour is white, and her father's name is Gelwan [Jelwan], the son of Hadba, and the colour of his mother is white. The whole are from the Nedgdi horses, celebrated amongst the Arabs.

> Sealed: The Shereef Abdullah
> Son of the Shereef Muhammad Ibn Aioon
> Shabaan 6, 1253 [Nov. 5, 1837]

Vyse was particularly pleased in getting the horse, and although it appears he judged horses according to English standards of perfection, he apparently was capable also of viewing the Arabs with an eye towards the classic Arab standard as we know it today.

. . . The colt in question is very low, barely 14 h., and has small bone, but is muscular, and so much furnished that his age has been doubted til repeated examinations of his mouth proved that his pedigree was correct. He shews blood, has fine action, is remarkably healthy, and has great courage, as he sometime since proved by leaping a gate 3'9" high and a boarded door seven feet from the gate and 5'6" in height; which he cleared with his forehand and body and broke through with his hinder legs without any other injury than a scratch below his stifle. The whole leap was about 18' in breadth. The horse has also good length for his size, but he has not the shape of a race horse; what his progeny might turn out is another question.

Several of the other horses showed blood and were of good substance, and height. The Shereef himself, when at the Pyramids, rode a five year old bay horse which had the appearance and action of an English hunter; and one of his attendants was mounted on an animal of unparalleled beauty and animation. Although of low stature, he was the strongest and most magnificent war horse I ever saw, but he was old and had been in the stud at Shoubrah. I saw also in the Shereef's stables a bay and a fine five year old grey mare, belonging to one of his sons, and one or two other clever horses, any of which I could have obtained with much less trouble, and with less expense, than the yearling. They were in better condition than those belonging to the Pacha, but in point of value could not be compared with the best of his stud, which I have already described to have been brought from Mecca; indeed, I believe that some of them were taken from the Shereef's stables.

It is to be observed, that most of the best and highest bred horses from Mecca and from the Hedjas, had great bone, and were of good size (like the grey and the chestnut Wellesley Arabians), they had also the finest muscular shape and indications of high blood; but with a few exceptions, particularly amongst the mares, they have not the length and character esteemed in England.

In addition to the studs mentioned, there were some outstanding stallions and mares belonging to the high dignitaries of the government. Akmet Pasha, minister of war and nephew of the viceroy, owned several Nejdi stallions of great beauty and twenty or thirty Arab mares of the most beautiful race. However, the stud was operated in the manner most prevalent at the time. Some of the governors of the provinces also bred horses, but they did so on a less grand scale than the Pashas of the royal family.

The "richest stud in Egypt, by the very superior quality of the stallions and mares," belonged to Abbas Pasha, wrote Hamont. When Mohammed Ali wished to make the gift of a horse to a consul general or some particularly worthy person in the political world, he chose from the stud of either Abbas Pasha or Ibrahim Pasha. They in turn supplied only common horses, not wishing to let go of their choice stock any more than did the viceroy himself.

The years of Mohammed Ali's reign were drawing to a close, however, and it was not long before both he and Ibrahim Pasha died. Fortunately for Egypt, the greatest Arabian horse breeder of them all stepped forward to rescue the priceless remnants of the studs and make them part of his own.

Abbas Pasha and his entourage.

PAINTING BY DE PORTES, IN THE COLLECTION OF D. B. MARSHALL

8

THE CELEBRATED STUD OF
ABBAS PASHA

ABBAS PASHA, grandson of Viceroy Mohammed Ali, became entranced with the bedouin horses in his early childhood. Born in 1813 and reared in the desert, he obtained a thorough foundation in Arabian horse lore in his formative years. His father, Tousson Pasha, died when Abbas was only three years old, and he was brought up under the watchful eye of his grandfather. Abbas became thoroughly familiar with the horses his father had obtained from Abdullah ibn-Saud during the truce, as well as those accumulated by his uncle, Ibrahim Pasha. By the time Abbas reached the age of twenty-three, he had developed a natural feel for horses and was already a connoisseur of the Arabian breed. Because of this, his grandfather placed him in charge of the administration of the horse-breeding stations.

It was heartbreaking for Abbas to witness the slow deterioration of Mohammed Ali's once incomparable Arabian stud. To preserve the bloodlines, he carefully studied the pedigrees and the offspring of particular stallions and broodmares, and from time to time he was able to obtain some of the best individuals and their foals. He was meticulous about keeping records of the origins and breeding history of his animals and spared neither time, money, nor his own security to acquire by whatever means necessary the best of his grandfather's and Ibrahim Pasha's horses. That he loved them with a passion beyond any breeder Egypt had known, except perhaps Sultan el-Nacer, was evidenced by the quantity and particularly the quality of his stud.

Through his deceased father's connections, but particularly through his own resourcefulness, Abbas formed friendly ties with the Arab princes and leaders, and in 1842 engineered the escape of Prince Faisal ibn-Saud from the Citadel of Cairo, where the Wahabbi prince had been kept prisoner pending payment of ransom money. News of the escape reached Mohammed Ali, but much to the surprise of all, instead of flying into his customary rage he supposedly said: "This is a trick of grandson Abbas, but there be some good reason for it." And indeed there was.

The story is related by Raswan, who claims to have heard it from Egyptian notables, that Faisal and Abbas had previously met while Abbas was still in his middle twenties at a time when Faisal was allowed some freedom of movement about the city. They discovered their mutual love of horses and discussed their knowledge and experience of breeding, as well as pedigrees and strains. Bedouin chiefs were invited to Cairo and scribes recorded the information which they provided Abbas and Faisal. Though still a captive, Faisal was treated with consideration due him as the Imam, or exalted spiritual leader, of the Wahabbis. The last great act of friendship of Abbas on behalf of Faisal was the planning of his escape to Nejd. For this Faisal was ever grateful, and he assisted Abbas in acquiring the pick of desert mares, among them the famed Jellabiyah known as Wazira.

What were Faisal's horses like? W. G. Palgrave, who visited the stud of Prince Faisal ibn-Saud in the early 1860s, gives an eyewitness account of the source which Abbas Pasha had so successfully tapped:

During this time I got a sight of the royal stables, an event much desired and eagerly welcomed. . . . Among all the studs of Nejed, Feysul's was indisputably the first; and who sees that has seen the most consummate specimens of equine perfection in Arabia, perhaps in the world.

. . . The stables . . . are situated some way out of town . . . [and] cover a large square space, about 150 yards each way, and are open in the centre, with a long shed running round the inner walls; under this covering the horses, about three hundred in number when I saw them, are picketed during night; in the daytime they may stretch their legs at pleasure within the central courtyard. The greater number were accordingly loose; a few, however, were tied up at their stalls; some, but not many, had horse-cloths over them. . . . About half the royal stud was present before me, the rest were out at grass; Feysul's entire muster is reckoned at six hundred head, or rather more.

. . . Never had I seen or imagined so lovely a collection. Their stature was indeed somewhat low; I do not think that any came fully up to fifteen hands; fourteen appeared to me about their average; but they were so exquisitely well shaped that want of greater size seemed hardly, if at all, a defect. Remarkably full in the haunches, with a shoulder of a slope so elegant as to make one in the words of an Arab poet, 'go raving made about it;' a little, a very little saddle-backed, just the curve which indicates springiness without any weakness; a head broad above, and tapering down to a nose fine enough to verify the phrase of 'drinking from a pint-pot', did pint-pots exist in Nejed; a most intelligent and yet a singularly gentle look, full eye, sharp thorn-like little ear, legs fore and hind that seemed as if made of hammered iron, so clean and yet so well twisted with sinew; a neat round hoof, just the requisite for hard ground; the tail set on or rather thrown out at a perfect arch; coats smooth, shining, and light; the mane long but not overgrown nor heavy; and an air and step that seemed to say 'Look at me, am I not pretty?' Their appearance justified all reputation, all value, all poetry. The prevailing colour was chestnut or grey; a light bay, an iron colour, white, or black, were less common; full bay, flea-bitten, or piebald, none. But if asked what are, after all, the specially distinctive points of the Nejdee horse, I should reply, the slope of the shoulder, the extreme cleanness of the shank, and the full rounded haunch, though every other part too has a perfection and a harmony unwitnessed (at least by my eyes) anywhere else.[1]

When it was known that Mohammed Ali was fatally ill, the government of Turkey decided Ibrahim Pasha should accede to the viceregency in the place of his father. Abbas supposedly emigrated to Arabia because of a quarrel between him and his uncle, Ibrahim, and he settled down among the Arabs of the Roala tribe. Abbas's absence was short and at the death of his uncle in 1848 he returned to Egypt where he was placed on the viceregal throne.

In the meantime, Abbas set about acquiring the choicest Arabians. In the Arab world, his emissaries, but particularly his mameluke Aly Gamal el-Din el-Shamashirgi Bey, known as El-Lallah, had begun their relentless search throughout the Arabian peninsula for the finest strains available. Journeying from one end of the desert to the other, the devoted Aly Bey gathered up prized mares and stallions from the most celebrated Arab studs. The owners of the studs were anxious to satisfy his master, Abbas Pasha, who was known to them through Faisal. In addition to selling many of their choicest horses, they made available to him the

1. W. G. Palgrave, *Central and Eastern Arabia* (London 1865), vol. 2, pp. 92–94.

ancient histories of the horses which Abbas had gotten from the studs of Mohammed Ali and Ibrahim Pasha. Abbas's love of Arabians and his determined quest to obtain horses having first-class pedigrees reached such an intensity that it is said he purchased, at prohibitive prices, almost all the Saqlawiyah Jedraniyah mares from the Anazeh Tribe, paying as much as 3000 Egyptian gold pounds for a single old mare. Lady Anne Blunt, co-founder of Crabbet Arabian Stud, mentions in her private notes of 1882 that Ibn Sudan had reputedly sold their last mare to Abbas Pasha just prior to the pasha's death: a bay mare, fifteen years old, for which he paid £1000, but she was apparently in such condition that she had to be transported in a wagon. Nevertheless the pasha was fortunate and got several foals from her. The Dahman Nejib, Dahman Shahwan, and Kunayhir strains came very dear, as did the Kuhaylan Mimrah, among others, the favorite of all being that of Dahman Shahwan.

Abbas established luxurious housing for his horses. According to manuscripts belonging to the family library of Prince Mohammed Ali, Abbas owned seven palaces by 1852. His stables were built in the near vicinity and housed his priceless collection of horses as well as the library documenting their pedigrees which Aly Bey—"El-Lallah"—was so faithfully recording. Abbas also succeeded in engaging the most select bedouins from Arabia not only to watch over and direct the management of his stud along strictly bedouin lines, but to check the accounts given of the horses' histories so as to preclude any chance of error. Four of these men were from Nejd, some twenty or thirty came from Anazeh, three from the Ateybe (Oteyba) tribe, and one from the Muteyr.

The reputation of Abbas Pasha's Arabians soon spread throughout the Arab and Christian world. Many poems and paintings were inspired by their beauty. His collection became the envy of kings and princes in Europe and Asia, and emissaries arrived from various parts of the globe to offer almost any price for just one of Abbas's priceless creatures. Eventually, at the peak of his fame, the pasha owned three large stables and had in his collection some one thousand purebred Arabians, the like of which had not been seen since the days of King Solomon. Some were stabled at Haswa, and at a place on the island of Roda, where the Bahrite mamelukes once held sway; others were at the viceregal residence at Abbassia; and some were at Dar el-Beyda, the magnificent White House stables situated amidst the desert and said to have cost the pasha some one million Egyptian gold pounds. It was built in a commanding position atop a hill—an immense group of buildings of pink and white marble where he could reside and keep watch over his horses and be away from the prying eyes of foreigners, whom he distrusted with a passion. A huge underground cistern was connected with stone troughs where the mares were taken to drink and water was hauled over fifty miles from the Nile River by camels and mule wagons. Camels' milk was provided and poured into troughs for the foals, as was the bedouin custom, and as many as three hundred camels were said to have been retained as a source of supply.

When the German king of Wurtemburg, William I, established his Arabian stud at Weil in 1817, he began collecting only desert mares and stallions. Realizing that the best were in Egypt, he sent his studmaster, Baron von Huegel, to obtain some Arab horses from Abbas Pasha in 1852. As a present for the viceroy he sent a pair of selected German coach horses. Von Huegel was not allowed to visit the stables of Abbasia where at that time about one thousand horses were stabled, for it was said that "Abbas Pasha feared the evil eye of a Christian." Von Huegel was so eager to see the legendary horses, however, that he made a secret trip on horseback into the desert before daybreak to see the horses when they were ridden across the barren sands for daily exercise.

Eventually, Abbas received von Huegel in audience, and although the viceroy usually was evasive in talking with strangers about horses, von Huegel succeeded in bringing the conversation around to that subject. Abbas began the discussion by asking about the general opinion of Europeans on the conformation of horses, and then proceeded to discuss the Arabian breed, asking where the Europeans obtained their Arabs and what qualities their Arabs possessed. After von Huegel had answered him, Abbas ended the conversation with the famous remark intended to discourage any rival, yet containing an element of truth: "Never for a moment must you believe that the horses born in your countries are genuine Arabs, for the simple reason that the Arab horse can scarcely retain its quality and characteristics for which it is renowned unless it breathes the desert air."

Nevertheless, as a present von Huegel received the brown stallion Hedban, foaled 1848 and bred by the S'baa Anazeh tribe. A very noble stallion with good conformation, his get were reputedly excellent. Unfortunately, he was used only for one breeding season due to his untimely death. Von Huegel also bought two grey mares, the supremely elegant Koheil Aguse and a mare of the Saklawi strain. Koheil Aguse became an important mare in the stud and her grandson, Amurath-Bairactar, went to Babolna (Hungary) and was most influential there. Another stallion, the grey Zarif, was obtained by Count Pueckler in 1852, and exported to Europe, while the gift horse Calif, whom Abbas gave to the U.S. consul for Egypt, was exported to the United States in 1860, although no descendants exist today.

A situation which obviously did not improve Abbas's love for the English, even though they were his advisers, was brought about, according to Baron von Huegel, by a faux pas committed by Queen Victoria. It seems that "the Pasha had presented Her Majesty with a grey stallion of the purest breed and of great size, but the animal (like all Arabs we may say en passant) was not esteemed in England, and was sold to India. The Pasha, on hearing the fate of his much prized animal, was extremely nettled, and sent into Arabia for the Bedouin who had bred him, of whom he inquired whether he should recognize the horse again. The Arab replied that he should know him out of a thousand. Whereupon the Pasha sent him to India in company of a trustworthy agent, and they returned at the expiration of a twelve-month with the high-bred grey, Saklavi Durbi, whom they had obtained at an expenditure of five thousand guineas. We expect the whole story is fabulous, but it is illustrative of the character of the Pasha."[2]

Historians, particularly the Europeans and English, were not kind to Abbas Pasha, and one finds him depicted as "swarthy, with a scanty beard, short and stout of figure, with a sensual face and cruel eyes. . . ." However, it is said that there was "both energy and intelligence manifested in his countenance when warmed into interest or animation on any matter that touched him nearly. Moreover his manners, like those of all high Turks, were bland and polished. . . . In his dealing with his own subjects he was despotic to a degree. His word was law and woe to the man who attempted to thwart him. He seemed to have inherited the cunning and treachery of the old pasha, but without most of the redeeming qualities which had succeeded in raising the country to a posi-

2. Translated from the original German for the author by Erika Schiele.

tion of importance. His life was one of sensualism, avarice, terror, and suspicion, and he was fearful of falling victim to the instruments which he himself employed."[3]

Ciaffar, a famous Abbas Pasha stallion.

ENGRAVING BY V. ADAM

Palgrave too made disparaging remarks about Abbas Pasha, his impressions having been gained during interviews with Emeer Meta'ab of Hayel.[4]

In this and in the following interviews with Meta'ab, who became more intimate day by day, I obtained a tolerably distinct idea of what I had heard about before, but only confusedly—I mean the strange Arab intrigues of 'Abbas Pasha. That prince had devised a scheme for not only rendering himself independent of the Ottomon Porte, but even of becoming in person sole sovereign of the Arabian Peninsula, by means of a double alliance, linked with the Bedouins to the north, and the Wahhabee to the south. In the view

3. *Twentieth Century Impressions of Egypt* (Lloyd's Greater Britain Publishing Co., London, 1909), p. 56.
4. Palgrave, op. cit., vol. 1, pp. 189–91.

of ensuring the sympathy of the former, he consigned his eldest son, then a mere child, to the well-known Feysul-ebn-Shaalan, chief of the great Ruala tribe, intending thus to have his heir brought up like one of the clan, and in all the perfection of wild ways and customs. Besides this singular measure, he sent abundant largesses to the other contiguous tribes; while any Bedouin who approached his palace was sure of a favourable reception, and was readily admitted to experience the effects of his lavish liberality, if one may term liberality what was in fact mere waste. Nay, the infatuated viceroy went to the extent of affecting the Bedouin in his own person and manners, would imitate the nomad style of dress, relish, or seem to relish, their fare, and live with them on a footing of sham familiarity, fancying the while that he was gaining their affection to his service.

It may be said in the way of apology for the extravagancies of 'Abbas Pasha, that others of more pretensions than ever were his to intellectual discernment, have now and then committed a somewhat similar miscalculation regarding the supposed importance of the Bedouin tribes, and the advantages to be derived from their alliance. But what rendered the Egyptian governor particularly inexcusable in his error, was the contrary example of his own uncle Ibraheem Basha, and the success which had attended him in an exactly opposite course of policy. The neglect of family lessons and hereditary experience is of all others the hardest to pardon in a ruler.

"The man who relies on Bedouin assistance is like one who should build his house on the face of the water," said Meta'ab to me, while describing the conduct of 'Abbas, and he said true. . . . "The Bedouins," thus continued the Emeer, the sense of whose words I give, though not the words themselves, ". . . are besides the mere creatures of the moment, to whom the present hour alone is something, yesterday and tomorrow alike nothing. . . . Their only real partiality is for the highest bidder; and while, to use their own expression, 'his food is yet in their bellies,' they may possibly do his work, but even that so far only as it is evidently profitable to themselves, and not over-dangerous either."

Considering Abbas Pasha's goal of creating the supreme stud, Palgrave's condemnation may be seen as his own inability to have understood the man and his motives.

A man devoted to Abbas Pasha, and to seeing the pasha's goal become reality, was the mameluke Aly Bey, who later became known as Aly Pasha Gamali (not to be confused with Ali Pasha Sherif). After his many sojourns into Arabia and beyond, he subsequently compiled all the information he and his associates had gathered relating to the genealogies of the Arab horse, and presented it to his khedive in a beautifully handwritten book illumined in gold leaf and inscribed in black, red, and blue ink. It contained the entire history of all Arabian strains and how they became known or received their principal names.

This manuscript was handed down through the family of Ali Pasha Sherif and is now in the possession of his great-grandson, Ahmed Sherif.

Sobha, a Hamdaniyah Simriyah mare of Abbas Pasha breeding.
By Wazir out of Selma, she was purchased from Ismail Pasha by
Mahmud Bey, who later sold her to the Blunts. Photographed at
Newbuildings in 1898.

COURTESY OF LADY ANNE LYTTON

It was published in part by Prince Mohammed Ali as volume 2 of his *Breeding of Purebred Arab Horses* (Cairo, 1936). Much of the translation was erroneous. The material was presented totally out of context and sequence, and consequently was almost impossible to understand. The prince himself did not translate it (he spoke Arabic badly, his first language being French), and he does not mention who did.

Lady Anne Blunt was also in possession of the manuscript at one time, for she mentions in her notes that she had made a rough translation of it but that the Arabic was full of blunders and gaps; even so, one could still follow a distinct story. Perhaps the colloquialisms were diffi-cult for her to decipher, for the part on the Dahman strain which appears in Lady Wentworth's classic book (the *Authentic Arabian Horse*) is in-complete and hard to follow. Lady Anne further mentions in her notes of January 28, 1889, that Ali Pasha Sherif had in his possession *ten books* of Abbas Pasha's stud, with a full account of the origins of all the mares —when, where, and from whom he bought them. It was to these books Ali Pasha referred when making out pedigrees for the horses which Lady Anne had bought from him. What happened to the other nine, nobody knows. Prince Mohammed Ali obviously had an additional one, or more, for volume 2 of his work also makes mention of certain lists which are not contained in the historical manuscript of the strains.

The original Abbas Pasha manuscript has now been completely translated by Gulsun Ahmed Sherif, great-great-granddaughter of Ali Pasha Sherif, in collaboration with the present author, and the 400-page work, a collector's item for serious students of the breed, is to be pub-lished in the near future.

Abbas Pasha died in 1854 at the age of forty-one, having reigned as viceroy of Egypt from November 10, 1848, to July 13, 1854. It is said that he was assassinated by two of his servants because of his extreme cruelty to those who worked for him. Lady Anne Blunt relates the story that he became infuriated with one of his grooms who forgot to have a horse shod, and as punishment ordered a red-hot horseshoe be nailed to the sole of the forgetful culprit's foot.

It should be borne in mind, however, that the modern history of Egypt has been recorded by those who were partisan, influenced by personal or political motives. In fact, the writer of an Eastern romance could well find many materials in the records of Abbas's short and—to most historians—unprofitable episode of Egyptian history.

Brought up in an era when European adventurers were descending on the Middle East in search of fortune and fame, and when intrigues within his own family were rife, one can perhaps forgive Abbas Pasha some of the cruel inconsistencies of character attributed to him by many historians.

Abbas trusted no one, and there is an interesting account of his buried treasure hidden at Dar el-Beyda. After the treasure was hidden, Abbas had the witnesses killed so the secret would not be divulged. Two men managed to survive, however: a treasury keeper or official of Abbas's court, and a European who somehow escaped on a mule. On his deathbed somewhere in Europe, the European minutely described to his wife the exact spot, telling her how the jewels and so forth were rolled up in a scarf, tied with a rope, and buried under one of the pavements. His widow and Miss James (a friend of Lady Anne's who

Two exquisite mares in the tradition of Abbas Pasha: *Ansata Bint Mabrouka (by Nazeer out of Mabrouka), a Saklawiyah Jedraniyah, and *Ansata Bint Bukra (by Nazeer out of Bukra), a Dahmah Shahwaniyah.

PHOTOGRAPH BY POLLY KNOLL

related this story to her), together with one of the princesses, returned Dar el-Beyda and located the spot described, but on digging they found only traces of what had once been buried there. Afterwards, when the treasury keeper or official of Abbas's who had witnessed the burying died, certain things were found among the goods which were known to have been in the buried lot, such as a jeweled sword hilt, but the Princess Zeynab would not undertake proceedings to obtain what was rightfully hers from the man's heirs. The khediveh mother later continued searching the palace, authorizing destruction of parts of it by dynamiting, but nothing further was located and the palace itself was damaged beyond repair and fell into ruin.

Ansata Abbas Pasha, descending in tail female from the original Saklawiyah Jedraniyah mare, Ghazieh, owned by Abbas Pasha.

One of the great romances in Arabian horse history is thought to be that between Abbas Pasha and the legendary Wazira mare, the most celebrated Jellabiyah in history, for whom he paid some £7000, and from some of the great Arabians of our time descend. This story is related in the following chapter, and indeed the rest of this book and the Arabian horses mentioned herein are a testimony to this man's talent, and his love for and devotion to the beauty and purity of the breed.

Time has proved that Abbas Pasha made an incalculable contribution to Egypt, and to the Arabian horse world in general. Historians have overlooked this aspect of his life, which was in fact his life, and condemned him on other economic and personal accounts. Perhaps this chapter, and the subsequent ones, will make up for the failure of most historical writers to accord this contribution its rightful place in their chronicles.

9

THE ROMANCE OF THE JELLABIYAH

A RAB LEGEND relates that in the spring the oysters rise to the surface of the sea, and when it rains, or if a heavy dew exists, the oyster drinks in one or more drops of water, which then turn into pearls.[1] The sages of Araby often likened their finest Arabian mounts to "pearls of great price," and with good reason. Although the isle of Bahreyn has been famed since Assyrian times for its "jewels of the deep," for the past three centuries its pearls have been complimented in value and repute by their poetic simili: the Arabian horses of the Al Khalifas, and particularly the famous Jellabi strain.

The Al Khalifas trace their origin to the great Anazeh confederation, the celebrated horse-breeding bedouin tribe that once inhabited the deserts of Iraq and later journeyed south to Nejd. The ruling Saud family of Saudi Arabia and the ruling house of Al Sabah of Kuwait are likewise descended and related, though kinship has not prevented them from fighting each other. With the advent of the Al Khalifas some of the finest horses of desert Arabia were brought to Bahreyn in the late 1700s. The horse as an instrument of war and protection from attack was as indispensable to them as it was to their peninsula brethren, against whom they frequently waged war, and breeding superior horses was an ingrained family tradition. The precious strains of Dahman Shahwan, Dahman Najib, and Kuhaylan Jellabi were fanatically preserved by the Al Khalifas, and it was Sheik Mohammed al-Khalifa, reigning from 1843 to 1867, who supplied Abbas Pasha with so many magnificent specimens of the breed, particularly those strains mentioned above.

1. James Belgrave, *Welcome to Bahrain* (Bahrain, 1968).

The history of the Jellabiyah mare's arrival on Bahreyn has been handed down orally and is still talked about among the Arabs of that tiny island. It was Abdullah ibn-Ahmed al-Khalifa who obtained her, either during his rule (1825–1843) or earlier. The story as told on Bahreyn varies only slightly from the history by Aly Bey in the Abbas Pasha manuscript. The manuscript version is presented here just as it was written, in the typical manner of Arab storytelling. The simplicity of presentation has not been altered.

THE HISTORY OF THE KUHAYLAH OF IBN JARSHAN, AND HER NAME IS AL HANIF, AND HER CHILDREN, AL ZAHIYAH AND AL JELLABIYAH

In the presence of Huzam ibn-Hathlin, the Sheikh of Al Ajman, those who were present at the majless at Al Hassa were asked about the Kuhaylah of Ibn Jarshan. Amir ibn-Shayi' of Al Hathlin, and he is a white-haired man, and Mani' ibn-Muajjil, who is a white-haired man and the paternal cousin of Huzam ibn-Hathlin, and Mesaoud ibn-Felah, the brother of Sirhan al-'Abd, the Ra'i of the Stud, replied that: "She is a Kuhaylah Ajuz, the first of Al Kuhayl and the dearest and most valuable[2] of the Arabs of Nejd, and she is to be mated in the darkest night.[3] And she originates from Ibn Jarshan of Al Baqoum and has relatives at Ibn Jarshan's. And it happened there was a *ghazu* [raid] on Al Baqoum, and they took the flock of sheep and camels of Ibn Jarshan. And when the news reached Ibn Jarshan that his flock of sheep had been taken and Al Baqoum terrorized, and that the sheep were not returned, he rode his mare, Al Kuhayla, and caught up with the raiders. And he admonished them:

> With my Kuhaylah
> And my tribesmen
> Horsemen eighty or archers eighty
> Canst escape us.
> Wish as you will
> But futile your desire
> To raid Rashid ibn-Jarshan
> For his mare
> Whose grazing lands are the desert
> Brings pride and glory to her master.

And he took back his sheep from the tribe on that day.

---

2. The word used to mean "valuable" was '*anaber*'—the plural form of the Arabic word for ambergris.
3. A phrase frequently used to indicate there was no question about her purity.

Preparing for a ghazu (*raid*).

And Mohssen ibn-Darjan al-Abd of al-Ajman bought from Ibn Jarshan a *safra* mare [white with a yellowish tinge], whose name is Al Dughaym, and he agreed to give the first foal to Ibn Jarshan. And Ibn Darjan mated her to Rabshan al-Moaydi of our horses, O Ajman, and she produced a *khadra* filly [white with a green tinge] whose name is Al Shohayba, which was returned as *methnawi*[4] to Ibn Jarshan. And Al Shohayba was brought from Ibn Jarshan by Sirhan al-Abd of al-Ajman. And her mother, Al Dughaym, went to Al Salateen of the people of Al Jawf in the south.

And Sirhan mated Al Shohayba to Kuhaylan al-Karay [Kray] the horse of Ibn Awlbah of the family of Ma'ayid of al-Ajman, and she produced a *shaqra* [chestnut (fem.)] filly whose name is Sayida. And she was given by Daydan, the brother of Sirhan al-Abd, to Saud. And she did not produce anything at Sirhan's.

And Sirhan mated Al Shohayba to the Saklawi Jedran horse of Ibn Qarawan of the family of Ma'ayid of Al Ajman, coming from the horses of Ibn Urayer. And she produced a *shaqra* filly which we call Shaqra Sirhan.

And we mated Al Shohayba to Al Saqlawi Jedran, the horse of Abdul Aziz al-Saud, and she produced a *safra* filly who is pidgeontoed [*hanef jawani*], so they called her Al Hanif. And Al Shohayba was killed under Sirhan al-Abd during a battle with the people of Al Bataniya No'man.

And we mated Shaqra Sirhan to the Saklawi Jedran horse of Al Saud, and she gave birth to an *ashqar* [chestnut (masc.)] which we used as a stallion at our place. And on the day of Al Radimah, he was felled together with Al Hanif.

Sirhan mated the aforementioned *shaqra* to Kuhaylan Buraysan, the horse of Ibn Selba of Al Ajman, and she produced a *shaqra*. And the *shaqra* daughter of Buraysan was bought from Sirhan by an Adawani, on the first day of Al Islam. And we do not know what happened to her. But the mother was felled during a *razzia* [raid] that Al Dawasser made upon us.

And we mated Al Hanif to the Saklawi Jedran horse of Ibn Selba which was related to the horses of Ibn Urayer, and she produced a *khadra barda*[5] [snow white] filly which Sirhan sold while she was still a filly to Ibn Jellab of Al Murrah.

And we mated Al Hanif to her brother, Al Ashqar, and she gave birth to an *azraq* [blueish gray (masc.)] horse who died at Zared when he was two years old.

And we mated Al Hanif to the Saklawi horse of Ibn Selba which was related to the horses of Urayer, and she produced a *hamra sabha mezyuna*

---

4. An agreement between seller and buyer whereby the seller receives offspring from the mare before the deal is consummated.

5. The colors given are those at maturity or after the true color has been established. *Khadra* refers to white with a greenish tinge, whereas *barda* means cold, or snow-ice coming from the sky.

filly [bay with a white blaze and very beautiful] which they called Al Zahiyah.

Then Al Hanif was accidentally mated at Al Ma'dar to a horse that was running free in the open—a horse of the family of Suleyman of Al Ajman, but he was not pure [asil]. She gave birth to an azraq horse and when he reached four years of age, Tarah sold him for 400 rials to Al No'man, the people of the south.

And we mated Al Hanif to an aswad [black] Kuhaylan of Ibn Wabera called Waalan, and she produced an asfar horse whose name is Zahyan. But one of Al Ajman felled him.

And we mated Al Hanif to her brother, Al Ashqar, and she produced a safra filly whose name is Modayli. And on the day of Al Radimah, Al Hanif, the mother, was killed; and her brother, Al Ashqar, was killed.

And the one which had been bought by Ibn Jellab, he acquired with methnawi. And he mated her to Al Ashqar, her maternal uncle, and she produced a shaqra filly which was owned in partnership by Ibn Jellab and Sirhan. And Sirhan took her, but she died at his place when she was four years old and without producing any color.[6]

As for the mother, she went to Ibn Jellab for six years, but she did not produce any color. So Sirhan argued with Ibn Jellab and he took the mare by force and called her Al Jellabiyah, after Ibn Jellab. And Sirhan mated her to Kuhaylan Zoayr of the horses of Ibn Saud, and she produced an asfar horse.

Then Abdullah ibn-Ahmed al-Khalifa asked for her, and her son, and Abdullah took them and gave twelve hundred rials for the mother, two No'mani camels and two free birds [falcons] and a slave and clothing for his people, and the gathering of that year [i.e., the right to gather dates and the profit therefrom]. And for the horse he gave 800 rials. And Al Jellabiyah went to Ibn Khalifa, and she is the daughter of Al Hanif. Then the strain of Al Jellabiyat was cut off from us.

Although the manner in which the Jellabi strain came into being was not of startling import, the individuals were obviously outstanding and the price paid for Al Jellabiyah by Ibn Khalifa was a large one for those times. And as history was to prove, she became ancestress of a most highly valued family in desert Arabia and was particularly influential in the stud of Abbas Pasha and subsequently the world. One has only to reflect on Carl Raswan's classic photos of Mahroussa, Bint Yamama, *Nasr, *Zarife, *Roda, *Maaroufa, *Fadl,[7] and others, and their Jellabi

6. This phrase was often used to express the fact that the mare had not produced any foals.

7. All but Mahroussa and Bint Yamama were imported to America; such importations are indicated by an asterisk preceding the horse's name.

heritage immediately comes to mind.

Truth is often stranger than fiction, and Raswan handed down a romantic history of the Jellabiyah's family which, he said, was related to him while he was living in Egypt by Prince Kemal el-Dine and Prince Mohammed Ali, as well as testimony from Emir Feysul ibn-Dauwish, a descendant of the Feysul connected with the following story, with whom he was acquainted in desert Arabia. This synopsis is summarized from Raswan's writings.[8]

The Jellabiyah produced foals for Ibn Khalifa, and gradually the strain increased and became one of the most sought-after in all Arabia. For a long time Prince Abdullah ibn-Saud coveted the Jellabiyat which belonged to Emir Feysul ibn-Dawish, chief of Muteyr. However, the stud was small and the prince could not afford to relinquish any without damaging his own herd. He had originally come into possession of them through Ibn Hathlin of the Ajman, friends and allies of his Muteyr tribe, for over the years it had been the custom to exchange horses among each other in order to perpetuate certain families. It happened one day, however, that Abdullah's tribesmen ambushed a party of Feysul's bedouins and made off with one of Abdullah's precious Jellabiyah mares. Upon arrival at the camp, Abdullah recognized the mare as belonging to Feysul and returned her to his enemy with due apologies. Even though they were blood-feud enemies, they had still exchanged horses and loaned each other stallions during times of truce.

Later, when Mohammed Ali had requested more than two hundred specifically selected desert steeds from Abdullah, of particularly valuable strains, Feysul heard about it and sent one of his slaves to Abdullah's camp with the same chestnut Jellabiyah which had previously been captured by Abdullah's tribesmen. Now she was in foal to Kuhaylan Krush, a stallion belonging to Feysul's bedouins. Prince Abdullah did

8. It must be pointed out that the Abbas Pasha manuscript does not mention the episode as related by Raswan, and this does seem strange since she was so illustrious a mare. Indeed one would have expected further elucidation from the scribes as to how she reached the Stud. It is possible, of course, that this could be contained in one of the lost nine manuscripts, but the one extant is so complete in detail regarding the strains that this seems an unlikely supposition. Further, there is a history of the Kuhaylah Jazia mare in the manuscript and it sounds amazingly like part of the Raswan story. One wonders whether Raswan could have confused the strains. The story on Bahrain is also at variance with the Raswan tale, but since nothing concrete can be proven at this writing, the Raswan version is presented with the suggestion that the reader keep a question as to the total historical validity of the tale.

not feel he could accept Feysul's generous gift, but the slave explained that Feysul had a reason for so doing: it was his intention to ransom her and thus save for Abdullah the five mares of the Hamdani strain which Mohammed Ali had demanded. Feysul realized that Mohammed Ali would prefer having one Jellabiyah rather than the five Hamdaniyat, for he had been trying to obtain for some period of time this particular family, but always in vain. Feysul and Abdullah preferred the Hamdani strain for sentimental reasons, as well as for its comparative rarity.

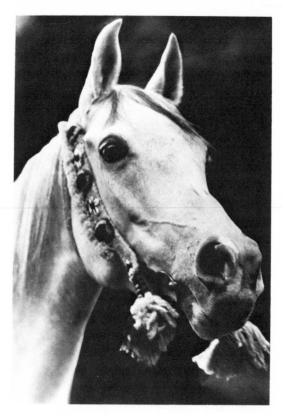

Mahroussa (by Mabrouk Manial out of Negma), one of the great Jellabiyah mares of all time.

PHOTOGRAPH BY CARL RASWAN

Prince Abdullah considered the idea, and finally accepted the Jellabiyah after he received consent from Abbas Pasha's father, Tousson Pasha, that the arrangement to retain the Hamdaniyat was agreeable.

The day of surrendering the horses arrived and it is said that Prince Abdullah claimed to have a vision as he turned over the leadrope of the Jellabiyah, suddenly exclaiming that he beheld a messenger of darkness and death in the likeness of Tousson Pasha seated upon the mare, and that Tousson's son would be the master of the mare which was now pregnant by the Krush stallion even before the foal was weaned from her.

Negma (by Dahman out of Bint Yamama).

PRINCE MOHAMMED ALI COLLECTION

Abbas Pasha was then only an infant of two and far too young to be master of the mare at that time, or even before her foal was weaned. Thus the Egyptian master of horses, who received the mare, initially paid little heed to the prince. But Abdullah continued and said that Tousson would indeed die if the Jellabiyah went to Egypt, but that if she remained in her native home of Arabia, Tousson would live. Abdullah's prophecy was ignored and taken for the babbling of a superstitious bedouin, and the Jellabiyah was soon on her way to Egypt with Tousson, who advised his father, Mohammed Ali, that she was to become the property of Ibrahim Pasha. But the prophecy of Abdullah was not to be reckoned with lightly, and three months later Tousson Pasha was dead of poison.

It was in 1816, when Abbas Pasha was three years old, that Ibrahim Pasha prepared to leave Cairo for a campaign in Arabia. The Jellabiyah he had received from Abdullah via Tousson had by now given birth to a handsome sorrel colt who was not yet weaned from his mother's side.

*H. H. Mohammed Ali's Hamida (by *Nasr out of Mahroussa),
imported in 1932.*

PHOTOGRAPH BY LOIS KINNEY

Astride the Jellabiyah, Ibrahim Pasha rode off to bid his brother's widow and young Abbas farewell; mounted behind him on another mare rode Srur, the bedouin slave who had accompanied the Jellabiyah from Arabia to Egypt by order of Feysul. Upon seeing his uncle, the young child Abbas rushed up to him, and taking a fancy to the Jellabiyah asked if he might ride her. Ibrahim obliged his little nephew and dismounted to lift the boy up on the mare's back, telling him that while he was away in Arabia fighting the war, Abbas would become the mare's master.

Later that afternoon Abbas was still astride the mare, following his uncle and a military detachment along a path near the Mokattam hills. When camp had been pitched one of the officers of the mounted troop stepped up to Ibrahim Pasha and asked that he be allowed to speak. The officer then revealed that he was the former master of horses for Tousson Pasha, and that Abdullah's psychic vision, the message which had been given to him in Arabia, must be fulfilled. The Jellabiyah and her colt must be sacrificed to save the royal family and Abbas from disaster.

Ibrahim Pasha chided the superstitious soldier, refusing his request. But then before anybody could interfere the crazed officer drew the pistols from his sash and shot the Jellabiyah and her beautiful colt point blank. Abbas crashed to the ground, but fortunately he was unwounded. The stricken mare, struggling to rise to her feet, momentarily occupied Ibrahim Pasha's gaze, but he quickly recovered his senses and taking a scimitar felled the demented officer in one fell swoop, cleaving him half in two.

Srur bent down and comforted the young child, and taking a daggar from his belt cut off a strand of the dead mare's blessed forelock. Carefully he folded it into a small amulet and then, placing it around the neck of Abbas, prophesied to the child that from then on the memory of the Jellabiyah would be with him, and he should become a peer among the masters of Ishmael's desert steeds.

Ibrahim Pasha, noting the touching scene and tenderness which Srur displayed towards his nephew, freed the slave and made him master of horses of his own stud. Srur then accompanied him to Arabia, and became to become a vital link in the chain of friendships which Ibrahim Pasha formed with the desert sheiks, particularly Feysul ibn-Dauwish of the Muteyr, and the chiefs of Harb, Ateybah, Ajman, and Beni Khaled.

In the meantime Abdullah ibn-Saud had been captured and killed, and his son Turki had also been killed, leaving Faisal ibn-Turki as prince of Arabia and leader of the Wahabbis. Faisal in due course set out to revenge the plunder of his grandfather's stud by Feysul ibn-Dauwish, and falling upon his old enemy, stripped him of a large number of his war horses and thus most of his broodmares.

Now desperate, Feysul ibn-Dauwish made a move to save his remaining small but precious stud of Jellabiyat by sending them off to Ibn

Above, *Maaroufa (by Ibn Rabdan out of Mahroussa) at age twenty-nine on the Babson Farm. Imported in 1932, she became the most influential Jellabiyah mare in America within straight Egyptian breeding programs. Below, Fay Roufa (by Fay El Dine out of *Maaroufa) in old age, a fine example of a classic Jellabiyah head.

Hathlin of the Ajman on Bahreyn Island, the original breeder of the strain. In the meantime Faisal ibn-Turki was ambushed by the Egyptians and packed off to the Citadel in Cairo, where fate willed that he and Abbas met. Afterwards, Faisal realized and regretted his vengeful raid against Feysul ibn-Dauwish and the irreparable loss suffered to the horseflesh on both sides. If given the opportunity, he told Abbas Pasha, he would try to make amends. Together they composed a message to Srur, the old slave who was then in Central Arabia, and with his assistance Faisal ibn-Turki and Feysul ibn-Dauwish became reconciled. Then Faisal, while in Cairo, ordered his stud manager in Nejd to return to Feysul any mares and foals which had been captured by his people from Feysul, and any foals which had since been born. Thus was Abbas instrumental in mending to some degree the damage done by his grandfather to horsebreeding in Arabia.

In 1842, upon Faisal's return to his capital at Riadh, he invited Feysul ibn-Dauwish of Muteyr to visit him. A festival was proclaimed, and among the visitors was Srur, Feysul's former slave. As a token of friendship Faisal ibn-Turki and Feysul ibn-Dauwish asked Srur to enact the ritual of blood sacrifice for their newly established brotherhood, and to cut the throat of a young lamb while it was placed across the withers of an aged white Jellabiyah mare, one of Feysul's original mares.

At this time Srur[9] asked Feysul if he could take leave to see the ra'i of Bahreyn, Ibn Khalifa, to bring back Feysul's stud of Jellabiyat which he had previously sent off to prevent them from falling into the hands of his new blood brother, Faisal. As fate would have it, however, Ibn Khalifa decided that he wanted to keep the mares and their foals and would not part with more than one animal at a time, and then only for the price of five thousand gold pieces. Ibn Khalifa, like Feysul and Faisal, was a fanatic breeder and although he held the horses in trust to protect their future and assure their preservation, they were creatures of God and therefore in trust to Him, not for the men who owned them.

9. Here the story varies with that told on Bahreyn, for there it is said Srur was a slave employed by Ibn Khalifa who he sent with the horses to Abbas Pasha, as in the tale previously related. Mrs. D. Al Khalifa says: "In those days as today, the rulers do not sell horses to each other. They exchanged and/or gave gifts to each other, but not money. . . . After Feysul's escape from the Cairo citadel, back in Riyadh, he received the Jellabiah from Mohammed here, and Feysul sold that mare to Abbas for a fantastic sum of money, and that is why she was so famous."

Furthermore, he had gone to considerable expense to maintain the animals.

The amount which Ibn Khalifa demanded was exorbitant, but the two "brothers" were determined to regain at least one of their priceless mares. Therefore they pooled their resources and some months later

El Maar (by Fay El Dine out of *Maaroufa), a champion mare and one of the finest *Maaroufa daughters.

Srur and Ibn Khalifa sealed an agreement. Srur left Bahreyn with two Jellabiyah mares, each with a new filly by her side and each by a different but original Jellabi stallion of Ibn Hathlin; the mares had been bred back to another Jellabi of Ibn Hathlin. But in order to talk Ibn Khalifa out of this prize package, since the two brothers had insufficient money to buy them, Srur made a supreme sacrifice: he gave his own son, Hamud, to Ibn Khalifa.

The old black slave delivered his priceless charge to Feysul, but in so doing asked one favor of his former master. Srur had never forgotten the day when the Jellabiyah mare had been shot from under her master, Abbas Pasha, and the love of the boy for the mare. Now Abbas was grown; twenty-six years had passed and Srur had seen his prophecy come to be. Abbas had established a supreme stud of desert horses. Thus, Srur asked Feysul to allow him to return to Abbas Pasha in Egypt with a true gift of desert brotherhood: one of the Jellabiyah mares and her filly, to recompense him for his childhood loss and the longing he had since felt.

Feysul ibn-Dauwish agreed to the old man's request and sent him off on his last journey by way of Mecca and Medina, to receive the blessing of Faisal for the mare and her filly. Faisal named her Wazira. She is registered as Wazira in the studbooks of Egypt, England, America, Poland, Russia, Germany, France, and anywhere else that her blood is preserved in the world today.

Meanwhile, Faisal ibn-Turki quietly recompensed Ibn Khalifa for Srur's son, and eventually the boy joined his father in Egypt where he became master of the horses to Abbas Pasha.

Such was the romance of Abbas Pasha and his Jellabiyah; altered to a degree or perhaps embellished by poets and authors over the years, but nevertheless firmly woven into the thread of Arabian history which binds human beings so closely to the Arabian horse. Indeed great personal sacrifices and devotion to an ideal are necessary for the preservation of anything worthwhile, and Abbas Pasha had proved to the world that they who best command the ideal, enjoy most the real.

The romance did not die with Abbas Pasha's passing in 1854: it lives on wherever one finds a stallion or mare of this strain today. Thanks to the Al Khalifas and Abbas Pasha, the select members of this strain still remain "pearls of great price."

Ali Pasha Sherif.

10

ALI PASHA SHERIF PRESERVES
THE LEGACY

A<small>BBAS PASHA</small> guided the Arab horse to unparalleled heights in Egypt, but when he was assassinated in 1854, his precious animals were inherited by his son, El Hami Pasha, a madcap youth of eighteen who showed little respect for his inheritance and gave away horses right and left to everyone who managed to approach him with a well-turned piece of flattery.

As a result of the young pasha's generosity, the German king William I was the recipient of the grey Arab stallion El Hami in 1858. Then in 1860 King William participated in a trade, exchanging with El Hami Pasha two horses and obtaining the grey Arab mare Zariffa and the grey Arab stallion Soliman—the latter by Gadir out of Voidna, born in 1852. Shortly thereafter the sale of the century began and lasted some three weeks at El Hami Pasha's Cairo stables. One account relates that some 90 stallions, 210 mares, and 180 colts and fillies went under the hammer, while another states that at the time of the sale only 350 animals were left.

A sale of this magnitude was a phenomenon in the horse world and naturally attracted the attention of horse lovers around the globe. Some people came just to look at these magnificent creatures that had achieved universal recognition, while others prepared to pay large sums to obtain whatever they could. And so although the sale took place at a time when money was tight, it realized good prices. The sale lasted three weeks and the bids were made in English guineas. On one day twenty-six horses fetched 5000 guineas; aged mares twenty years old were sold at prices ranging from 180 to 250 guineas, while colts and fillies went from 300 to 700 guineas each. The French government bought eighteen stallions and mares, the Australian government five stallions, the Italian government twenty animals all told, and the German government eight stallions. German records indicate that Baron von Huegel, representing the king of Wurtemburg, purchased at the auction the grey Saklawi Jedran stallion, Gadir, born 1847; the brown Sadhan, born 1858, the grey mare Dachma El Chahouan; and two mares in foal: the grey Saklawiyah Jedraniyah, Doueba, and the grey Saklawiyah Moreghiyah, Moreghia. Gadir was said to be an outstanding specimen while Sadhan received little acclaim. The three mares apparently did not prove productive or successful in the stud, however, for nothing remains from them. And von Huegel paid well for what he got.

Von Huegel's records indicate that the remainder of the horses were sold to different persons in Egypt in lots of two and three, except that a "young man, Ali Bey, President of the Court of the Chamber of Commerce, bought 40 horses during the auction." In addition to the collection of superb Arabians Ali Bey already possessed as a result of his father's governorship of Arabia and the purchases he had made directly from Abbas Pasha, it was obvious that Egypt had another savior of her legacy at hand. Thus many of Abbas Pasha's most celebrated and beloved horses were soon gracing the elaborate new stables which Ali Bey built for them at his ornate palace on the beautifully shaded boulevard of Sharia Abd el-Aziz, not far from Abdin and Bab el-Louk in Cairo. The palace was built in the 1830s when Egypt was making her first tentative overtures to Europe, in the flush of her triumph over the mameluke tyranny, longing for progress and greatness, as well as freedom, but ignorant of what these consisted in. It was a mighty memorial of those days, in conception as in execution, typical of the epoch, splendid in its main features. The palace, surrounded by a walled garden, dominated the whole street.

The approach to the gateway of the mansion was wholly suited to the state and condition of so powerful a pasha. The parapet, to the right hand, and then to the left, formed with the road that paralleled it an access as nearly personal and private as could be insured in the heart of a city. Descending the brief slope of the roadway, one halted in front of a huge gate. In it was a smaller gate for the admittance of lesser persons who could not drive into the pasha's courtyard in full state in a carriage. Within was the great vaulted arch of the entrance, and beyond that, the long courtyard; and at the end of this courtyard stood a wall near which were two spreading banyan trees. In any other environment one might have wondered at their size, at the expansion of their countless intertwining roots and the area of their broad-leaved shade. Lady Anne

Bint Helwa (by Aziz II out of Helwa), a Saklawiyah Jedraniyah mare bred by Ali Pasha Sherif, was purchased by the Blunts for Crabbet.

COURTESY OF LADY ANNE LYTTON

Blunt never failed to note these marvelous trees at each visit. However, in this environment they were to most minor details, and the eye was just as easily attracted by the entry to yet another courtyard, more distant, prefaced and guarded by vines that clambered all over the wall and archway that bounded it.

When one entered the first courtyard, the size of the building and the extent of its precincts gradually asserted themselves. On either side were the two wings of the palace, which had some 500 windows. Opposite, on the other side of the courtyard as one faced it were the stables, where were the great high white-washed stalls that housed the pasha's priceless collection of Arab horses. The garden was as great as the palace, and in it were large rosebeds and areas covered by vines on pergolas. Two tall cocoa palms dominated everything and harmonized with the long expanse of grey building. Indeed the whole scheme was grandiose in intention and a fitting background for the world's finest collection of desert steeds then existing.

Ghazala "Bint Bint Helwa," founder of a dynasty all her own. Bred by Ali Pasha Sherif, she was purchased with her dam December 14, 1896, by the Blunts, who later sold her to Spencer Borden.

Ali Bey learned to love horses early in life. Born in Egypt, he attended the same school as his father, El Sayed Mohammed Sherif. At the age of twelve, El Sayed Mohammed was brought from Albania to Egypt by Mohammed Ali, with whom he found favor and who obtained admittance for him to the school at Khanka, not far from Cairo, where the sons of pashas and princes were educated. Eventually El Sayed Mohammed became an important administrator in Mohammed Ali's regime, filling various government posts and later becoming governor of Arabia, including Lebanon and Syria. El Sayed Mohammed instilled the love of horses and horsemanship in his son through association with desert chieftains, as well as through Abbas Pasha and the royal family. Ali Bey was sent to the French staff officer's school in Paris where he completed his education, and when he returned to Egypt he was commissioned as an artillery colonel in Mohammed Ali's Egyptian Army. After the death of his father, Ali Bey received the title of Ali Pasha Sherif, becoming president of the Chamber of Commerce and subsequently president of the legislative council. In this capacity he served throughout the reign of Khedive Mohammed Tewfik, father of Khedive Abbas Pasha Hilmi II.

Ali Pasha's sons likewise inherited his love for horses, particularly Ibrahim Bey, who owned the largest stable of racehorses in Cairo, the cost of which nearly brought about his own financial ruin. It is still related by the Sherif family how Ali Pasha, insisting that his children become excellent horsemen, tested their skill often by placing a coin between their knee and the saddle. If it fell during their equestrian exercises, they received a whipping for their failure.

Both Abbas Pasha and Ali Pasha Sherif showed favoritism toward the strains of Dahman Shahwan and Duhaym al-Nejib, Saklawi Jedran of Ibn Sudan and Saklawi Jedran of Ibn Zobeyni (the superb grey stallion, Wazir, combined both these strains), as well as Kuhaylan Mimreh, Kuhaylan Jellabi, Kuhaylan Nowak of the Debbe strain, and Wadnan Hursan. At the height of Ali Pasha's stud, he had assembled some four hundred of the finest Arabians in the world. However, the horse plague invaded Egypt and wiped out many valuable strains, and only those which he had removed to Upper Egypt were saved. Wazir, the most celebrated horse in Egypt and unbeaten on the track at all distances, escaped the plague's ravages and continued to breed mares until he died in 1890. Lady Anne saw the famous horse in 1881 and remarked that "Vizir is still there looking better than any of the other horses. I remark that the black on the muzzle in his case completely covers the lips. He is quite white (not fleabitten). The Shueyman (fleabitten) is also well and a good horse, but I prefer Vizir (Wazir) who combines the Sudan and Ibn Sbeni strains of Segl. Jedran."

Lady Anne Blunt, who was later to obtain many of Ali Pasha Sherif's famous horses, stated that despite the setback of the plague, the stud carried on and remained world famous. She further records in her diary her first meeting with the pasha at the theater in Cairo on November 24, 1880. "Ali Pasha came into the box and staid some time talking to Wilfrid [Scawen Blunt] and me about his horses and at the first word or two one could perceive he understood all about Bedouin ideas of race and was imbued with them. He wanted us to visit his stud." Her diary continues:

On Thursday very tired. . . . But we had a great pleasure, the greatest we could have, that of seeing some purebred Arabians. By appointment we were at Ali Pasha's house at two. He received us and showed us his horses first then a few mares and a half dozen foals and afterwards directed us to go to see the remaining mares at Abassieh.

Of the horses most were white or grey—the first "Shueyman Sebaa" and of that breed—handsome with fine head, not very good shoulder—the second called "Vizir" [Wazir]—a Seglawi Jedran of Ibn Soudan, fine all round —18 years old but with no appearance of age. His head in shape reminded me of both Kars and Basilisk (sire: S.J. of Ibn Sbeni). The third a young horse and still darkish grey, Wadnan Khursan. There were about five more; one a white Seglawi Jedran of either Ibn Sbeni or Ibn Soudan (I have a confused recollection of the name), very good, a fine shoulder—all the horses have splendid legs except a handsome Dahman Shahwan chestnut with 4 white stockings who has badly curbed hocks—4 years old only and used for breeding in spite of the defect. (N.B.—Mesaoud's sire, Aziz.) Ali Pasha made no allusion to the hocks but said that this horse had been used for the stud at 3 years old, for he had been curious to see whether the 4 white legs would be inherited. He does not like 4 white legs. The marks have not been transmitted and we afterwards saw a foal (filly 15 days old) from a splendid Seglawieh Jedranieh, Horra, own sister to Vizir, mare—white—which has but one small patch of white just above one hind foot. The chestnut horse was good *except* the hocks—fine long neck, well-arched and head a little like Canora's. In the desert, at Abassieh, we saw 2 bay Duhaymah Nejib mares difficult to choose between. The more interesting at first is a 5 year old—bright full bay (like Kars) with 2 white hind feet, small star. Her crest, wither and shoulder exaggerated like the portraits of the Godolphin Arabian. She is a picture and at a little distance very like Kars. The other mare was darker bay and altogether I think the best—legs stouter and more muscle— she is 6 or 7—a daughter of a celebrated D. N. mare called Norah who died of the disease when this mare was 2 years old. The first bay is a grand-daughter of Norah. Both of these are daughters of Vizir.

Since our visit to this stud, Ali Pasha has promised to let us have in writing a list of his different strains—those he now possesses and those he lost at the time of the disease. Several of them are probably quite extinct as he got them from Abbas Pasha who had swept the whole of Arabia for specimens of the particular breeds he fancied.

Some nine years later events transpired which led Ali Pasha Sherif to sell ten of his precious horses. The Blunts record that the sale was made because of political and financial difficulties, while the Sherif family maintains that the pasha was wealthy to the end and left land, money, and also property in other countries to his heirs, including a castle in Italy. The Blunts based much of their information on that related by an agent of the pasha's, P. Flemotomo, and it is obvious that some of his

Mesaoud, a Saklawi Jedran of Ibn Sudan, was bred by Ali Pasha Sherif and purchased by the Blunts in 1888. Imported to Crabbet in 1891, he was sold in 1903 to Russia. He became one of the most influential stallions of all time.

COURTESY OF LADY ANNE LYTTON

information was erroneous or self-serving. Nevertheless, Flemotomo was
an intermediary for the Blunts and he obtained for them a list of the
horses to be sold and spoke for them to the pasha. The pasha despised
the English in general, having suffered political persecution at their
hands, but he continued to remain cordial to the Blunts, understanding
that they were sincere and dedicated to establishing a fine stud.

In her notes of January 17, 1889, Lady Anne mentions liking Ibn
Sherara. She further adds: "Wilfrid is of the opinion, and I think he is
right—that a Seklawi, one of those white Seklawi's of Ali Pasha Sherif's,
has certain points not found elsewhere and therefore it would be well
to buy one from the Pasha." At this time they were founding their
Sheykh Obeyd Stud, and planned to buy a stallion and two mares for
its foundation. The horses Ali Pasha listed for sale were (the comments
in quotation marks are remarks made by the Blunts):

1) A daughter of the Jellabieh, the chestnut, white forefeet, age 5.
Sire: Wazir.

2) A daughter of Makbula, the chestnut (Jellabieh), age 2. Sire:
Aziz II. "Very pretty filly."

3) A daughter of Aruseh, age 11, Nowakyeh. Sire: Harkan.

4) A son of Yemameh, the younger, chestnut colt, Seglawi Soudan.
Sire: Aziz. "Very fine, showy colt, four white legs." [This horse was
the celebrated Mesaoud.]

5) A son of Zarifah, the grey, younger, Seglawi, age 5. Sire: Aziz II.

6) A son of Zarifah, the grey, elder, Seglawi Semni, age 6. Sire:
Aziz II.

7) A son of Helweh, grey, Seglawi Ibn Soudan, age 5. Sire: Aziz II.

8) A son of Yamameh, the elder, Seglawi Seudan, age 4. Sire: Aziz II.

9) A son of the Jellabieh, the chestnut. Sire: Wazir. "Very handsome colt, all chestnut."

10) A son of Bint Azz (Momtazeh), bay, Dahman Shahwan. Sire:
Aziz II.

Within a week Mr. Flemotomo had obtained notes from Ali Pasha
Sherif about the horses the Blunts desired. Mesaoud, the chestnut colt
Judith (later Lady Wentworth) wanted so definitely, was priced at
£60. He proved to be one of the greatest bargains of all time and the
foundation or "rock" upon which Crabbet built its world-famed stud.
The "very pretty filly" priced at £80 (daughter of Makbula) was

Khatilah, and the other chestnut colt, at £100, by Wazir, was Merzuk. Ibn Sherara was not for sale, although the pasha agreed to put a price of £200 on him. At this time Lady Anne took special note in her diaries of her concern that "I am afraid Ali Pasha's stud will soon be a thing of the past—it must come if he once begins to break it up and is in the hands of creditors, it cannot last long." Again, this seems inconsistent with reality, when one considers the huge fortunes inherited by Ali Pasha Sherif's children.

Two days later Ali Pasha Sherif agreed to take £220 for the three horses and offered to sell Ibn Nadir, a very handsome grey stallion who was blind in one eye; the one which both Lady Anne and Wilfrid Scawen Blunt considered "the finest of the lot" despite his age of eighteen years.

By the twenty-seventh of January the Blunts went to see the horses and had Zeyd, their Muteyr bedouin friend, ride several of them. Unless Ibn Nadir could be purchased they decided they did not want grey! The decision was made in favor of the three chestnuts. Lady Anne thought the three well worth having, and wrote: "The pick is, of course, the Seglawi Soudani son of Aziz—he is four white legged and high up to the knee but surprising handsome. For a defect there is a certain lightness of hock inherited from Aziz but nothing wrong. The Jellabieh filly is the lightest of bone—the Wazir colt—Jelaby—also has very good strong hocks and is full of fire—three chestnuts will look well."

By this time foreigners had received word that Ali Pasha would sell some of his horses, and even the Polish breeders became interested in buying this select stock. Prince Roman Sanguszko had been a visitor to the pasha's stud and mentioned in a letter written in 1897 to Wilfrid Scawen Blunt:

I perfectly remember Ali Cherif who, when I was last in Cairo, was neither old nor Pasha; his name was Ali Bey, son of Cherif Pasha (it was in 1862) and already then possessed a well-known stud which I have visited and especially some admirable mares. I had wanted to buy one, for which he was asking 10,000 francs in gold—but I was told that she was already old and that she had never foaled. She was black and of great beauty.

Count J. Potocki was also in contact in 1890 with the Blunts, who offered to act as intermediaries in assisting him to purchase from Ali

Pasha Sherif. The pasha had decided to sell the two stallions, Mahruss and Aziz II, but he was asking the price of £800, which the count considered ridiculous considering the horses' ages. He proposed 500 louis for both, but went off to India to see if he could find anything cheaper and more to his liking. He apparently did not luck out, for in a letter of February 12, 1890, he wrote from Bombay that he would pass through Cairo to conclude his business with the pasha if the horses were still for sale. But he still quibbled over the price and was willing to offer 10–12,000 francs. The dickering went on, but the count still

In front of Ali Pasha Sherif's stables, a groom poses with
El Kharsah.

COURTESY OF AHMED SHERIF

persisted in offering only a trifling difference in worth from the price asked by the pasha. Finally, when he decided he would buy the horses, the pasha had become fed up and refused to sell. The count then bought an Indian racing Arab who was not only a failure at stud but turned out to be savage; he killed a groom and had to be put down.

On the fifteenth of January, 1897, an auction of the sixteen horses remaining in the Ali Pasha Sherif stud was held, and Lady Anne attended. The sale began at 10 o'clock sharp under the omnipresent blue Egyptian skies. It was a momentous day. Fate was with Lady Anne and she obtained Ibn Nura for £30—"the horse is magnificent—pity age 20"—and Badiaa for £70, plus an additional £5 in auction costs. She missed purchasing the orphan and the Bint Bint Jamila chestnut twenty-month foal which went for £45/6—"a mistake, but no use lamenting"—and also missed out on Bint Azz. The latter went for £40 because two of Lady Anne's friends told her not to bid as it was not bonafide bidding—and the dealer, Amato, got her. Most of the buyers were Egyptians, and Mahmud Moharram bought the last two fillies and two colts, with Mohammed Khadr buying the Makbula filly.

Three days later Lady Anne was moved to write the following letter to the *Times*, but for some reason it was never sent. Her granddaughter, Lady Anne Lytton, found the letter in the Sheykh Obeyd herdbook, penned in Lady Anne Blunt's own hand. It is reproduced here in its entirety as a tribute to the man she so greatly admired:

Sir:

I feel sure it will interest readers of the Times in many parts of the World to learn that the last remains of the once celebrated stud of Ali Pasha Sherif at Cairo have just been dispersed under circumstances to lovers of the Arabian horse, somewhat pathetic. This unique stud traced its origin to that famous collection of pure Arab mares and horses made by Abbas I, Viceroy of Egypt some 50 years ago, to obtain which he ransacked the desert of Arabia and broke down, by the enormous prices he offered, the traditional refusal of the Bedouin breeders to part with their best mares. In order to achieve his object Abbas employed native agents, Arabs from Nejd of high birth and position whom he retained in his service at Cairo and treated with all possible consideration and who in return served him faithfully in a business he considered the most important of his reign. He thus got together some 290 mares with stallions to match, the absolute pick of the Desert which still are spoken of there with wonder and regret as the most authentic collection of pure blood ever made outside the Peninsula. These he established as a breeding stud in a fantastic desert home he created for them halfway between Cairo and Suez, placing them in charge of his Nejd Bedouins and causing them to be treated in all respects as Bedouin horses are in their own country. All was done regardless of cost and vast sums were expended, for in the Suez desert there is neither water nor horse pasture and everything had to be conveyed to them from the Nile valley, 50 miles away, a train of several one hundred laden camels being constantly employed for the purpose while as many more she-camels supplied them as the Bedouin custom is with their milk. The ruins of the Viceroy's desert palace of Dar el Beyda in connection with this establishment, and which at a distance look as large as Windsor Castle, are still to be seen from the abandoned post road which formerly carried the Indian Mails to Suez, and the immense reservoirs of hewn stone wherein the Nile water was stored—a desolate and romantic spot in this actual year of grace as anything there is so modern in the world. Nevertheless at Abbas' death in 1854 the whole of his desert establishment was broken up. The Palace, which had cost a million to build, was abandoned to the bats and owls, and the priceless stud was sent by his heirs to the hammer. At the public auction in that year great prices were realized and King Victor Emmanuel transferred a *moiety* of the stud to Italy where it flourished till his death in 1879 when it was again sold and to the great loss of the Italian Government, finally dispersed. The other *moiety*, however, and as the Arabs affirm, the most valuable, remained at Cairo, the best mares and stallions having been bid for and bought on the advice of Hashe, Abbas' chief Bedouin groom, and who best knew the ins and outs of the pedigrees, by Ali Pasha Sherif, then a young man of high family, the largest landowner after the Viceregal family in Egypt, and as great an enthusiast as Abbas himself had been about horses. Under the new management and transferred to Cairo, the stud maintained itself for 20 years and more in full efficiency, and continued to be recognized still as beyond question the first and most authentic Arab stud out of Arabia. Ali Pasha made it his one hobby and delight. The broodmares were seldom seen abroad, being kept secluded in their harem like the Eastern princesses they were, but the horses were a feature in the Cairo streets. They were entered from time to time in the local races and generally won, the horse Wazir being the most prominent of those that were put in training. The Pasha was too much of a Grand Seigneur to sell, but he gave away royally to Sultans, Kings and Eunuchs, and the finest stallion now in Abd el Hamid's stables in Constantinople is an old one of his breeding. They were nearly all pure white, the fortunate colour of the East. Then misfortune came. With the Khedive Ismail's downfall the reign of gold in Egypt ended and Ali Pasha in spite of his immense landed possessions became indebted with his master. The horse plague followed and swept off half his breeding stock in a single year, and little by little and year by year, since 1882, something was shorn from the magnificence of the Stud which was not replaced. Outwardly the Pasha maintained a brave appearance. He was one of the great functionaires of Tewfik's Court, he was in credit with the British Agency, he was even entrusted with the sublime function, under Lord Dufferin's Charter, of presiding over the Legislative Council. But indoors there was a sad lack of money and the debts were estimated at a quarter of a million sterling. Then came the scandal of the Pasha's arrest two years ago on a charge of slave buying, a somewhat cruel advantage was taken of an old fashioned Turkish gentleman by modern official zeal, and then as its consequence his formal interdiction as one no longer capable of managing his own affairs or distinguishing between *meum* and *tuum* [yours and mine]. Last of all the public sale of his effects by order of his legal guardian in the interest of his creditors. His beloved stud, woefully diminished in numbers but still scrupulously pure in blood was the latest of all Ali Pasha's possessions to which in his senility he clung, and it is related of him that for some weeks he defied his guardians and the law, and sat day by day at a window of his palace armed with a Winchester repeater[1] threatening all and sundry who should approach to seize it. It was a sad spectacle when at last the few high born descendants of a race secluded for 49 years were led into the light of day and put up to common auction by a common Italian salesman. The broodmares were still beautiful and with the marks of their high breeding, though from long inbreeding and lack of vigorous conditions of outdoor life somewhat fragile and insubstantial. Half starved too by the penury of the old Pasha's establishment they realized small prices at the bidding. Seven of them, I am glad to think, have been added to the credit of England and the Crabbet Stud, as also one of the three aged stallions, a venerable but splendid ruin. *Sunt lachrymae rerum* [there are tears for things], and especially at this hour of evil omen for all Eastern sublimities, we cannot but be saddened at the final disappearance of what was in its day a noble thing, a type of Oriental magnificence passed away forever.

On the twentieth of January, 1897, Lady Anne was taking her customary ride into the desert when Abd el-Hamid Bey, a son of Ali Pasha Sherif, arrived, offering to sell his mare. She was a daughter of Bint Fereyha by Aziz II, grey, very strong and rising five years of age. The transaction was agreed upon and £50 was paid to the pasha's son, who told her Ali Pasha Sherif himself would see her if she would call to ask for the *hojjas* (pedigrees) of the horses bought directly from His Excellency. Lady Anne made note that they had now secured the larger

1. Again, this sounds like a Flemotomo fabrication, since Lady Anne did not witness the event herself.

part of what remained of the pasha's stud, that is, Bint Helwa and her foal, Bint Fereyha, two daughters of Bint Fereyha, Badiaa, Makbula, Bint Bint Jamila and the two stallions, Ibn Nura and Ibn Bint Nura, together with three horses acquired previously—Anter, Sherif, and Ibn Mahruss.

Ahmed Sherif, great-grandson of Ali Pasha Sherif, poses with
*Gamilaa, a *Morafic daughter imported to America by
Douglas Marshall.

Despite Ali Pasha's antipathy for the British, he apparently maintained friendly relations with Lady Anne, as did his sons. She was one to inspire confidence in the face of incredible odds, and it was with great sadness that she noted in her diary entry for February 26, 1897, that a friend had met crowds and police and soldiers and was told Ali Pasha had died and was being buried. "Poor Ali Pasha—Mutlak [her stableman] has a good heart and grieved for his old master."

March 26 saw the remnants of Ali Pasha Sherif's horses go under the hammer at the serai. Lady Anne attended with her daughter, Judith, and Mutlak. The auction was delayed and did not begin until long after 9 o'clock. Aziz II was the first horse to be brought out at a £20 bid in, but was taken back unsold. The two-year-old filly, Bint Bint Azz, a grey, brought £29, Ibn Johara £32, Ibn Zarifa el-Saghir £27, and el-Kebir £26. Ibn Bint Nura el-Saghir fetched £56, el-Kebir £43, Ibn Bint Jellabieh Feysul £55, Ibn Bint Nura es-Shakra £44, Ibn Makbula £63, Ibn Bint Azz el—Saghir £60, Johara Bint Helwa (Seglawieh) £80, Bint Horra and foal £125, Bint Nura es-Shakra £106, and Bint Makbula £255. Of these she bid up to £31 for the grey three-year-old Ibn Johara, a splendid colt which had been sick with a cold, and later she regretted not having gone to £35. She obtained Bint Nura and foal and Bint Nura es-Shakra, and regretted not having bought the chestnut Ibn Bint Jellabieh Feysul, who was four years old and very beautiful, but she feared to add to the number of stallions they had already acquired. Mutlak went home with the two mares and the foal, and Lady Anne was delighted to have gotten them. She very much liked Johara, the Saklawiyah half-sister of Bint Helwa, although she did not consider her quite up to the other two. Had there not been an unpleasant scene the day previous (apparently between Judith and Wilfrid against her), she might have bid and got her, she noted in her diary.

A few remnants were still for sale by Ali Pasha Sherif's sons, and on the April 8 Lady Anne went to see Ibrahim Bey Sherif, who had bought the mare Johara Bint Helwa, but was now willing to sell her for more than the £80 he paid. Ahmed Pasha had offered £100 for her, and Lady Anne was willing to give £120, although she was distressed "because Wilfrid and Judith were so averse that it was not worth disputing about." In a poignant note, she mentions that she could almost regret having purchased the Ali Pasha mares because Judith, her sole heir, did not value them.

However, Lady Anne persevered, and Sunday, April 18, found her trusted *sais*, Mutlak, arriving with the chestnut mare, Johara. Her diary notes that "this is indeed an Easter gift for me and she is so beautiful, surely not too dear at £120—and now the Stud is complete." And she added that she hoped her pleasure in having the own sister to Bint Helwa would be shared by Wilfrid and Judith.

Many of the horses which were purchased by the Blunts they sent to England where they had established their prestigious Crabbet Arabian

*Ansata Ibn Halima with owner Don Forbis and *Morafic with trainer Tom McNair. These are two of the most famous modern Egyptian Arabians in the world, descended from stock bred by Ali Pasha Sherif.

PHOTOGRAPH BY SPARAGOWSKI

Stud; the others remained at the Sheykh Obeyd Stud in Egypt until Lady Anne's death in 1917. While many of the choice Ali Pasha Sherif horses did go to the Blunts, others had from time to time been given to members of the royal family, before the pasha's supposedly dire straits forced him to sell, and of course many of the sale horses also went to Egyptian notables. Thus even though Lady Wentworth asserts that Egypt was bankrupt of original stock, such was absolutely not the case —as we will see even more clearly in the subsequent chapters. Nevertheless, the world owes a debt of gratitude to the farsightedness of the Blunts, and particularly to Lady Anne.

It does seem incredible, in retrospect, that such magnificent studs could have met with such tragic ends in the land of the Nile; but then many of the most celebrated Arabs ever bred in Egypt came to America, and were almost equally dispersed through the inability of the American breeders to realize the worth of the priceless gems they had obtained. In their ignorance, they crossbred almost all the Egyptian mares with other bloodlines instead of retaining a large percentage of straight Egyptian bloodlines for posterity. Only the Babson farm had sufficient foresight to breed some of their stock strictly within the Egyptian line. Had Dickinson and Brown followed suit, America and the world would be better off for it.

But American breeders were not alone in their blissful ignorance. European countries were equally neglectful. Lady Wentworth, who inherited the Crabbet Arabian Stud from her parents, did not bother to preserve the Ali Pasha Sherif bloodlines in any straight form, and eventually Blunt desert-bred stock (Azrek, Rodania, Queen of Sheba, Basilisk, etc.) and the Polish Arabian Skowronek predominated the pedigrees, and then the Wentworth "superhorse" came along. Lady Anne's fears were not without foundation. But now, in the early seventies, the stampede is on to recreate the classic Arabians of Abbas Pasha and Ali Pasha Sherif in their highest form, and breeders the world over are establishing Arabian breeding programs based exclusively or predominantly on Egyptian bloodlines.

It is said that Ali Pasha Sherif kept copious herdbooks and manuscripts about his stud, but they have unfortunately been lost. They were at one time in the hands of Hussein Bey Sherif, according to the present Sherif family, but he loaned them to the late King Fouad, after

The foundation of the modern Jellabi strain, following the story in the Abbas Pasha manuscript. Mares are listed in full caps, stallions in lowercase.

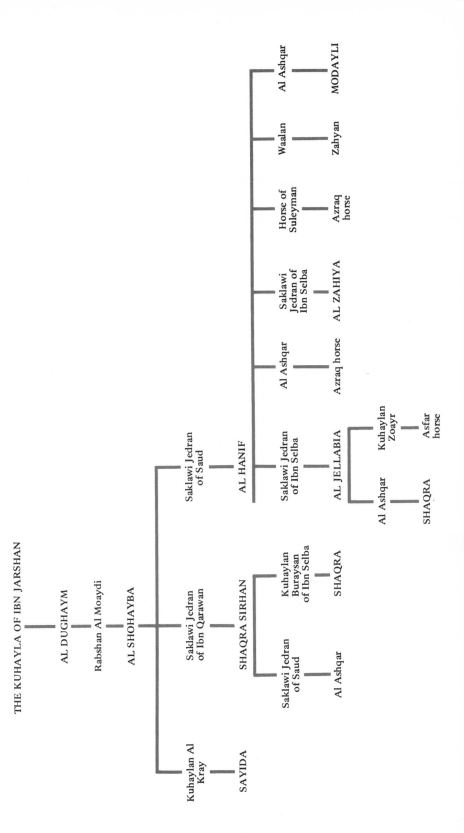

THE KUHAYLA OF IBN JARSHAN

AL DUGHAYM

Rabshan Al Moaydi

AL SHOHAYBA

Saklawi Jedran of Ibn Qarawan

Saklawi Jedran of Saud

Kuhaylan Al Kray

SAYIDA

SHAQRA SIRHAN

Saklawi Jedran of Saud

Al Ashqar

Kuhaylan Buraysan of Ibn Selba

SHAQRA

AL HANIF

Saklawi Jedran of Ibn Selba

AL JELLABIA

Al Ashqar

SHAQRA

Kuhaylan Zoayr

Asfar horse

Al Ashqar

Azraq horse

AL ZAHIYA

Saklawi Jedran of Ibn Selba

Horse of Suleyman

Azraq horse

Waalan

Zahyan

Al Ashqar

MODAYLI

which they disappeared. Raswan published a manuscript in his *Raswan Index* which he attributed to Ali Pasha Sherif, but Arabs of note who have translated it seem to think it has little or nothing to do with Ali Pasha Sherif's Arab horses.

Although many of these priceless herdbooks and recordbooks have disappeared, records have been handed down through the last century by the Blunts and the Egyptian royal families, but particularly through the Royal Agricultural Society (R.A.S.), which we will discuss in a later chapter. What happened to these irreplaceable documents remains a mystery, but like many archaeological treasures of ancient Egypt, they may still be unearthed at some future time. In the meantime, modern breeders can content themselves with the fact that certain Egyptian pedigrees are some of the longest, if not the longest, on record in the Arabian horse world today.

The love of Ali Pasha Sherif for the Arabian horse was unequaled during his era, and fortunately it did not pass from his family with his death. Among his descendants today is Ahmed Sherif, well-known Egyptian breeder and active member of the Egyptian Jockey Club for many years, and his daughter Gulsun, an avid Arabian horse enthusiast and breeder who has jockeyed her father's horses in the "gentleman" races in Egypt. To them was entrusted the priceless Abbas Pasha manuscript which has been handed down through the family for generations. It is one of the rarest documents of all, and one which Ali Pasha Sherif would be pleased to know has survived in his family.

11

THE BENEFACTORS

〉〉〉

M ANY PERSONS have been dedicated to breeding the Arabian horse in Egypt throughout the centuries. However, those special bene-factors of the breed within the past hundred and fifty years are etched most strongly in our minds because their horses are within reading distance in our modern pedigrees. Foremost among all breeders were the royal families of Egypt, certain wealthy pashas, and sheiks of the desert tribes. Private studfarms were founded by very affluent men and women. And the Royal Agricultural Society was established, which today under the name of The Egyptian Agricultural Organization remains *the* protector of the breed in Egypt. Those most prominent in this historical era will be presented in reasonably close chronological order, with the exception of the Royal Agricultural Society, which because of its scope will be dealt with separately in the following chapter.

THE TAHAWIYA BEDOUINS

Much has been said about the desert-bred Arabian horses of the Tahawiya bedouins of Egypt, yet little has been written. The Tahawiya are members of the Hanadi tribe who were among the foremost Arabian horse breeders in the Egyptian desert for centuries and are certainly deserving of a place in the pages of Egypt's Arabian horse history.

We have already mentioned the bedouins, the factions of tribes which crossed into Egypt in remote times from Arabia and the Sinaitic peninsula, some of whom still preserve a tradition of the district from which their ancestors came. Among them were the powerful Beni

Suleim, from whom are descended the Hanadi branch or tribe. They inhabited the province of Beheira in Upper Egypt and lived a typical bedouin life, frequently warring with neighboring tribes, and enjoying a reputation as fine Arabian horsebreeders and cavaliers. When Napoleon's troops landed at Fort Marabout in 1789 they were attacked by the Hanadi, "the fiercest Arabs of these deserts," whose horses "moved with the rapidity of lightning." Napoleon's savants said that Musa abu-Ali, the chief of the principal tribe of the Hanadi, could muster at least three or four hundred horses, and more than double that including those of his allies. Although "peace" was declared with the French on July 4, 1789, when sheiks of the Hanadi, Awlad Ali, and Beni Una met with the French delegation, yet some eight thousand bedouin horsemen comprised the left wing of the mameluke army at the Battle of the Pyramids against the French. The French weaponry and their disciplined troops were more than a match for the bedouins, however, and when the sheiks saw that the battle was lost, they disappeared into the desert from whence they came.

With the rise to power of Mohammed Ali shortly thereafter, the Hanadi found favor with him by supporting his military campaigns as mercenaries and, according to certain accounts, formed the personal bodyguard of the pasha himself. Shefei, the sheik of the Elawat section of the Hanadi, served with approximately two hundred of his men throughout the Syrian campaigns of Mohammed Ali. He thus gained the pasha's favor to such a degree that he was appointed to control half the tribe, and they were deeded choice lands in the province of Sharqiya. Ibrahim Pasha sent many of the Hanadi to Syria expressly to keep the Anazeh tribe in check near the region of Aleppo. Here they settled, building their villages of beehive-shaped earthen houses, and becoming half-cultivators of the soil. The Blunts came into contact with them here in 1876 when they purchased the Kuhaylan Ras el-Fadawi horse, Darley. He had been bred by Seyd Ahmed, sheik of the Hanadi, who at that time was breeding horses on shares with Mattar ibn-Sbeyni of the Fedaan Anazeh.

With the death of Mohammed Ali and Abbas Pasha's succession to the throne, Amir el-Shafei found himself in a precarious position. An informer had told Abbas Pasha that the Hanadi were plotting to seize the country. Abbas promptly determined to arrest the whole family, it is said, and actually imprisoned two of its members in the Citadel. The rest of the tribe fled to Syria. Eventually the imprisoned ones were released and the tribe returned to Egypt under the reign of Ismail Pasha. But there are still kinship ties between the Hanadi in Syria and the Hanadi in Egypt, and this fact has been a vital asset to both in horse breeding.

Sheik Teleb Rageh al-Tahawi holds a Tahawiya mare at his farm in the Sharkieh province.

Shafei was succeeded by his son, Tahawi, a man of turbulent temper and strong character who would brook no opposition from anyone. Eventually he usurped considerable authority and became a man of such striking personality that a clan developed adopting his name and obscuring that of the tribal ancestress, Hind. A plot against him succeeded, however, and he was murdered at a meeting of some of his tribe despite having been warned of the treachery.

One of the "white-haired men of the tribe" today is Sheik Rageh el-

Tahawi, age ninety-seven when interviewed in 1969. He nostalgically remembers when the Tahawiya mares numbered three thousand. Now perhaps 15 percent of that number remain, for many of the Tahawi lands
have been taken and their influence reduced since the revolution in 1952.
Many of the Tahawiya's horses originated from the Anazeh tribe, whose
main territory was in the Jezirah of upper Syria. The favored strains
perpetuated among the Tahawiya were: Saklawi, Dahman, Abeyan,
Muniqi, Hamdani, Shueyman, Kuhaylan el-Mohssen, Krush, Khars
Tamri, and Halawi. Sheik Rageh mentioned that he liked all the strains
and held no particular preference. He affirmed the fact that the
Tahawiya had remained entirely independent in their breeding programs, always returning to the desert for their stock and not using any
horses within Egypt when outcrosses were required, even though such
notable studs as those of Mohammed Ali, Ibrahim Pasha, and Abbas
Pasha existed.

It was rumored however that the Tahawiya once incorporated some
Ali Pasha Sherif blood into their stock, and this does not seem unlikely.
The Tahawiya actually supplied some of the renowned Egyptian breed-
ers with horses, or acted as agents for bedouin sheiks in the desert of
Arabia and Syria with whom they were in close contact. Lady Anne
Blunt purchased Tihawieh, one of her foundation mares for the Sheykh
Obeyd Stud, from Ghadir Aamr el-Tahawi. This was a chestnut
Kuhaylat Ajuz out of a grey Kuhaylat Ajuz of the strain belonging to
Ibn Maajil of the Roala tribe, her grand dam a Kuhaylat Ajuz purchased
from Misbah of El Maajil of the Roala; her sire, a bay Muniqi Sbeyli,
the property of El Haj Saoud el-Tahawi. Lady Anne maintained good
relations with the Tahawiya breeders, and it is noted that the Ali Pasha
Sherif mare Yemama (the Jellabiyah dam of Yashmak, etc.) was given
on December 8, 1906, to El Shefei el-Tahawi, to keep on shares with
Mutlak, her sais. The Tahawiya also were donators to the Royal Agricultural Society when it was implemented, but nothing remains of their
stock in Egyptian Agricultural Organization (E.A.O.) pedigrees, nor
was it used to any extent.

Prince Mohammed Ali was a great admirer of these Tahawiya
bedouin sheiks, and in his booklets published in 1936 he paid tribute to
them because they had done so much for racing and hawking in Egypt.
"The Chiefs of this tribe are real gentlemen, fine fellows, good characters
and great sportsmen. They love horses and they own some magnificent

specimens. They keep up hawking and hunting the gazelle with their horses. They train their horses for racing and very often win on the race courses of Alexandria and Cairo. I feel I owe these few words of praise to these people, for those who love horses and sport must appreciate all they are doing to keep up the qualities and reputation of the Arab and bedouin horses."

One of Egypt's most distinguished racehorse trainers, Sheik Abd el-Aziz el-Sabek, who is said to be over a hundred years old, remembers the old-time Tahawiya horses and regrets the passing of the outstanding purist breeders such as Abdul Hamid Rageh el-Tahawi, Abu Saud el-Tahawi, Mohammed abu-Mugalli el-Tahawi, and Nasr Ismayde el-Tahawi. "The Tahawiya were good horsemen," he said, "and used to breed pure Arabs, having brought their foundation stock from Arabia. Sheik Abdul Hamid was well known; he did not buy his stock from merchants, but went straight to the desert to obtain new blood. One of the most famous stallions was Dahman 'Amr from the Sabaa bedouins near Deyr ez-Zor in Syria.[1] Abdulla abu-Saud el-Tahawi brought the horse to Egypt. Then Mohammed abu-Megalli obtained some large Saklawi and Dahma mares and these when crossed with Dahman Amr got big horses. These were often refused at the Classification Committee meeting by Dr. Branch, the R.A.S. stud manager, even though they were pure Arabians. Abdulla abu-Saud el-Tahawi never mated his horses to anything but bedouin-bred stock. The Sabaa horses were not beautiful; many mares had big heads and long noses and didn't carry their tails well. Classic type was not a considering factor in acquiring horses for the track." The sheik also felt, however, that all too often an outstanding winner on the track was subject to being accused to impurity simply out of jealousy and spite.

The Tahawiya horses possessed appreciable size and height and were well ribbed up, having substantial bone and usually long necks. Heads were somewhat long and often straight in profile. There is a resemblance to those early desert-bred Arabians pictured in Arabian books some fifty to a hundred years ago, particularly the Davenports. When crossed with the more "elite" lines of the Royal Agricultural Society, the results have been gratifying and have given the offspring additional refinement and elegance.

The Tahawiya were also famous for their saluki hounds, the noble

1. This horse is influential to this day in Tahawiya pedigrees.

hunting dogs of the pharaohs and the Arabs. The first salukis imported into England in 1895 were bred by the Tahawiya and said to be of the finest stock and of the same breeding as those in the kennels of the shah of Persia. These dogs founded the breed in Great Britain, where it was recognized in 1922; it was recognized in 1927 in America. The saluki first came to Egypt through trade with the Arabs, according to tradition, and it is from ancient Egypt that we find some of the earliest records of the breed—for example, the tomb of Rekhmire, grand vizier of Thutmose III. Records of them are also found at Hierakonpolis as early as 3600 B.C.

Today the Tahawiya bedouins live the settled life of agriculturalists in the Sharqiya province, but they are still breeding outstanding racehorses. Their stock remains in great demand for the racetracks of Egypt and the Middle East and there are many beautiful and classic types among them. It is indeed unfortunate, however, that within the last thirty years or so they too, like so many of their bedouin brethren, have succumbed to the temptation to use some foreign blood in their breeding stock to produce faster horses for the short-distance races held on the Middle Eastern tracks. The days of raiding and warring among the tribes have long since passed away, and a new raison d'être is guiding the reins of the once celebrated war mares.

LADY ANNE BLUNT AND WILFRID SCAWEN BLUNT'S SHEYKH OBEYD STUD

Arabian breeders the world over have a uniqueness which somehow sets them apart from other horse people. Perhaps they are unique because the tradition behind this particular breed creates among its protectors the fervent desire to continue its perpetuation at all costs; perhaps the magnetic character and incomparable qualities of the Arabian horse draw certain types of people to it. The Blunts were unique in their time, and Lady Anne was assuredly one of those brave people who was sustained by the desire to enjoy the adventurous and contribute something worthwhile to the world at a time when frontiers in the real sense of the word were just opening up.

The sojourns of the Blunts in the Arab world and among the bedouins were chronicled at home and abroad, and by 1878 they had es-

tablished their prestigious Crabbet Arabian Stud in England with foundation horses they had secured during their precarious desert journey.
However, their trip to Egypt in 1879 changed their life immeasurably,
affecting them as it does so many travelers and historians who become

Lady Anne Blunt and her favorite riding mare, Kasida.

COURTESY OF LADY ANNE LYTTON

entranced by the spirit of the land, its ancient monuments and tranquil climate. Two years later they purchased the forty-acre Sheykh Obeyd garden near Heliopolis, "the city of the sun," where they established part-time residence and where Lady Anne eventually lived until her passing in 1917. Today the farm subsists as an orchard; the guest house, now in disrepair, is the only building in evidence. Nearby the blocks of Lady Anne's beloved house and stables litter the ground, a rubble heap clattered upon by migrant black goats or stumbled over by the felaheen. Yet the shadow of the past hovers over the remains if only in the scent from flower blossoms and from the grace of a towering minaret slenderly rising between the trees and the horizon. The call to midday prayers drifts religiously along on the desert breeze, then a spiritual quiet descends.

In the days when Lady Anne was in residence an Oriental calmness and serenity pervaded the estate—gardens of fragrant flowers, oranges, olives, apricots, and roses in bloom provided a picturesque setting for the priceless collection of desert steeds she and her husband were accumulating. The residence itself was an old Egyptian villa which had been modernized, and the Blunts employed the same architect who had worked for Prince Ahmed Pasha and created his beautiful establishment. From the flat second-story roof Lady Anne could quietly observe the sunrise and sunset steal over her "garden grown, which just divides the desert from the sown." Life was not always peaceful, however, and mention is made in her diaries of brigands and robberies, and the great necessity for a careful watch. Her neighbor, Ahmed Bey Sennari, kept a regular arsenal of weapons and she describes vividly his pride in them as well as his horses.

Loving Arabian horses as they did, the Blunts plunged forthwith into the heady atmosphere created by Egyptian Arabian breeders and became devout students of this Egyptian heritage. Here they came into contact with the superb Arabs of the classic type bred by Ali Pasha Sherif, his son Ibrahim Bey Sherif, Prince Ahmed Pasha Kemal, Ahmed Bey Sennari, and other princes and private breeders in the Nile Valley, and they frequently called upon these gentlemen with whom they struck up close acquaintances. They could not help but be influenced by such horses as were constantly paraded before their eyes. Their enthusiasm grew by leaps and bounds, particularly Lady Anne's, for she was constantly expressing admiration and excitement over every lovely horse she appreciated. One finds exclamations over such beauties as Ahmed Bey Sennari's bay mare, Muniet el-Nefus, whom she called "*the Hamdanyeh*," while one of his supremely beautiful mares, Bottla (Batila), she considered "*the the the* pick" of his horses. The celebrated grey stallion Kehilan Musenneh she thought "is certainly a good horse and as his owner said with pride, so gentle . . . 'kind', that if he gets loose he never does any harm." Such were her impressions of horses which today we recall in the pedigrees of our most famous Arabians. Through her observations, some of them are brought to life for us.

The primary objective of the Blunts, however, became that of collecting from the stud of Ali Pasha Sherif; as we have seen, they were able to buy not only directly from the pasha, but also from other breeders who had his bloodlines, and also from the daira after his demise. With perseverence and tenacity they collected some of Egypt's finest Arabians, shipping some of them to the Blunt estate, Newbuildings, and later to Crabbet while leaving others at their Sheykh Obeyd Stud. It is obvious that these Ali Pasha Sherif acquisitions were responsible for upgrading the two studs, improving upon the desert-bred horses they had acquired during their travels among the Arab tribes in Arabia and Mesopotamia. Few travelers in the world could come close to matching their understanding of the Arabian breed, and after spending much time and money in obtaining desert-bred stock direct from the tribes, the final appraisal of the best Arabian horses in the world was summed up in a note of Lady Anne's:

Judith was painting Mesaoud in the afternoon. In the evening we rode three mares, they were first the two new ones and then the bay Managhyeh. Our two mares [Sobha and Safra] made the smart Managhyeh look quite plain. I don't know what it is, or rather I don't know how to put into words that indescribable air of distinction which marks the horses and mares of Ali Pasha Sherif's, or rather I would say of Abbas Pasha's breeds, the breeds collected by him—for in the case of our two new mares their dam was never actually Ali Pasha's property, she having been bought by Mahmud Bey at that same sale by auction (in 1878 I think), at which Ali Pasha bought up mares then in the hands of Ismail Pasha but who had formed part of Abbas Pasha's stud. So it is, however—the moment one sees other horses beside them—when *moving* one sees the *style* of the Abbas Pasha collection.

The Crabbet Stud was eventually to become world famous, primarily due to its fabulous Egyptian collection and, in later years, to its successful promotion in the show ring by Judith Blunt, known as Lady Wentworth. However, the greatest credit for its excellence goes to Lady Anne, for she oversaw the purchasing, importation, breeding, and maintenance that kept alive the original venture. She studied the strains, pedigrees, and history in the backgrounds of all her horses, and her copious notes (which comprised her "Book of Fragments" in *The Authentic Arabian*), would doubtless be of great value to students of the breed when and if they are made available. They were "left away" by

The Sheykh Obeyd Stables.
COURTESY OF LADY ANNE LYTTON

Lady Wentworth and her immediate children cannot claim them. Perhaps a future generation, such as the Earl of Lytton's family, will take an interest in seeing that they are some day published intact.

Many of the horses from Sheykh Obeyd are found in modern Egyptian and Crabbet pedigrees. To illustrate the extent and immeasurable value of the stud, we list some of the foundation stock below based on Lady Anne Blunt's Sheykh Obeyd herdbook. Thirteen mares and two stallions are listed in Part I, covering "the first attempt" at creating the stud, and 38 mares and 14 stallions are listed in Part II,

which is comprised primarily of horses descending from the collection of Abbas Pasha I and bred by Ali Pasha Sherif. Every horse listed was bred by Ali Pasha Sherif unless otherwise noted. The symbol x means "out of," and an asterisk preceding a name indicates that the horse was imported to the United States and registered with the Arabian Horse Registry of America.

Azz (Bint Bint Azz), white Dahmah Shahwaniyah, by Ibn Nura x Bint Azz.

Mezna, chestnut Dahmah Shahwaniyah, by Antar (Ibn Muniet El Nefus) x Meshura. Bred by the Khedive Abbas II at Koubba.

Sahab, white Dahman Shahwan, by Kaukab x Azz (Bint Bint Azz). Bred by Osman Sherif, son of Ali Pasha Sherif.

Bint El Bahreyn, bay Dahmah Shahwaniyah of Ibn Khalifa. Bred by Sheik Aissa ibn-Khalifa of Bahrain.

Dalal, bay Dahmah Shahwaniyah, by Jamil x Bint El Bahreyn. Bred at Sheykh Obeyd.

Badiaa, brown Dahmah Nejibah, by Aziz x Mumtaza.

Bint Nura Es-Shakra (Bint Bint Nura), chestnut Dahmah Nejibah, by Aziz x Bint Nura.

Ibn Mahruss, chestnut Dahman Nejib, by Mahruss x Bint Nura.

Abu Khasheb (Ibn Bint Bint Nura), grey Dahman Nejib, by Mahruss x Bint Nura.

Bint Helwa, white Saklawiyah Jedraniyah of Ibn Sudan, by Aziz x Helwa.

Ghazala (Bint Bint Helwa), white Saklawiyah Jedraniyah of Ibn Sudan, by Ibn Sherara x Helwa.

Bint Horra, white Saklawiyah Jedraniyah of Ibn Sudan, by Aziz x Horra.

Johara (Bint Helwa Es-Shakra), chestnut Sakawiyah Jedraniyah of Ibn Sudan, by Aziz x Helwa.

Ghazieh (Bint Bint Horra), bay Saklawiyah Jedraniyah of Ibn Sudan by Ibn Nura x Bint Horra.

Ghazwa, chestnut Saklawiyah Jedraniyah of Ibn Sudan, by Feysul x *Ghazala. Bred at Sheykh Obeyd.

Ghadia [Radia], grey Saklawiyah Jedraniyah of Ibn Sudan, by Feysul x *Ghazala. Bred at Sheykh Obeyd.

Jemla [Jamila], grey Saklawiyah Jedraniyah of Ibn Sudan, by Jamil x *Ghazala. Bred at Sheykh Obeyd.

Aida, bay Saklawiyah Jedraniyah of Ibn Sudan, by Jamil x Ghazieh. Bred at Sheykh Obeyd.

Feyda [Fayda], bay Saklawiyah Jedraniyah of Ibn Sudan, by Jamil x Ghazieh. Bred at Sheykh Obeyd.

Ghadir, grey Saklawi Jedran of Ibn Sudan, by Feysul x *Ghazala. Bred at Sheykh Obeyd.

Ghareb, bay Saklawi Jedran of Ibn Sudan, by Feysul x Ghazieh. Bred at Sheykh Obeyd.

Roda (Bint Bint Roda), bay Saklawiyah Jedraniyah of a strain from the Abbas Pasha collection, by Sabbah x Bint Roda. Bred by Prince Ahmed Pasha Kemal.

Bint Roda, fleabitten grey Saklawiyah Jedraniyah of a strain from the Abbas Pasha collection, by Jamil x Roda. Bred by Prince Ahmed Pasha Kemal.

Bint Bint Jamila El-Kebira, a grey Saklawiyah Jedraniyah of Ibn Sbeyni, by Aziz x Bint Jamila.

Bint Fereyha (entered in Ali Pasha Sherif's register as Bint Fereyha El-Saghira), white Saklawiyah Jedraniyah of Ibn Sbeyni, by Aziz x Fereyha.

Fasiha (Bint Bint Fereyha El-Kebira), grey Saklawiyah Jedraniyah of Ibn Sbeyni, by Ibn Sherara x Bint Fereyha.

Fulana (Bint Bint Fereyha El-Saghira), brown Saklawiyah Jedraniyah of Ibn Sbeyni, by Ibn Nura x Bint Fereyha.

Wujra (Bint Bint Fereyha), grey Saklawiyah Jedraniyah of Ibn Sbeyni, by Ibn Nura x Bint Fereyha. Bred at Sheykh Obeyd.

Bint Jamila, white Saklawiyah Jedraniyah of Ibn Sbeyni, by Shueyman x Jamila.

Aziza, chestnut Saklawiyah Jedraniyah of Ibn Sbeyni, by Aziz x Bint Jamila.

Wubbr [color not noted], Saklawi Jedran Ibn Sbeyni, by Ibn Sherara x Bint Fereyha.

Jamil, chestnut Saklawi Jedran of Ibn Sbeyni, by Aziz x Bint Jamila.

Ferid, bay Saklawi Jedran of Ibn Sbeyni, by Feysul x Bint Fereyha. Bred at Sheykh Obeyd.

Yemama, bay Kuhaylah Jellabiyah, descended from the mares and horses brought from Arabia by Abbas Pasha I and of Ibn-Khalifa origin.

Yashmak, fleabitten grey Kuhaylah Jellabiyah of the Khalifa family, by *Shahwan x Yemama.

Makbula, white Kuhaylah Jellabiyah of the Khalifa family, by Wazir x Makbula [el-shakra].

Manokta (Bint Makbula Es-Saghira), grey Kuhaylah Jellabiyah of the Khalifa family, by Nasr x Makbula.

Jellabieh (Bint Bint Jellabiet Feysul), white Kuhaylah Jellabiyah of the Khalifa family, by Ibn Nura x Bint Jellabiet Feysul.

Kasida (Bint Makbula Es-Shakra), chestnut Kuhaylah Jellabiyah of the Khalifa family, by Nasr x Makbula.

Kerima, chestnut Kuhaylah Jellabiyah of the Khalifa family, by Aziz x Makbula.

Atwa, bay Kuhaylah Nowakiyah of the Debbe family, by Jilfan x Daifa. Bred by Nazir Agha.

Bint Noura, bay Kuhaylah Nowakiyah of the Debbe family, by Dahman x Noura. Bred by Prince Ahmed Pasha Kemal.

Sabah, bay Kuhaylah Mimrehiyah, by Rabdan x Om Shebaka. Bred by Prince Ahmed Pasha Kemal.

Antar, grey Hamdani Simri, by Aziz x Sobha.

Abeyyan (Saadun), bay Abeyan Sherrak, by Abeyyan x Abeyyah Sherrakiyah. Bred by Sheykh Mishara ibn-Saadun of the Montefyk.

Despite their common love of horses, the personal problems of the Blunts reached such a pitch that in 1906 they separated, and the stud was divided between Crabbet and Newbuildings Place. Alone, Lady Anne returned to Sheykh Obeyd in 1915 where she remained for two years until her death at the age of eighty.

A courageous traveler, brilliant scholar, and completely unselfish person, Lady Anne shunned publicity despite her renown. Her two books, *Bedouin Tribes of the Euphrates* and *Pilgrimmage to Nejd*, stand today as classics of the Arabian horse world, and much information contained in Lady Wentworth's *Thoroughbred Racing Stock* and *The Authentic Arabian Horse* was owed to her mother's copious notes. Having traveled many of the routes followed by Lady Anne and her husband, one can only marvel at their fortitude, especially when one compares conditions in those lands at the time of their journey with those today—though they remain at present precarious.

Time has passed and times have changed, yet Lady Anne Blunt's name is still held in veneration by the Egyptians, for her scholarly knowledge of the Arabic language and understanding of the Arab people and their horses endeared her to them. The "noble lady of the horses," as she was known by the nomads of the desert, now rests at Abbasieh beneath the Egyptian soil she loved so well.

STUDFARMS OF THE ROYAL FAMILY

With the passing of Ali Pasha Sherif, one would be inclined to think that breeding of Arabians in Egypt was ruined, if one believed either Wilfrid Scawen Blunt's comment that the Crabbet purchase "left Egypt

The Koubbeh Stables of Abbas Pasha Hilmi II.

without any first class stud . . . ," or Lady Wentworth's insinuations in her *Authentic Arabian Horse*. However, such was not the case. Although a stud of a size comparable to Ali Pasha's did not exist again in Egypt until the creation of the Royal Agricultural Society, the royal families still maintained great interest in horse breeding. Their farms were on a smaller scale than the pasha's, but nevertheless they had obtained over the years many of the best Ali Pasha Sherif horses as the foundation stock for their breeding establishments and there remained in Egypt horses every bit as good as, if not better than, those shipped to Crabbet. The Khedive Abbas Pasha Hilmi II, who was dethroned when British officials became administrative rather than advisory, maintained an outstanding stable of Arabians and possessed various gift horses from desert sheiks in Arabia as well as from Ali Pasha Sherif, who gave him among others the lovely dam of Mesaoud, Yemama. The khedive was also one of the donors to the Royal Agricultural Society's studfarm, and Lady Anne Blunt also obtained horses from him. However, he was not dedicated to the breed as was his namesake, Abbas Pasha I, and eventually his interest waned in the face of political problems and other diversions.

PRINCE AHMED PASHA KEMAL
AND PRINCE YOUSSEF KEMAL

One of the most enthusiastic collectors of elite Arabians was Prince Ahmed Pasha Kemal, who obtained most of his horses from Ali Pasha Sherif and direct from the desert of Arabia through the services of Fahad Abdullah, an Agheyleh sheik, who also purchased horses for Ahmed Bekri and Ahmed Sennari Effendi. The prince kept several palaces and stables, and the Blunts were in frequent touch with him about horses and other matters. In 1889 during one of their visits to his Berkeh farm where the berseem was cultivated, they saw his horses and mares out grazing. They were particularly taken with an old Kuhaylat Ajuz chestnut mare from the Roala, whom they likened to their desert-bred Rodania mare; and a little white Saklawiyah mare from the horses of Ali Pasha Sherif (Roda) they considered very beautiful. The celebrated bay Saklawi Jedran stallion Jamil, who was out of an Ali Pasha Sherif mare, was also there and they were most impressed with his foals.

Prince Ahmed also kept the famed Sabbah, a grey Muniqi Sbeyli stallion who was influential in early pedigrees, and whom the Blunts used as a sire.

Prince Ahmed maintained superb stables and his racehorses were very successful on the Egyptian tracks. His horses were to play an influential part in the Blunt and R.A.S. breeding programs, as well as those of Prince Mohammed Ali and Prince Kemal el-Dine. His only son and heir, Prince Youssef Kemal, also maintained a keen interest in Arabs for a time, and after his father's death in 1907 he inherited the horses. An ardent polo player, Prince Youssef kept a splendid string of polo ponies. He maintained some Arabians, but held an auction on January 9, 1908, where a number of his and his father's horses were sold. Prince Ahmed seems to have been overshadowed in modern historical records by Prince Mohammed Ali and Prince Kemal el-Dine, but his own contribution is not to be overlooked. Indeed, he played a major role in the overall Egyptian Arabian scene. Among the celebrated horses of Prince Ahmed were:

Dahman, white (fleabitten) Dahman Shahwan, sired by Kehilan Mesenneh, and out of Ferida, the superb white Dahmah Shahwaniyah mare from the strains of Abbas Pasha I's collection. She was the property of Ahmed Bey Sennari, and after his death she was taken by Prince Ahmed, and later by Prince Kemal el-Dine.

Sabbah, a grey Muniqi of Ibn Sbeyel bred by Ahmed Pasha, his dam a Muniqiyah Sbeyliyah from Ibn Maajil of the Roala, obtained through the Tahawi family who brought her to Egypt from El Dukki ibn-Someyr, sheik of the Waled Ali tribe in the Hamad. His sire was the old white Saklawi Jedran which Ahmed Pasha had gotten from Ali Pasha Sherif. Sabbah [swimmer] was so-named because having fallen as a foal into a *sakieh* (well), he swam.

Rabdan, a grey Kuhaylan Rabdan bred at Matarieh by Prince Ahmed, his dam the Kuhaylah Rabdiyah brought from Arabia by Ibn Bassam, his sire Dahman, the white (fleabitten) Dahman Shahwan bred by Prince Ahmed Pasha, and whose sire was Jamil, the dark bay Saklawi Jedran bred by Prince Ahmed.

Jamil, a dark bay Saklawi Jedran sired by the old chestnut Seglawi Jedran of Ibn Sbeyni, and out of Sobha, a white Saklawiyah

Jedraniyah from Ali Pasha Sherif.

Seglawi Jedran, "the old chestnut Saklawi Jedran," brought from Ibn-Sbeyni of the Mehyed Fedaan (Anazeh) to Prince Ahmed.

Seglawi Jedran, "the old white Saklawi Jedran," of a strain from the collection of Abbas Pasha, got from Ali Pasha Sherif.

Roda (Bint Bint Roda), a white (fleabitten) Saklawiyah Jedraniyah of a strain from the collection of Abbas Pasha I. Sire, Sabbah; dam, Bint Roda (by the dark bay Jamil x Roda of Ali Pasha Sherif).

Bint Roda, a white (fleabitten) Saklawiyah Jedraniyah (dam of Roda, above).

Om Shebaka, a brown Kuhaylah Mimrehiyah mare bred by Prince Ahmed at Matarieh; her dam Fereyha, the original mare, Kuhaylah Mimrehiyah, brought from Arabia to Prince Ahmed; her sire, the old chestnut Saklawi Jedran. The name Om Shebaka (meaning "that which has the properties of a net") came from her having an affliction of the skin which left a pattern like a net.

Noura, a bay Kuhaylah Nowakiyah of the Debbe family, from Ali Pasha Sherif.

PRINCE KEMAL EL-DINE HUSSEIN

One of the most influential breeders in the early 1900s was Prince Kemal el-Dine, heir and successor to the throne of Egypt. When his father, Sultan Hussein, died in 1917, the prince had no ambition to take his place or that of Abbas II, nor was he attracted by the prospect of being a dummy king under the orders of succeeding British generals or ministers—and he declined the throne. It was then offered to Fouad, who was the next son of Ismail, thus reverting to the old order of succession. The prince was an avid sportsman, maintaining several splendid palaces and hunting lodges throughout Egypt, as well as superb stables for his Arabs. Henry Babson, one of the American Arabian breeders who bought horses from the prince, recalled that "the Prince was destined to become the next king, but he had been poisoned and had gone off to Europe. . . . He was a great explorer and we visited his hunting lodge down the Nile. There was a huge map in the lodge showing places in North Africa where he had explored and hunted, and big game heads hung all over the walls."

Although Mr. Babson unfortunately did not meet the prince, Dr. A. E. Branch, who attended the horses of Prince Kemal el-Dine, Prince Mohammed Ali, and the Royal Agricultural Society, showed him through the stables. From among the entire herd Dr. Branch selected Serra as one of the finest mares in Egypt, and he especially wanted Mr.

Prince Kemal el-Dine Hussein, his saluki dog resting at his feet and his hunting falcon on his arm, after a successful hunting expedition.

Babson to take her daughter to America. Thus he interceded on Mr. Babson's behalf and "Bint Serra" by Sotamm was acquired. She was Mr. Babson's favorite mare of the importation. A tail female descendant of the elegant Saklawi Jedran Ibn Sudan strain (through Horra) of Abbas Pasha lineage, she descended in direct male line from the famous Saklawi Jedran stallion Zobeyni. Her son *Metsur, by Rustem, accompanied her to the U.S., but he died shortly after his arrival and before he could be used at stud.

Another export from the prince's stud was Ibn Fayda, by Ibn Rabdan x Feyda (Fayda) of Lady Anne Blunt. The prince presented him in 1929 to Sidi Tabet in France. However, exports from the prince's stud were not numerous and *Bint Serra remains the most famous mare associated with his name.

There was great rivalry between the two princes over their horses, it is said, and Mr. Babson recalled that he did not care for the horses from Prince Kemal el-Dine's stable as well as those of the Royal Agricultural Society or Prince Mohammed Ali. The prince was also a donor to the R.A.S. and often borrowed horses from them for his own breeding program. The famous picture of Ibn Rabdan taken by Carl Raswan was photographed at the prince's magnificent estate while the stallion was on loan to him.

No records remain of this outstanding stud, except for the references in the Egyptian studbooks.

PRINCE MOHAMMED ALI TEWFIK

The most splendid of the royal studs in the early 1900s was that of Prince Mohammed Ali, the prince regent of Egypt. The prince was an outstanding horseman and scholar, and his *Breeding of Purebred Arab Horses*, published in Cairo in 1935/1936 in two volumes, is valued in Arabian horsemen's libraries everywhere. In the preface of the first volume he records: "All my life I have lived among horses and loved them. When I was only six years old I had a pony to ride which was as powerful as a stallion. My guardian was an old Georgian Pacha, who was sent more than twenty times to Arabia to buy the finest horses for my ancestor—Abbas Pacha the First. Abbas had a stable of horses finer and more beautiful than any since the days of King Solomon. The Pacha used to tell us stories all day long of his travels, praise what he bought, and also taught us the beauty of horses.

"I have been to horse shows all over the world and have seen the Circassians and many other Oriental Siberian Nomads in Siberia; the Indian horseman, the Gauchos of the Argentine, the Cowboys in U.S.A., the Australians, and everywhere I always took the keenest interest in the horses and horsemen. And with this experience I have been breeding Arabs for thirty-five years."

The prince maintained fabulous stables at Koubbeh, Shoubra, Mataria, and on the island of Roda in the Nile. His palatial Manial stables at Roda bore the stamp of the most opulent Arabesque architecture. The ornate palace and buildings housing his priceless oriental carpets, tapestries, Korans, and art treasures, as well as his hunting trophies from expeditions throughout the world, were set amidst lush botanical gardens. All was surrounded by a high wall with buttresses and two impenetrable brass-ornamented gates. Indeed it reflected the grandeur and wealth of royalty, and provided a spectacular background for his prized collection of Arabian horses.

The foundation stock which he chose were mostly of Ali Pasha Sherif derivation, but particularly descendants of Abbas Pasha's renowned Jellabiyah mare which the prince bred to a perfection not since duplicated. The matriarch of his stables was the lovely white Bint Yamama, which established for him that special "type"—a certain look by which great breeders are made. Two of Bint Yamama's well known progeny were *Nasr (by Rabdan), the exceptionally graceful white stallion later imported to America by W. R. Brown, and Negma (by Dahman El Azrak), a beautiful grey broodmare who produced for the prince the exquisite *Roda (by Mansour), imported by W. R. Brown in 1932 together with her handsome half-sister *Aziza (by Gamil Manial). Negma also produced one of the great mares of all times, the legendary and much photographed Mahroussa (by Mabrouk Manial) who became the dam of the famed American imports *Fadl and *Maaroufa (by Ibn Rabdan), imported by Henry Babson in 1932; *H. H. Mohammed Ali's Hamama (by Kawkab); *H. H. Mohammed Ali's Hamida (by *Nasr), closely linebred and a superior individual; and the handsome stallion *Zarife (by Ibn Samhan), imported by W. R. Brown. These were some of the finest Arabians ever bred anywhere in the world, and their influence upon American breeding programs has been inestimable. W. R. Brown, owner of Maynesboro and one of the foremost and best-traveled American authorities on the Arabian breed in his time, described Mahroussa as the most beautiful mare he ever saw. Raswan's photographs immortalized her, a rightful heiress to the title "drinker of the wind."

Two other stallions of this line, bred by the prince, were also influential in another quarter of the world. Khafifan, a handsome white full brother to Mahroussa, was sold to the Polish breeder Count Potocki, and became a leading sire of race winners in Poland, and Jasir, a powerful masculine white stallion, was sold to the Princess of Weil in Germany, where he headed the Marbach national stud for many years. His blood remains most influential to this day.

The premise that it is quality, not quantity, that counts in a breeding program was aptly illustrated by the prince, whose breeding aims were described by Lt. Col. Sidney Goldschmidt in his book, *Skilled Horsemanship,* published in 1937:

But then the selection of sire and dam at this great stud is not on orthodox lines. The Prince has made a collection of old prints and drawings showing the traditional Arab horse, the horse of poetry and romance. These serve as his guide, and it is his aim to breed to this standard. Every sire and dam as well as their progeny, are studied with this ideal before him, and the tests are applied with almost mathematical precision. Any that fall short in the minutest detail are ruthlessly weeded out and sold.

Photographs of some of the horses placed alongside old prints show how surely he is approaching his goal. In reply to an unguarded question as to the utility of a stud of horses that were never ridden, we were told that the attainment of an ideal has no utilitarian object, and just as we in Europe hang beautiful pictures on our walls to look at and admire, so he has his beautiful horses. I must say that those we saw, especially those that had already spent their maturing months in the desert, excelled in beauty any work of art it has been my good fortune to see.

As the prince advanced in years, however, he decided to disperse his stud and at the time regretted that nobody in America would purchase his beloved Negma, who was now well on in years and doubtless a poor breeding risk. A Scot, T. G. B. Trouncer, didn't think so however and took her. She rewarded him by producing a beautiful filly, Gazala, by Registan, who won a number of races after having first produced twins.

The prince was a small man, distinguished in bearing and appearance and displaying polished Turkish manners. By some who knew him he was thought to be rather penurious, surrounding himself in luxury, but not particularly giving. He spoke French as his first language, and very little Arabic. He never married and thus left no heirs. With his passing the curtain rang down on what was left of an era of opulence. His once magnificent estate is only partly preserved as a museum today, and badly preserved at that. The other half has been taken over by a French tourist agency, and ugly modern cottages and a swimming pool have been erected in the midst of the once lush and pridefully tended botanical gardens. The priceless collection of pictures and paintings was thrown into the attic during the 1967 six-day war, and gathered dust until somebody recently found a place for them elsewhere. The fabulous library of equine books fortunately was bequeathed to the E.A.O., and eventually a research library should be constructed to house the collection.

Indeed the old order yieldeth, as the prince remarked, but in so doing a certain element of magnificent and Oriental splendor has vanished with it.

PRIVATE STUDFARMS SINCE 1930
T. G. B. TROUNCER'S SHEIK SUDAN STUD

Thomas Geoffrey Beauchamp Trouncer, a Scot, became entranced with Egypt and her Arabian horses and retired to life in the desert during the 1930s, settling down at his twenty-three-acre studfarm, Sheikh Sudan, surrounded by groves of Khanka's heavily laden date palms. Trouncer lived along with his horses, most of them descendants of Abbas Pasha and Ali Pasha stock which he obtained through the prominent breeders already mentioned. He kept no radio or telephone, and his only companion was an old Sudanese servant. Although something of a recluse, he nevertheless took keen interest in racing his Arabian horses on the Egyptian tracks, and it was he who owned the beautiful and outstanding R.A.S.-bred stallion Sid Abouhom, recorded as Nabeeh in the studbook. Trouncer used him successfully as a sire, but when the R.A.S.. manager noticed what fine foals the stallion was getting, he requested and was able to obtain him for their own stud once again.

Mr. Trouncer is survived by his groom, Mohammed Refai, who lives but a short distance from what remains of the Sheikh Sudan farm, now an Army base. A slight man with a giant smile, he nostalgically recollected his thirteen years with the kindly Scotsman. "Of all the horses Mr. Trouncer owned," he recalled, "Kasbana was his favorite. I remember once she gave twins by Registan." Registan was a son of Skowronek,

*H.R.H. Prince Mohammed Ali poses at the entrance to his
fabulous palace gardens.*

the famous Polish Arabian, and was imported into Egypt from Crabbet. Kasbana was out of Prince Kemal el-Dine's fine mare Serra, and according to the records and photos which Mr. Trouncer bequeathed to his good friend Ahmed Sherif, she was thus a descendant of the celebrated Abbas Pasha mare Horra.

For quite some period of time Trouncer bred only elite Arabs, using stallions such as Sheikh El Arab among others owned by the Royal Agricultural Society to service his mares. In his later years he swung more toward the racing type of Arabian and owned several horses of unknown pedigree, including the racing stallion Sharkasi. Sharkasi had an excellent record on the track and subsequently became known as a good sire of racehorses. He was said to have come from Upper Egypt, and indeed he was typical of the horses in that region. There was a rumor that Trouncer offered £200 to anyone who could ascertain the pedigree of the horse, but nobody stepped forward to provide one. Nevertheless the horse proved a popular sire with the local racing breeders and when Trouncer passed away in 1957, racing enthusiasts requested the E.A.O. to buy Sharkasi and stand him at local stud, so they could avail themselves of his services in the production of racehorses.

In 1957 an auction was held and the remainder of Trouncer's herd went on the auction block. All the records that remain of his beloved horses are contained in the small printed pamphlet which was given out to those attending the auction. Like records and herdbooks of other prominent breeders, his too disappeared.

AHMED PASHA HAMZA: THE HAMDEN STABLES

A native of Egypt and a descendant of the Billi bedouin tribe, Ahmed Pasha Hamza in his late seventies is a warm-hearted gentleman who has always been devoted to his country and his Arabian horses. During a moment of reflection he recalled how as a child he loved to spend hours riding at his tranquil farm in Tahanoub, a serene village nestled among the palms some fifty miles north of Cairo. School in England occupied a few of his early years, but when he returned to Egypt he devoted much time to improving his lands and the rural felaheen community. A beautiful yellow stucco mansion was constructed at Tahanoub amidst the fragrant gardens where flourished jasmine, fol, tuberoses, geraniums, bitter oranges, and other plants which furnished precious oils for the essences of perfumes that his Jasminoil company exported to world-famous perfume houses.

After his farm was well established, Mr. Hamza entered politics and filled the post of minister of supply and later minister of agriculture un-

Ahmed Pasha Hamza and Sheik Abd el-Aziz el-Sabek, together with Mahasin, Hamdan Stables' foundation mare.

der Farouk, who also bestowed the title of pasha upon him. In the interim, however, he had never lost his enthusiasm for Arabian horses. Like every young man of his station, he learned to ride dancing horses, and then he became interested in breeding pure Arabians and also in racing them. He laughs when he recalls the visit of his good friend, the late King Abdul Aziz ibn-Saud of Saudi Arabia, who attended an exhibition of dancing horses at Mr. Hamza's request. "Horses are for war, not dancing!" the king exclaimed.

The foundation mare of Mr. Hamza's herd was acquired from his good friend Mr. Trouncer—an elegant grey two-year-old filly named Mahasin. A truly magnificent mare with great black eyes like the gazelle which keeps her company, she has an international pedigree of distinction. Sired by Sheikh El Arab, the Royal Agricultural Society's leading stallion of his time, she was out of the excellent bay mare Kasbana which Mr. Trouncer had obtained from Prince Kemal el-Dine. Kasbana was by Registan, an imported stallion from Crabbet Park which was sired by Lady Wentworth's famous Polish Arabian, Skowronek, and out of a Rodania mare. Thus Mahasin combined the best of Polish, Egyptian, and old Blunt lines, in addition to the ultra-refinement provided by the Egyptian side of her pedigree (the all-important tail female line).

Shortly thereafter Mr. Hamza acquired three more foundation mares, also greys, from Sheik Abdul Hamid Rageh el-Tahawi. These mares, Futna, Folla, and Bint Barakat, were of desert breeding. Their progeny did extremely well on the racetrack.

When the days of Egypt's monarchy slammed to a close and King Farouk was deposed, the magnificent collection of Arabians from his Inshass Stud was auctioned off. Mr. Hamza heard that Hamdan, the senior herd sire, was to go through the sale and determined to buy him for his stud. But the Hamdan of that day scarcely resembled the prancing white stallion who had often bedazzled visiting world dignitaries; instead, Mr. Hamza recalls, a pathetic creature was brought forth to the auction block—his ribs noticeably protruding. Mr. Hamza decided to buy Hamdan despite the horse's advanced age and pitiful condition, but it was debatable whether he could be brought back to usefulness as a sire after he had been so badly neglected by the army. Nevertheless, Hamdan, which means "the thankful," was delighted with his new home amid the gardens at Tahanoub, and with loving hands attendant upon him and ample feed, he regained health and vigor and once again became his bold aristocratic self. He was put to stud again and got several outstanding individuals, among them Bint Muneera, Fol Yasmeen, Bint Folla, and Okt El Fol. So attached did Mr. Hamza become to Hamdan that he named his stables in honor of him.

Stablemates of Hamdan were Mozzafar (Wanis) and Emam (Amlam), both sons of Balance, the famous racing stallion of the R.A.S. All three stallions produced outstanding racehorses, but for classic beauty the Hamdan sons and daughters were generally unsurpassed. Later a Nazeer son, Korayem (Ibn Fakhri), was obtained, thus bringing additional beauty and strength plus a fine racing record to Hamdan Stable's stud battery.

Other horses for racing purposes were also acquired, of less renowned bloodlines and racier type, but Mr. Hamza concentrated on maintaining the beautiful and known pedigreed lines. Hamdan Stables flourished until one morning Mr. Hamza woke up to find himself under sequestration by the new pro-socialist Nasser regime, a fate that befell many of Egypt's wealthy families. Powerless to withstand the onrushing tide of disaster or to visit his farm, his horses were auctioned off. Hamdan, once again neglected, was sold by the sequestrators to the zoo, where he was to be slaughtered and fed to the animals. Providence intervened once again, and at the last moment he was saved through the intervention of an American horse lover who was resident in Cairo, Sarah Loken, and Douglas Marshall of Texas, who provided the wherewithal to maintain the horse. A rack of bones whose tail had already been chopped off just below the last vertebra, to signify he was for slaughter, Hamdan hardly resembled the noble creature for which Farouk had once refused an offer of $120,000. Hamdan appeared thankful indeed to be spared such an ignominious end and gained in strength and spirit; he spent his remaining days at the studfarm where he was born in 1936, and finally was laid to rest in 1967.

Eventually the sequestration was relaxed and Mr. Hamza, considerably less wealthy in land and fortune but determined to regain his horses at all costs, was able through the help of friends and family to reacquire many of his former herd, as well as to make some new purchases from the government studfarm, run by the Egyptian Agricultural Organization. Today Mr. Hamza's stud, which comprises about eighty horses, is the only one of any size in Egypt still belonging to an individual private breeder of elite Arabs. The horses listed in the first (and at present, the only) volume of his studbook fall into three categories: (1) straight Egyptian Arabians bred by or descending only from Royal Agricultural Society/Egyptian Agricultural Organization stock; (2) Polish-Egyptian-Crabbet-Blunt lines (to Skowronek); and (3) horses of Tahawi and Anazeh desert breeding. A mixture of unknown or unpedigreed bloodlines used mostly for racing purposes was not included in the book. The Hamdan Stables herdbook was published in 1969 so that at least one private studfarm in Egypt would leave a printed record for posterity. It has since become a collector's item; only one thousand copies have been printed.

Other Egyptian breeders contemporary with those previously mentioned also contributed much to the Egyptian Arabian scene: among them were Mohammed abu-Nafie Pasha; Mr. Kasdughli, a Greek who bought many Blunt horses; the Sherei family; El Itribi Pasha; Mohammed Taher Pasha; and other notable wealthy men who maintained small but select stables either for breeding racehorses or for breeding classic Arabs just for the pleasure of riding or dancing them. But the most significant contributors were those already noted.

Aside from the major farms which have come and gone, and which still remain, there are a number of smaller breeders who are struggling to maintain Egypt's ancient Arabian horse heritage on a less grand scale. Madame Dagny el-Barbary maintains a beautiful farm not far from the Great Pyramid of Gizeh, and carefully and lovingly raises a few Arabians of E.A.O. bloodlines. Other breeders have supported the racing scene and kept up interest in this "sport of kings" when kings are no longer fashionable: among them are Gamal Fouad, the late Rajah Coutran, the Tahawi clan, and Kordy Radwan. Despite the questionable purity of their stock many of these racing breeders are to be commended for carrying on programs and supporting racing at a time when everything within the country is economically geared against it.

In bringing this chapter to a close, we must mention the El Badia stables belonging to the very powerful governmental minister El Sayed Sayed Marei, a lover of horses as was his father before him. American-educated and a clever administrator, he held the vital post of minister of agriculture throughout most of Nasser's rule, which in itself was a feat of brilliance and political genius. It was Marei who intervened several times to save the Egyptian Agricultural Organization's studfarm from being wiped off the government budget as a luxury item. With the renewed interest in Egyptian Arabian horses, the farm has now become a source of hard currency through its increased sales abroad at a time when Egypt's foreign currency credits are low. The minister has always maintained horses of his own for racing and riding—some from the E.A.O. studfarm, which he purchased directly in their local auctions, others from the Tahawi and various breeders throughout Egypt. His farm today functions as a collection point for horses of good Arab type, most of which are offered for sale to meet the demand of Arab amateurs.

Until recently there has been no Arabian horse registry in Egypt. The Royal Agricultural Society/Egyptian Agricultural Organization maintained its own herdbook and published it as such. A General Stud Book for racehorses has also been established under the auspices of the Jockey Club. Now that small groups of individual breeders want to breed and maintain only purebred Arabians, those descending strictly from authentic stock of the R.A.S./E.A.O., the accepted stock of the royal families, and certain desert-bred lines, a special register has been created by the government under the direction and supervision of the E.A.O. (but not as a part of it). Whether this becomes a respected and effective instrument yet remains to be seen, but it should encourage private breeding of Arabian horses to a much greater extent. At present, the Egyptian Agricultural Organization is the surest source and fountainhead of the breed in Egypt.

12

THE ROYAL AGRICULTURAL SOCIETY
PROTECTOR OF THE BREED

THE YEAR 1892 marked another milestone in Arabian horse history when the Egyptian government began to take special interest in horse breeding because it needed good horses for the army and the police. It therefore set up a Horse Commission, which was the forerunner of the Royal Agricultural Society, founded in 1908 under the patronage of King Fouad. At that time the purest Arab horses were in the possession of the royal families and through their generosity the society obtained a number of select mares and stallions, most of them descendants of original Abbas Pasha and Ali Pasha Sherif stock.

In order to increase the quantity of its herd, the society decided in 1918 to purchase some twenty Arabs of strong Ali Pasha Sherif lineage from Lady Wentworth's Crabbet Stud in England. Except for a few individuals, they used these Crabbet imports to service horses in the provinces in the hope of upgrading the local stock. They apparently did not consider these imports of equal quality to the lines which had been preserved in Egypt. The Greek-Egyptian trainer Kosta Panayees, whose father was a leading trainer of race horses in the early 1900s, has explained that these horses bred in England at Crabbet from Egyptian stock were very large and that the Egyptians could not reconcile the change. A few were chosen for racing, but they were not very successful. "Not much is remembered about them or what was done with them," he has commented.

As the society's herd increased, the need for more land became ap-

*Stallions out for morning exercise trot down the main entrance
to the Egyptian Agricultural Organization's El Zahraa Studfarm.
Gassir (by Kheir out of Badia) takes the lead.*

parent and a palm-fringed sixty-acre desert studfarm in Ein Shams, just outside the city limits of Cairo, was constructed for the purpose. Modern stables have subsequently been erected over the years and large sandy paddocks provide adequate space for the horses to move about freely. Horses were maintained at the two farms of Bahteem and Kafr Farouk. Although the stud was under the direction of the Royal Agricultural Society, which was supported by wealthy Egyptian notables and the royal family, it nevertheless required competent and dedicated people to manage the breeding program and all the facets involved.

DR. A. E. BRANCH

The implementation of the R.A.S. studfarm fell to Dr. A. E. Branch, an outstanding veterinarian, a Scot, and a graduate of the Royal College of Veterinary Medicine and Surgeons in Great Britain. His knowledge as a horse breeder and veterinary was profound and both Prince Mohammed Ali and Prince Kemal el-Dine called on Dr. Branch to solve many of their problems. He assisted them loyally in various phases of their breeding programs and was totally devoted to his work of improving the classic beauty and quality of the Arabians in his charge, and in the country as a whole. He was also a member of the Jockey Club's Classification Committee, and it was not unusual for him to incur the wrath of various owners for refusing a horse which did not measure up, in his eyes, to the classic standard of the breed. Branch was often chided by racing trainers for his "beautiful" Arabians which he took such pride in at the R.A.S. stud, and finally he became fed up with the trainers' derision and determined to put an end to it. Selecting two of his best colts, both by Ibn Samhan and out of the very classic mares Farida and Bint Radia, he put them in training. Both turned out to be excellent racehorses; Balance, out of Farida, burned up the tracks, setting records as a matter of course, including one still held for the mile. Radi, out of Bint Radia, also ran admirably—and Branch thus proved, much to the discomfiture of various racing owners and trainers, that the classic Arabians of the R.A.S. could do as well as or better than some of the "countrybreds" they owned. Balance was eventually returned to the stud, where he became the sire of outstanding racehorses and a number of fine broodmares which were retained for the breeding herd (e.g., Nefisa, Zaafarana, and Yaqota).

When the late Henry Babson first went to Egypt and decided to found his studfarm on Egyptian bloodlines, he was forced to deal with Dr. Branch. Mr. Babson, in a nostalgic moment during an interview at his now famous Babson farm in Illinois, recollected his first confrontation with the gruff Scotsman. Upon entering the society's neatly manicured grounds, Babson and the friend who accompanied him were faced with a walk down a long corridor. They could see Branch sitting in a chair at the far end, but he never acknowledged their presence even though he heard their footsteps coming toward him. Finally when they stood before him he looked up and growled, "What do you know about Arab horses?"

Broodmares spend the days in sand paddocks.

"Not much," Mr. Babson had the foresight to reply.

"That's good," retorted Branch, and from then on assumed a more congenial manner. Before the visit was over, Mr. Babson came to regard highly the doctor's knowledge as a breeder. Branch took great delight in lining up a group of mares and their progeny separately, and then asking his visitors to say which foals belonged to which mares, just to see how much they did (or did not) know about Arab horses.

Dr. Branch was honest, forthright, and totally dedicated to his work. He was greatly respected by the Egyptians and will always be remembered for his contribution to Arabian breeding in Egypt at a most critical time in its history.

DR. AHMED MABROUK

A very capable Egyptian veterinary followed Dr. Branch. Dr. Ahmed Mabrouk was in charge of the stud from the mid-1930s untill 1941, and did an able job as administrator. His quest for possible additions of pure Arabians to the society's herd took him to Arabia, Bahrain, Iraq,

The late Henry Babson and the grand old monarch, Fay El Dine
(by *Fadl out of *Bint Serra).

Syria, and Lebanon, but he realized as a result of his journey that Egypt reigned supreme in breeding classic Arabians, and he did not see much wisdom in acquiring inferior stock just because it was pure. In his book *Journey to Arabia*, published by the R.A.S. at Cairo in 1939, he described his search and published pictures of many horses he saw at the studs of celebrated sheiks. Although many of the photographs are of poor quality, the horses having been photographed in unorthodox poses and wrong perspective, one nevertheless is provided with a rare collection of pictures through his efforts and the book has become a collector's item.

Up until Dr. Mabrouk's time most of the stud records had been maintained in English by Dr. Branch. However, Dr. Mabrouk began an additional recordkeeping system in Arabic, and his original herdbooks form the basic record system of the Egyptian stud today.

DR. AMEEN ZAHER

Dr. Mabrouk was assisted during his administration by a clever young colleague, Dr. Ameen Zaher, who later attended Michigan State University and wrote a thesis on Arabian horses for his doctorate. Dr. Zaher returned to Egypt in an advisory capacity to the R.A.S., and

Left to right: *Dr. Ibrahim Zaghloul, Dr. Mohamed El Marsafi, E.A.O.; Mrs. Danah al-Khalifa of Bahreyn; Dr. Ameen Zaher, E.A.O., Mrs. Valerie Noli-Marais of South Africa, and General Moafi, President of the Egyptian Jockey Club.*

his thesis was published as a book entitled *Arabian Horse Breeding and the Arabians of America.*

Dr. Zaher has for many years devoted much time and energy to the Arabian horse program of the R.A.S./E.A.O., and has held such responsible positions in the government as under-secretary of state. He is now in charge of many facets of the government's poultry industry. As a result of his travels in this connection, he has visited many Arabian studfarms in Europe, and was instrumental in getting the Hungarian Stud at Babolna interested in the Egyptian Arabian horses. Through his efforts with the German breeder Dr. Nagel, a significant number of Egyptian Arabians have left the E.A.O. for Hungary and Germany.

Dr. Zaher remains very active as technical adviser to the E.A.O. studfarm. He also holds positions with the Jockey Club of Egypt and is currently Egypt's representative to the World Arabian Horse Organization. His name is always found on the active list of various horse-related projects within his country, and he has been associated with the Arabians of the R.A.S./E.A.O. longer than any of the current officials. He enjoys recalling the famous horses he has been privileged to know over the years, including his enjoyable visits to American studfarms when he was living in the United States.

DR. ABDEL ALIM ASHOUB

Dr. Mabrouk was replaced by another well-qualified and very enthusiastic Egyptian veterinarian, Dr. Abdel Alim Ashoub. His administration during the years when the world was at war proved to be a challenging one, yet the stud continued to flourish. Under his direction was compiled the first printed *R.A.S. Studbook* (in both English and Arabic editions), an admirable work of fact and photos which has become a collector's item in Arabian circles. It was during Dr. Ashoub's tenure as manager that the beautiful mares Moniet El Nefous, Bukra, Maisa by Shahloul, and Wanisa, Halima, Yosreia and El Bataa by Sheikh El Arab were foaled. Quality, if not quantity, was preserved despite wartime conditions.

At this time Fouad Abaza Pasha was director-general of the society, and through his intelligent management and dedication to the Arab horse, efforts were made to see that the horses received whatever was required to keep them properly. Sufficient stud colts were raised and kept each year to maintain a basis of fifty active stallions which were distributed throughout the twenty-three districts of Egypt from November to May each year. The plan followed was similar to the old American Remount Organization maintained by the U.S. Army. Twice a year the society held a show at its headquarters in Gezira and purebred Arabs were shown and competed for prizes. Thus the breeding program kept moving ahead and enthusiasm was never lacking despite the war in Europe and on Egypt's western flank.

Fouad Abaza Pasha, a former Director-General of the society, on Shahloul (by Ibn Rabdan out of Bint Radia), one of Egypt's most influential sires.

After the war, however, the administrators of the R.A.S., and particularly its president, Mohammed Taher Pasha, considered it would be a wise move to employ an outstanding European horseman to head the stud and through advanced Western methods to bring some new ideas in stud management to the farm. Dr. Ashoub had been promoted to head of the animal breeding section of the society and thus the stud was still under his supervision.

GENERAL TIBOR VON PETTKO SZANDTNER

Fortuitously Mohammed Taher Pasha, himself an excellent horseman, learned at this point that General von Szandtner, former head of the once-renowned Babolna Stud in Hungary, was homeless. The years in the wake of the Second World War were desperate ones for this world-famous horseman. His life's work at Babolna had been destroyed; his home and property were lost. He was living in Sweden when he received a phone call from Taher Pasha asking if he would take over the Kafr Farouk Stud. The general did not hesitate a minute to give an affirmative reply.

In 1949 von Szandtner went to Cairo to take up his duties; indeed life in the desert was a contrast to the green pastures and luxurious stables at Babolna. Although he was sixty-three years of age and ready for retirement, he and his courageous wife started their new life with enthusiasm despite the obstacles that faced them in a strange land. Thus he began his new work with only one known quantity—the Arabian horse. With prudence and tenacity he introduced his proved theories into the old establishment. He was allowed to build new stables and lay out new paddocks where broodmares and foals could move about more freely, now that the stud was expanding. Pedigree and type were his guiding principles in establishing the program. From various districts throughout Egypt where the society maintained stallion depots, he collected stallions of society breeding and at length after intense investigation and rigid scrutiny he chose two grey stallions, Nazeer and Sid Abouhom (Nabeeh), to head up his stud battery, in addition to a few other stallions still at the main farm. He became captivated with the Mansour blood because Nazeer and Sheikh El Arab, even though he never saw Mansour or the latter alive. However, Sheikh El Arab, a head sire in the forties, had stamped his mark on many of the mares before the general's arrival. Dr. Ameen Zaher spoke of this stallion as being "an extremely fine type of Arabian of the very best blood. . . . his offspring are amazingly like him and he is considered one of the most pre-potent sires in existence." Indeed, the general eventually got some of his best horses by breeding Nazeer to Sheikh El Arab daughters—doubling the Mansour blood. Oddly enough, the general was unknowingly selecting on the very lines espoused by Abbas Pasha's scribe: the Dahman Shahwan and Kuhaylan Mimreh, together with the Saklawi. Sid Abouhom (Nabeeh) was also most influential in the general's selection; he was a well-balanced and very elegant white stallion, proven on the racetrack and a sire of great quality. His sire, El Deree, was said by Dr. Zaher to be "one of the best Arabian stallions that ever lived," and his dam, Layla, was out of the dam of Sheikh El Arab.

Within a few years the stud had improved by leaps and bounds; the horses gained in quality, beauty, and conformation without losing any of their extraordinary nobility. The farm was kept immaculate, flowers bloomed gaily in the gardens, and the corral fences were kept sparkling white.

From 1949 to 1959 von Szandtner devoted all his time and energy to breeding and improving the horses. When King Farouk was deposed, the R.A.S. was renamed the more democratic-sounding Egyptian Agricultural Organization and the name Kafr Farouk was changed to El-Zahraa. At that time the general became responsible for selecting what remained of the ex-king's horses. He screened them rigidly, breeding them apart at another farm until he decided which ones to approve for incorporation with the old society herd. His personal herdbooks, still at the E.A.O., and also kept by his wife, reflect his thoroughness, for he graded every single foal and mature horse from nose to tail, recording their assets and defects in early life and at maturity with unfailing accuracy.

The world began to take note of what he had done, and foreign buyers began visiting Egypt again. The Germans purchased four outstanding horses: two stallions and a mare by Nazeer, and one Sid Abouhom daughter. Ghazal (Nazeer x Bukra), who headed the stud at Lutetsburg and later was sold to Carl Domken, was said to be "unmatched by any stallion in Germany." Hadban Enzahi at Marbach has done a most credible job as a sire. Even the Soviet Union obtained the stallion Azmy by Sid Abouhom to incorporate in the Tersk Stud's breeding program. Richard Pritzlaff of New Mexico was the first Amer-

Dr. Marsafi and his harem of beauties, worth a king's ransom: Mona, Moniet El Nefous, and Mabrouka.

ican to bring from Egypt an important group of horses since the importations made in the thirties, and he became a great admirer of the general, who helped select his horses.

The late General von Szandtner regarded his last task in life as that of preserving the classic Arabian horse of the desert, and impressing upon Arab breeders of his era that El Zahraa remained the fountainhead of the purest Arab blood for Egypt and the world. The realization of this aim was his testament to the Arab breed he loved so well.

DR. MOHAMED EL MARSAFI

Administration of El Zahraa was taken over in 1959 by a very keen and skilled Egyptian veterinarian, Dr. Mohamed El Marsafi, who was also director of the animal breeding section of the E.A.O. He had the great advantage of having been associated with Dr. Mabrouk, Dr. Zaher, Dr. Ashoub, and General von Szandtner, and was thus well equipped to deal with all phases of the breeding program. And of course he possessed valuable knowledge of the old and new horse-breeding programs as well as familiarity with the individual horses of the preceding thirty years. Dr. Marsafi deftly picked up the reins and under his firm direction the breeding program continued to move forward, nearly doubling in size within a few years. New buildings were erected to house the increased number of broodmares and other buildings were turned over to stable young stallions that were for sale or were to be sent to the depots. Under his direction the second Egyptian studbook was published, and a third is now completed. Plans for a new library were also made under his supervision, and eventually the magnificent collection of books bequeathed by Prince Mohammed Ali to the R.A.S. will be kept there and made available to serious students of the breed for research purposes.

Despite the undiminished quality of Egyptian Arabians over the years, until Dr. Marsafi's administration their popularity abroad had been very insignificant. Except for scattered interest by the Germans and a few exports to America by the Queen Mother, Nazli, no really important or world-shaking Arabian news had been made by Egypt since the early thirties. The Pritzlaff horses were still unadvertised and little known to American breeders. Yet within a short period of time the popularity of Egyptian Arabians in America was to reach a propor-

Young horses learn to jump at El Zahraa.

tion beyond the Egyptians' wildest dreams, and its effects were far-reaching. It began, as usual, through an ironic twist of fate.

FROM EGYPT TO AMERICA

When my husband and I arrived at El Zahraa in 1959, General von Szandtner had only been retired and Dr. Marsafi placed in charge some two weeks previously. We had been searching throughout the Arab world for several years, trying to find a nucleus of classic Arabian horses from which to build a breeding program, only to be disappointed at every turn. In comparing notes with Dr. Marsafi and Dr. Zaher, we learned that they too had been visiting the same areas looking for a classic well-bred stallion that past year, and even on the same days in Damascus and Aleppo, but to no avail. Thus a note of mutual interest was struck, and when it was time for us to depart Dr. Marsafi, after consultation with Dr. Zaher and the director general, Ahmed Afifi, agreed to sell us three outstanding yearlings by Nazeer, even though the general had culled and sold everything the farm had for sale prior to his departure. Little did Dr. Marsafi realize what a commotion these three youngsters would cause in America and the world, and that by his generosity in releasing them he was fanning the flames of an almost dead fire into brightness once again. Another one of those strange "Eastern tales" was beginning.

When Ibn Halima, Bint Zaafarana, and Bint Mabrouka arrived in America, photographs of the three yearlings together appeared in newspapers and Arabian horse magazines, and immediately people from across the U.S. thronged to see them and wrote letters of enthusiasm to us, wanting to learn more about the bloodlines behind these imports. The word had previously been spread in America that Egypt no longer had any beautiful Arabian horses. How then did these beautiful creatures appear? And were there more of them? In the meantime, von Szandtner had learned these three yearlings had been sold, and wrote to a good friend that had he remained at the farm he would never have let them go! I wrote articles for Arabian magazines describing the Egyptian Arabians of the present day bred by the Egyptian Agricultural Organization, previously known to Americans as the Royal Agricultural Society, and it was not long before the words "Egyptian Arabians" were heard often in horse circles.

In the meantime the three imports had settled down to a quiet life and lush bermuda grass in Oklahoma. They had been registered with the word Ansata prefixed before their Egyptian names; we chose this word as a ranch name because it was symbolic of ancient Egypt. The Ansata Crux or Key of Life, which appears frequently in Egyptian relief or sculpture, symbolized the reproduction of seed and the reproduction of living things of their own species. The reproduction of living things was to the early Egyptian mystics the greatest mystery that they could observe and direct in its action. The notion developed that the capacity of each species to reproduce itself continually was proof that there was something immortal in the seed. The symbol therefore became a sacred emblem of the continuity of life, or immortality. It was to prove an apt choice.

The Ansata Crux, known as the hieroglyph ankh, *as it appears in the registered trademark of the Ansata Arabian Stud.*

Egypt has had her royalty and splendid studfarms, but America was now to inherit this legacy and take the lead in production of Egyptian Arabians. The mass exportation began when Douglas Marshall, already an Arabian fancier and champion of the Arab cause in the political world, became acutely aware of the need for Egyptian bloodlines and determined to establish a large herd in America which would restore in quality and quantity this strain's rightful place on the American and world scene.

Marshall had come to know the Arab lands during World War II where he saw active duty as an Air Force pilot. When he returned to civilian life in Texas as an executive partner in Quintana Petroleum Company, he established an Arabian herd selected from Arabian breeders in the United States. His interest in Egyptians was particularly aroused after purchasing *Moftakhar, a handsome white Egyptian stallion who had been imported in the fifties by Charles Votey, Jr. Marshall began returning to Egypt and the Arab countries once again, and between 1961 and 1965 he acquired through the cooperation of Dr. Marsafi and the E.A.O. officials a very select group of broodmares and the magnificent Saklawi Jedran stallion, *Morafic. The Arabian horse show world in America was soon acclaiming these beautiful Egyptian imports shown by the Marshalls' talented trainer, Tom McNair. Marshall kept importing and Gleannloch was soon the largest Arabian breeding farm of Egyptian bloodlines outside of Egypt. Other breeders also purchased horses and in 1970 two planes carried the largest single exportation ever made at one time: thirty-three Arabians were shipped to eight American and Canadian breeders. Through the kindness of Mr. Marshall,

*Ansata Ibn Halima, *Ansata Bint Mabrouka, and *Ansata Bint Zaafarana when they were chosen by Donald and Judith Forbis at El Zahraa in 1959. This picture appeared in publications across America after they were imported, and stimulated renewed interest in Egyptian bloodlines.

Dr. Marsafi was able to accompany the shipment. It was the highlight of his life to visit Arabian farms in the States and to see first hand how his breeding program in Egypt fared against the American-bred competition. He also visited the long-established Babson Farm in Illinois and was happy to see the descendants of the early stock flourishing.

The circle was not closed, however, until November, 1971, at the

*In 1970 a chartered DC-8 and a DC-6 hauled the largest shipment of Arabian horses out of Egypt to North America. Here Douglas Marshall holds *Ibn Hafiza while Don Forbis makes the tie-down. Tom McNair, in the background, prepares to board the jet.*

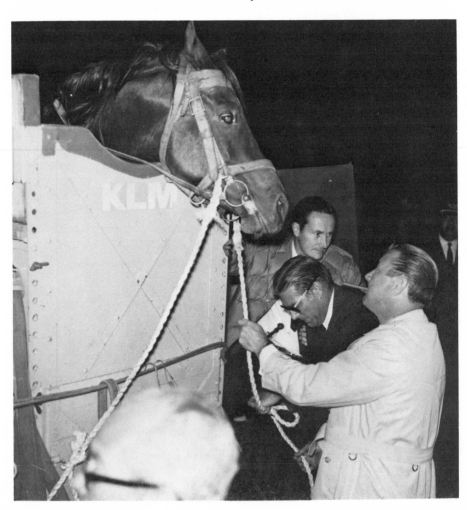

U.S. National Championships Arabian Show held in Oklahoma City. Here gathered under one roof were champion Arabians from the United States and Canada—the largest and most competitive show since the inception of the Nationals in 1958. The National Futurity classes for three-year-old fillies and colts were handily won by Marshall's breeding: Il Muna, a lovely double Nazeer daughter by *Morafic, became National Champion Futurity Filly, while Reserve went to another *Morafic daughter, Dalia. The National Champion Futurity Colt was the flashy chestnut *Morafic son, Dalul, owned by Dr. John Coles of Canada.

There was much speculation about the coveted title of National Champion Mare, but it was no great surprise to the crowd when the brilliant chestnut show mare, *Sonbolah, was acclaimed the winner. Bred by the E.A.O. under Dr. Marsafi's direction, selected and imported by Douglas Marshall for Serenity Farms in Canada, she had been renamed * Serenity Sonbolah and campaigned successfully for two years.

But the most sought-after title of the show is that of National Champion Stallion, and with eighty-three champions in the lineup, it was the toughest competition ever. Who would win it? Few spectators in the audience that day will ever forget the magnificent silvery grey stallion who pranced into the arena—neck arched proudly, flaring nostrils expanded, snorting confidently with ears pricked towards the judges and the competing stallions assembled in the ring against him. The crowd was with him—indeed, he personified the classic Abbas Pasha horses so beautifully portrayed by Victor Adam. The judges were with him too, and when the results were announced to the hushed audience, cheers went up from the crowd. Ansata Ibn Sudan had won! His sire was *Ansata Ibn Halima; his dam, *Ansata Bint Mabrouka—two of the yearlings Dr. Marsafi had generously sold to us in 1959. Egyptian breeding swept the show, as other E.A.O.-bred horses won U.S. Top Ten honors. Indeed the overall results gave Dr. Marsafi cause to be proud.

Today Dr. Marsafi is active in every phase of Egypt's Arabian horse industry; he advises private breeding establishments when they request information from him; he is a member of the Federation of Dancing Horses, serves on the Jockey Club Classification Committee, and remains director of the animal breeding section of the E.A.O. Unceasing in his efforts to see that the Arabian horse remains a heritage of Egypt and a source for the world, he has formed a major link in the chain of his country's Arabian horse heritage.

13

THE CLASSIC ARABIAN

W HAT CONSTITUTES the "classic" Arabian horse? The dictionary defines the word "classic" as meaning of the finest or highest class or rank; serving as a standard, model or guide; adhering to an established set of artistic or scientific standards and methods. We may therefore consider the "classic" Arabian to be the *ideal* representative of the breed.

Attitude and physical qualities must be taken into account when considering the ideal Arabian; in fact, the inner qualities must come first: love, courage, dignity, gentility, honesty, spirit, loyalty, grace, intelligence, and willingness to please. Without these transcendent values, the physical form cannot function and inspire.

The Arab of the desert did not consult books in creating the classic Arabian horse—the universe and the principles of nature were his library. Harmony was his guide. The rapport established between the Arab and his horse evolved through shared interests, shared loyalties, shared consideration—and shared results. All the real (intangible) qualities we admire in the Arabian horse today are a result of a long heritage established through companionship and mutual respect.

In every breed of animals there is an official physical standard of perfection toward which breeders strive. No Arabian can be a good Arabian without being a good horse; he must be sound in all respects. However, being a good horse is not sufficient. A horse cannot qualify as a first-class or "classic" Arabian without having the distinctive characteristics of the breed. That is, he or she must *look like* an Arabian. *Type should come first* in the judge's or breeder's final selection, for without it the breed loses its identity.

Type refers to basic form. The entire horse must be taken into consideration in determining proper type. However, the head is the hall-mark of the breed and is a vital factor in deciding whether an Arabian is of good or bad type. An Arabian with poor head type will never belong to the first rank. Bone and skeletal structure further determine type because the construction of the Arabian is fundamentally different from that of other breeds of horse. Elegance in appearance should never be lost sight of as it is indicative of the subtle strength peculiar to true desert-bred animals.

The knowledgeable breeder or judge will evaluate a horse *by its assets*, not by its faults. Judging of Arabians cannot be done by scoring individual faults alone; it must leave much to the personal equation of the judge, to his or her sense of harmony and the fitness of things. Judging or evaluating properly is not so much a science as it is an art.

When a horse is exhibited and the immediate general impression is good, then the judge should look for faults. If the overall impression is bad, the judge should seek the good points, for they can be found in even the poorest specimen. And better a horse with several minor faults distributed throughout his structure than one with a single gross fault sharply in evidence.

Faults are considered to be deviations from the standard. The ideal is an imagined picture of something which is close to perfection; a model or dream image. The horse who appears almost exactly true to the ideal, however, will have some fault(s), for the perfect specimen has not yet been attained. The Arabian horse described in the following standard is an ideal which in flesh can only be approximated.

General Appearance Majestic, dignified, especially noble and courageous. Temperament spirited but docile and affectionate. Head, neck, and tail carried high; eyes flashing with life and fire. Proud carriage, lithe, quick, graceful and elegant; harmoniously proportioned, having a smoothly muscled body whose form is essentially one of utility. Skin fine and supple, the coat close, fine, silken and brilliant; mane and tail long and glossy. Fine-boned. In action naturally balanced, smart and free with an airy step.

Skeleton The Arabian is a separate species, *equus arabicus*. Space does not permit complete detail, but in general the Arabian is known for the quality of the bone, which is as dense as ivory, the short wide tapering concave skull with larger brain case than usual, the large circular eye sockets, and the fact that it often has fewer vertebrae in the back and tail (seventeen and sometimes eighteen pairs of ribs rather than the usual eighteen of the Thoroughbred and nineteen of the common horse; sixteen tail vertebrae instead of eighteen and five lumbar vertebrae instead of six).

Color and Markings Bay, grey, chestnut, and black. Foals are born bay, chestnut, or black and gradually turn varying shades of grey to white, if they do not remain solid colored. White foals at birth are exceedingly rare. There are many shades of grey, including "fleabitten"—grey with chestnut or almost black speckling. Duns, roans, piebalds, and palominos are not true Arab colors.

The most common markings are stars, strips, snips, and blazes; coronets, pasterns, fetlocks, socks, or stockings are seen on the legs. Normally all white markings have pink skin beneath. Body spots are not desirable in America, but are common in England through Crabbet breeding.

The Classic Arabian, Dahman, in the collection of Abbas Pasha.

ENGRAVING BY V. ADAM

Skin, Coat, and Hair   Skin fine and supple; black; pink under white markings. Coat silk and satiny, brilliant and glossy. Legs should be clean of hair at the fetlock joints. Mane, tail, and forelock fine and long, and may have a slight wave, but should not be coarse and curly.

Height and Weight   14.1 to 15.1 hands at withers, with occasional individuals over or under. At maturity the Arabian usually weighs from 800 to 1000 pounds.

Action   Smart, free, naturally balanced action. A picture of harmony in motion. At the walk, fast and free, hind feet sometimes overstep the front track by 8 to 12 inches. At the trot action is extremely brilliant almost "floating." The front limbs move with unrestricted shoulder and knee action; the hock action is powerful, hocks moving sufficiently wide apart, well raised and brought forward with a swinging stride. At the canter action must be smooth and collected, not jerky or stilted. At the gallop, action is very free and light with long ground-covering strides.

Faults   Any deviation from the standard is a fault; however, some faults are more serious than others. Convex head, lop ears, roman nose, small eye, shallow jaw, ewe neck or short stiff angular neck, mutton withers, shallow ribs, goose rump, narrow hindquarters, short choppy action, weak hocks, badly carried tail, or lack of overall balance and harmony are particularly serious. Space does not permit a more detailed account, and reference books are readily available regarding both acquired and hereditary unsoundnesses.[1]

The classic Arabian described in this chapter is the ideal toward which Egypt has been striving for the past thirty-five hundred years. As a result, the entire Arabian horse world has benefited. The following chapters on foundation horses and the establishment of strains within the breed will enable breeders and students to better understand the background of horses in modern pedigrees, and also will provide a pictorial evaluation of many pedigrees.[2] Although the Arabian has been bred in Egypt for centuries, written pedigrees trace the breed only to the early 1800s, yet these are the longest and most historical pedigrees extant in the entire Arabian horse world!

1. Publications by the Arabian Horse Registry of America, 7801 E. Belleview Ave., Englewood, Colorado 80110, and The Arab Horse Society of England are particularly useful.
2. *The Reference Handbook of Straight Egyptian Horses,* of pictorial and historical value, is available from The Pyramid Society, 1936-500 Jefferson Bldg., Houston, Texas 77002.

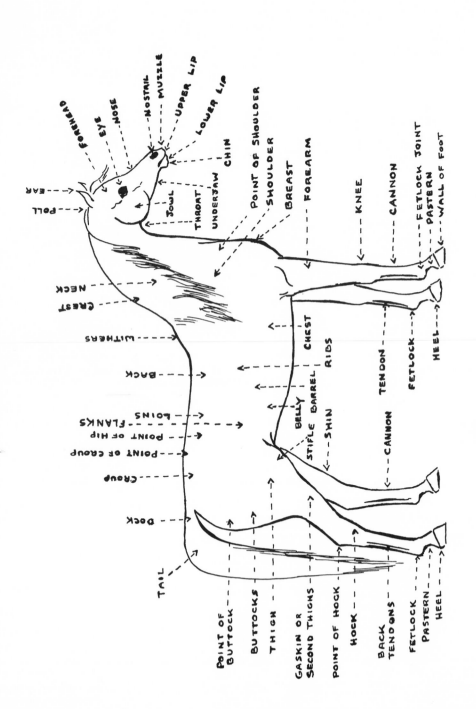

POINTS OF THE ARABIAN HORSE

SYMMETRY AND BALANCE

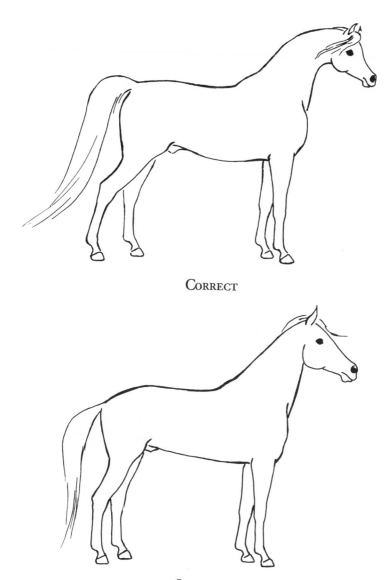

CORRECT

INCORRECT

Head disproportionate; hindquarters light. Compare stiff angular shape (neck, hindquarters, tail set) with flowing rounded outline in illustration above.

THE ARABIAN HEAD

CORRECT

Head Pyramidally shaped skull, profile straight or (preferred) slightly concave below the eyes; spare and lean, broad at cheekbones.

Ears Small, alert, pricked close together, flexible (smaller in stallions than in mares), beautifully chiseled, sharply outlined, tips curved slightly inwards; thin and well hollowed.

Forehead Large, flat, prominent.

Eyes Dark, large, blunted oval in shape, well opened, expressive, brilliant. (Blue eyes are a grave fault.) Comparatively short distance between eyes and muzzle. Good width between the eyes. Placed low in skull. Lower edge set almost horizontal when head in normal position.

Nostrils Large, extended when in action. Parallel to profile when in repose. Delicate, very flexible, and capable of enormous expansion.

Muzzle Small, delicate, firm and finely tapered; lips close and firm, mouth long.

Shaft of underjaw Straight (not convex).

Jowls Deep, wide between the branches which should remain decidedly distinct down to the chin and should cut well into it.

INCORRECT

Big lop ears; light deep-set pig eyes, white haws; rise over nose; small nostril; short mouth; brooding underlip (pendulous lip); convex underjaw.

MOUTH

CORRECT

A perfect "bite" is absolutely necessary.

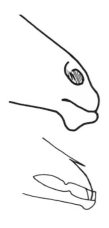

INCORRECT

Undershot.

INCORRECT

Overshot (parrot mouth).

NECK AND THROATLATCH

CORRECT

Neck "Curved like a palm branch," long, set on high and running well back into the withers. The setting of the neck onto the head requires the top of the neck to be powerful, the muscles wide behind the ears, the throat clean and loose. A stallion should have a fine stallion crest, which he will curve like a swan when excited. The mare's neck should be long and light, and also arched.

Throatlatch Set in a curved arch.

INCORRECT

Neck Short, thick, upside down.
Throatlatch Undefined, angular.

SHOULDER AND WITHERS

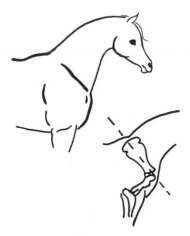

CORRECT

Shoulder Sloping, long, clean and flat, free in movement, well laid over with muscle.
Withers Moderately high and well defined.

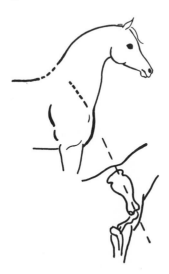

INCORRECT

Shoulder Short and straight.
Withers Low ("mutton withered"), flat, and ill-defined.

CROUP, LOINS, AND BACK

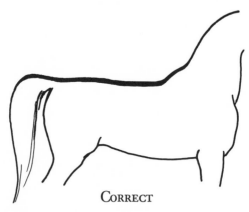

CORRECT

Croup Long, level, same height as withers.
Loins Short and strong.
Back Short and level. The back should be well muscled on each side of the spine. Mares may have longer backs than stallions, and somewhat deeper, particularly after carrying several foals.

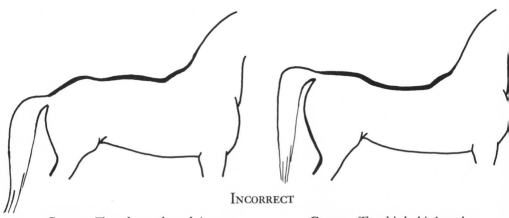

INCORRECT

Croup Too short, sloped (goose-rumped).
Loins Dipped.
Back Roached, like a cow.

Croup Too high, higher than withers.
Loins Weak.
Back Too long and low.

COUPLING

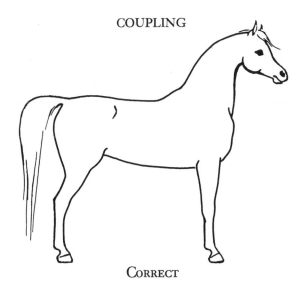

CORRECT

Short back, long undercarriage.

INCORRECT

Left, too short—horse appears "leggy" and too high off ground. *Right*, too long—horse appears too close to the ground.

TAIL SETTING AND CARRIAGE

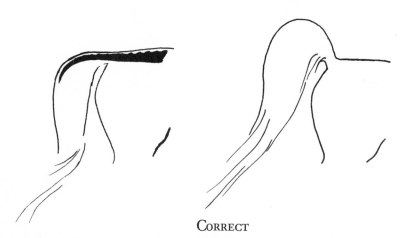

CORRECT

Left, natural setting. *Right,* elevated carriage when excited or in action, carried high, sometimes over back.

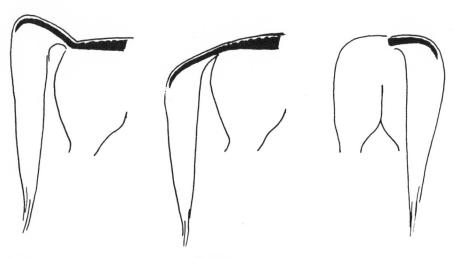

INCORRECT

Left, too high at natural stance. Indicates "gingering." *Center,* too far forward or too low. *Right,* carried to one side. Particularly objectionable when badly twisted and dock of tail shows.

CHEST, BARREL, AND FLANK

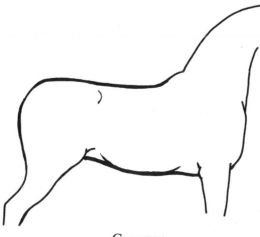

CORRECT

Chest Long, wide, muscular, deep, with ribs well sprung.
Barrel Deep and rounded. Deep through the girth—lots of heart room.
Flank Wide and deep.

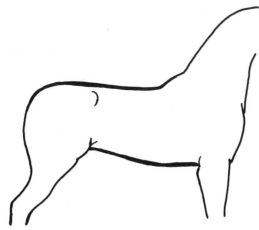

INCORRECT

Chest Drawn up (above elbow), not deep enough.
Barrel Flat, "slabsided."
Flank Narrow.

BREAST

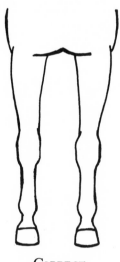

CORRECT

Moderate width.

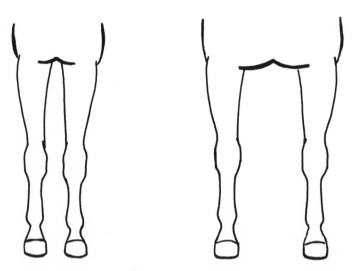

INCORRECT

Left, too narrow. *Right,* too wide. Narrowness tends to cause hoof to strike opposite leg; extreme width inhibits smooth, comfortable movement.

ATTACHMENT OF FORELEGS

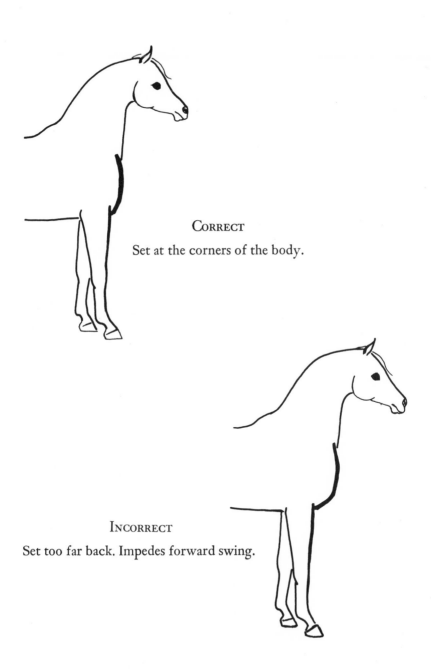

CORRECT

Set at the corners of the body.

INCORRECT

Set too far back. Impedes forward swing.

FOREARMS AND CANNONS

CORRECT

Long, broad, well-muscled forearms. Cannons short. Bone should be of ivory density and iron strength; back tendons vertical, the sinews well divided into two bars, the inner one standing out sharp and straight.

INCORRECT

Cannons long. Forearms short and narrow.

FORELEGS

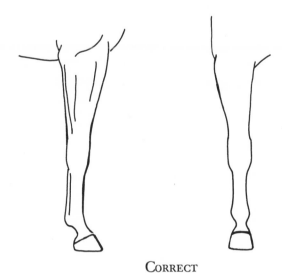

CORRECT

Tendons straight, whole leg parallel, knees large and flat.

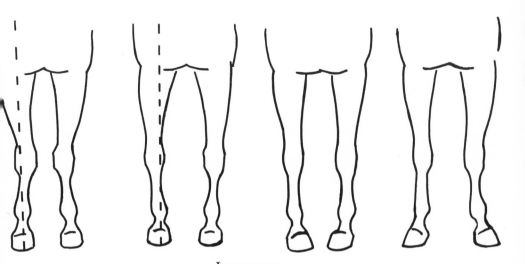

INCORRECT

Left to right: Knock-kneed; bow legs; toed-in (pigeon-toed); toed-out (splay-footed).

FORELEGS

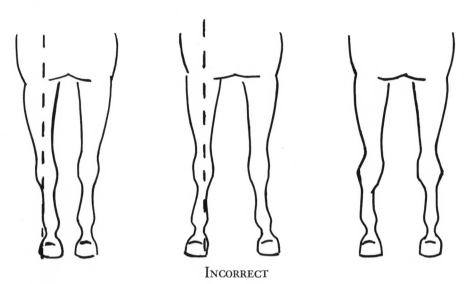

INCORRECT

Left to right: Base narrow (feet too close together); base wide (feet too far apart); off-set knees (bench-kneed).

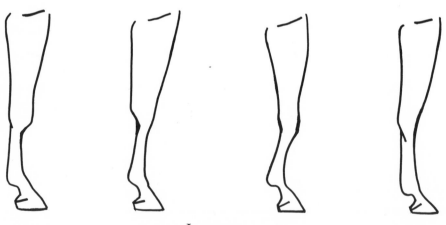

INCORRECT

Left to right: Cut out under knees; tied in at the knees; over at the knee (buck-kneed); back at the knee (calf-kneed).

HINDQUARTERS AND HINDLEGS—*Side View*

CORRECT

An imaginary perpendicular line from the point of the buttocks should touch the center edge of the hock, cannon, and pastern. Hocks large and flat with points well developed. Hips deep (from point of hip to point of buttock).

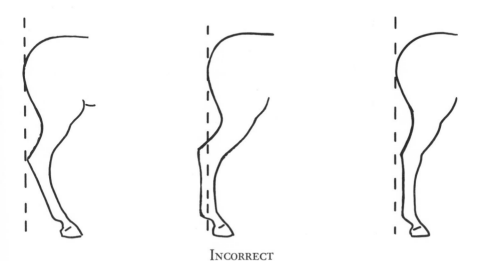

INCORRECT

Left to right: Sicklehocked (standing under); hocks too far back (standing out); hocks too straight.

HINDQUARTERS AND HINDLEGS—*Rear View*

CORRECT

Hips wide, deep, round; broad and flat and well filled up, appearing wide and tabular from behind. An imaginary perpendicular line should drop from the point of the buttocks, passing through the center of hock, cannon, fetlock joint, and hoof. Deviation from these imaginary lines indicates faulty conformation and structure which usually predispose the horse to blemishes and unsoundnesses.

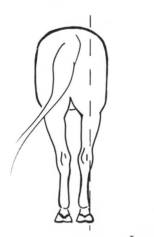

INCORRECT

Left, base narrow (standing close at hocks and fetlock joints). *Right,* base wide (wide at hocks and feet). Hips fall off (rafter-hipped).

THIGH, STIFLE, AND GASKIN

CORRECT

Thigh and gaskin wide and strongly muscled with great length from stifle to hock. Stifle strong and well defined.

INCORRECT

Thigh and gaskin narrow; gaskin too short; stifle weak.

PASTERNS

CORRECT

Flexible, of medium length. Normal front hoof and pastern axis approximately 47 degrees (hind nearer 50 degrees).

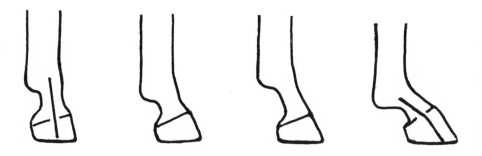

INCORRECT

Left to right: Too steep (greater than 50 degrees in front or greater than 55 degrees behind); too short and stiff; too long and weak; coon-footed (foot axis steeper than pastern axis—a most undesirable trait).

FEET

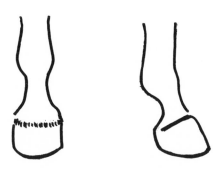

CORRECT

Circular, dense, smooth and hard, comparatively large. Mares usually have larger feet than stallions. Small pony feet and contracted heels and feet are very objectionable because they do not withstand stress.

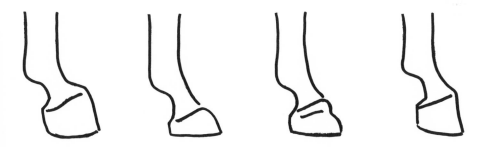

INCORRECT

Left to right: Blocked up foot; shallow hoof; bad hoof; "mule" foot.

"No hoof, no horse."

14

FOUNDATION HORSES OF THE
ROYAL AGRICULTURAL SOCIETY
AND THE INSHASS STUD

DESPITE THE disappearance of many records and herdbooks of bygone studs, information has survived through pedigrees and notes made by the breeders of the Victorian age as well as later arrivals on the scene. When the Royal Agricultural Society was founded, herdbooks were created that listed in English all acquisitions, with the name, birthdate, color, sire and dam, breeder, and price paid. These herdbooks remain at the E.A.O. office in Cairo. Unfortunately, even though when Prince Mohammed Ali died and the E.A.O. was bequeathed his vast library of horse books, his herdbooks and scrapbooks were not among them. Neither have the studbooks of the other princes been found.

The first Royal Agricultural Society studbook, published at Cairo in 1948, was entitled *History of the Royal Agricultural Society's Stud of Authentic Arabian Horses*, and was written by Dr. Abdel Alim Ashoub. A blue paperback book, it contains invaluable photos of early horses and historical information about the Arab horse in general, and records the majority of the foundation stock and Arab horses bred by the society from the year of its founding up to and including 1947. The horses are listed according to the *strain of the dam*, regardless of the sire's strain, and it is essential when researching pedigrees in this book to pay strict attention to the strain. Exact duplication of names is frequent, yet the horses may be of a different strain, color, marking, and age.

Ghadia (Radia) by Feyuil x *Ghazala El Beida; a Saklawiyah Jedraniyah, she was foaled March 3, 1904, at Lady Anne Blunt's stables and presented to the R.A.S. in March, 1917. This photograph was taken when she was twenty-five years old.

PHOTOGRAPH BY CARL RASWAN

Dalal (Dalalah), by Rabdan x Om Dalal; a Saklawiyah Jedraniyah, she was foaled October 15, 1903, at the Mataria stables of Prince Ahmed Kamal Pasha and was owned by Prince Mohammed Ali, who presented her to the E.A.O. in February, 1923.

PRINCE MOHAMMED ALI COLLECTION

Bint Gamila (by Ibn Nadra x Gamila), a Hadbah Enzahiyah, was foaled November 4, 1911, at the late Khedive Abbas Pasha Hilmi's Koubbeh Stables, and was received by the R.A.S. in January, 1914.

COURTESY OF E.A.O.

Khatra (by Sabbah x Doga), a Kuhaylah Mimrehiyah, came from the stables of Prince Ahmed Kamal Pasha and was owned by Prince Mohammed Ali. Khatra was the dam of Gamila Manial, an R.A.S. foundation mare.

PRINCE MOHAMMED ALI COLLECTION

The difficulty over the spelling of names is a persistent problem. One finds different English spellings in Egypt, as well as in other countries, for one specific horse. For example, we find the name of the mare Nafaa spelled Nafa, Nafea, Nafia, or the name Gamila spelled Jamila, Jameela, Gameela—yet there is only *one* Arabic spelling. Likewise there are numerous English interpretations of the strain names, although they too are spelled only one way in Arabic. Dialect also plays an important part in Arab pronunciation.

The Egyptian Agricultural Organization published volume 2 of the Egyptian Arabian Studbook, which registers the horses bred by the society from November 1, 1947, through December 31, 1965. This book follows a different format, clearer perhaps, but less profound and not as well presented as the first volume. In a separate section are listed those horses of the late ex–King Farouk's Inshass Stud which came into the society's possession. Not all the Farouk horses are listed, however, many having been sold locally at auction or before the society kept a record of them. Most horses not listed in the E.A.O. studbook can be found in the Inshass herdbook, which is published. Volume 2 also catalogs the horses according to tail female[1] family, as in volume 1; compilation of pedigrees is thus made on a similar basis. However, there are a number of errors in the book and while some have been corrected, it remains for others to be noted in volume 3.

The late Lady Wentworth, in her *World's Best Horse*, declared that out of four hundred horses registered in the R.A.S. studbook (vol. 1) *all* the foundation mares and twenty-five of the foundation stallions are pure Blunt-Wentworth stock, and 385 out of the 444 registrations are pure or partly pure.

A closer view of the record indicates that in actuality two root mares, Radia "Ghadia" and Jamila, were purchased from Lady Anne Blunt in Egypt, but both mares were of pure Ali Pasha Sherif blood. Durra was also obtained in Egypt by Dr. Branch after Lady Anne's death, and this mare descended in tail female from a mare given to Khedive Abbas Hilmi II, and desert-bred stock imported by the Blunts. Two other root mares, both rich in Ali Pasha Sherif blood, were purchased from

---

1. Tail female is the very bottom line of a pedigree tracing to the original foundation mare. In Arabian pedigrees, a horse always takes the strain of the mare; never the sire. For example, the sire may be a Kuhaylan Jellabi, the dam a Dahma Shahwaniya. The resulting foal would be a Dahman Shahwan (or Dahma Shahwaniya, depending on the sex).

Crabbet Park, England. These descended in tail female from Blunt desert-bred stock purchased outside of Egypt during their extensive travels. Thus of the sixteen mares, only two were related to original Blunt stock in the direct female line, and only one through the male line, a total of three out of sixteen. The balance of the root stock came from sources mentioned below, and while some ancestors may have been bred by Lady Anne, or in her possession at some time while she lived in Egypt, they nevertheless were overwhelmingly of Abbas Pasha/Ali Pasha descent.

Of the forty-eight foundation stallions, eighteen were purchased from Crabbet; however, all contained strong crosses to the Blunt's imported Ali Pasha Sherif stock which they had shipped from Egypt to England, This was, of course, the reason the Egyptians bought the horses—not because they wanted original Blunt desert blood but because they wanted to regain some strains of their own which had been scattered. The stallion Jamil [Blunt] obtained from Lady Anne in Egypt was of straight Ali Pasha Sherif stock.

After obtaining the Ali Pasha Sherif horses from the auction of his stud in 1897, the Blunts held a large auction of their own at Crabbet Park, where they disposed of the majority of inferior stock previously acquired in order to make room for their prized Egyptian imports. The actual percentage of original Blunt stock (their personal desert-bred selections) in today's Egyptian pedigrees is relatively small, though not without significance, and today's Crabbet-bred horses of England are markedly contrasting types as compared to the society's Egyptians, despite the high percentage of Egyptian breeding in the former.

Lady Wentworth's statement in the same book that the Polish Arab Skowronek was "full of Abbas Pasha blood" has been proved erroneous.

In studying the R.A.S./E.A.O. studbooks one finds that the below-mentioned strains are still being perpetuated in tail female line at El Zahraa, with the exception of the now irreplaceable Kuhaylan Mimreh. The Kuhaylan Jellabi no longer exist through the society's foundation stock, although there was until recently a line to it in the Inshass herd. The Dahman family tracing to Bint El Bahreyn has been reduced virtually to ashes, except for one sole survivor in the female line at this writing. The horses of each of these strains were distinctive, irreplaceable types.

The sixteen foundation mares of the R.A.S. as recorded in the 1948

Farida (Saklawi II x Nadra El Saghira), Dahmah Shahwaniyah, foaled April 11, 1921, at Prince Mohammed Ali's Manial stables, purchased by the R.A.S. December 18, 1921.

COURTESY OF E.A.O.

Nafaa El Saghira (by Managhi Sebeyli x Nafaa El Kebira), a Kuhaylah Mimrehiyah (not Kuhaylah Nowakiyah, as noted in the R.A.S. studbook), was bred by Prince Youssef Kamal and presented to the R.A.S. by Mohamed Abu Nafie Pasha in May, 1915.

PHOTOGRAPH BY CARL RASWAN

Jamil (Blunt), by Aziz x Bint Jamila El Beida, was a Saklawi Jedran bred by Lady Anne Blunt. He was foaled in 1896 and received by the R.A.S. in March, 1917.

COURTESY OF LADY ANNE LYTTON

Gamil (Manial), by Saklawi II x Dalal, was a Saklawi Jedran. Bred by Prince Mohammed Ali, he was foaled April 15, 1912, and bought by the R.A.S. in February, 1923.

COURTESY OF E.A.O.

Kheir (by Ibn Samhan x Badaouia), a Saklawi Shiefe, was bred by Lewa Ibrahim Khairi Pasha and purchased by the R.A.S. in May, 1928.

COURTESY OF E.A.O.

Kazmeen (by Sotamm x Kasida), Kuhaylan Jellabi, bred by Crabbet and purchased by the R.A.S. in September, 1920.

PHOTOGRAPH BY CARL RASWAN

studbook are listed below, and in addition, noted in brackets, are a few other mares which were presented to or purchased by the Society but which are listed only in the herdbooks. (The symbol "x" means "out of.")

Saklawiyah Jedraniyah Ibn Sudan: Radia, Jamila—from the Blunts' Sheykh Obeyd Stud; Dalal (Om Dalal), from Prince Mohammed Ali. All descended from precious Abbas Pasha stock.

Saklawiyah Jedraniyah: ["Hanem" Bint Bint Carmen from the khedive's Koubbeh stables, by Senari x Bint Carmen who was by Saklawi I x Carmen "Hallabieh" from Abou Amin Halabi, bought 1895.]

Dahmah Shahwaniyah: Obeya, Shamma, Bint Obeya—from the Khedive Abbas Pasha Hilmi II; Farida—from Prince Mohammed Ali. These four mares descended from the famous broodmare El Dahma of Ali Pasha Sherif. Durra, another branch descended from Bint El Bahreyn, a gift to Khedive Abbas II from the ra'i of Bahreyn.

Hadba Enzahiyah: Bint Gamila, Bint Hadba El Saghira—from Khedive Abbas Pasha Hilmi II; these mares descended from the mare Venus "Shekra Zefra," imported from Arabia by Hassan Agha in 1893.

Kuhaylah Mimrehiyah: Gamila Manial [Rezkeya, from Prince Mohammed Ali and later sold to Prince Kemal el-Dine], Zariffa II, also sold to Prince Kemal el-Dine, Doga by Dahman x Freiha, from Prince Mohammed Ali [Nafaa El Kebira, (also spelled Nafea, Nafa, Nafia], Nafaa El Saghira, from Mohammed Abu Nafa Pasha.[2]

Kuhaylah Jellabiyah: Aroussa, from Prince Mohammed Ali, descending from the Jellabiyah of Abbas Pasha.

2. Nafaa El Saghira was recorded in vol. 1 of the R.A.S. Studbook as Koheila Nowakiya. In 1962, while the author was perusing the handwritten Arabic herdbook of Dr. Mabrouk, together with Dr. Soliman, the El Zahraa veterinarian in residence, it was discovered that Dr. Mabrouk had cataloged her as a Mimrehiyah. This was in contradiction to the published R.A.S. Studbook, but it appeared Mabrouk was right. Raswan, after this incident was brought to his attention, said his notes had been incorrect and that indeed Nafaa was a Mimrehiyah, and that there were two Nafaa El Saghiras. No record of two exists anywhere other than Raswan's statement, for only Nafa Kebira and Nafa Saghira are entered in the original handwritten herdbooks. Raswan's statement that one Nafa Saghira is spelled "Nafa" and the other "Nafaa" does not, according to the Egyptian authorities, hold water. There is no record in Arabic or English of two Nafa El Saghiras.

Rustem (by *Astraled x Ridaa) was a Kuhaylan Rodan from the Crabbet Stud, imported to Egypt by Prince Kemal el-Dine.

COURTESY OF LADY ANNE LYTTON

Michaan, a desert-bred Kuhaylan Ajuz stallion from Saudi Arabia, was presented by Sheik Fawzan el-Sabek to the R.A.S. He is shown standing in front of the main office building of the stud, with various officials behind him. Michaan was an outstanding racehorse.

COURTESY OF E.A.O.

Kuhaylah Rodaniyah: Bint Rissala, and Bint Riyala, from Crabbet Stud, descending from the Blunts' foundation mare, Rodania.

Kuhaylah Nowakiyah: [Noura, by Jamil of Prince Ahmed, a Saklawi Jedran, out of Noura, bay, of Ali Pasha Sherif.]

Foundation stallions of the R.A.S. totaled forty-eight. Only the stallions most influential in modern Egyptian pedigrees are mentioned here. Eighteen stallions were purchased from Crabbet, the majority of which were sent to stallion depots for use in the provinces; the rest were purchased from royalty and prominent Egyptian breeders.

Saklawi Jedran Ibn Sudan: Jamil [Blunt] from Lady Anne Blunt, Hamran, from Crabbet Stud, Samhan and Gamil Manial from Prince Mohammed Ali. All four descended from Abbas Pasha stock.

Saklawi Shiefe: El Deree, a desert-bred stallion from Saudi Arabia, originally in the khassa of King Fouad and presented by him to the society; Kheir, descending from a desert-bred mare, purchased from Lewa Ibrahim Khari Pasha.

Hadban Enzahi: Nabras, desert-bred, purchased from Mohammed El-Itribi Pasha.

Kuhaylan Jellabi: Kazmeen, from Crabbet Stud, tracing to Abbas Pasha's Jellabiyah.

Kuhaylan Rodan: Rustem, from Crabbet, tracing to the Blunts' Rodania.

Kuhaylan Mimreh: Mabrouk Manial and Hadban, from Prince Mohammed Ali.

Kuhaylan Ajuz: Michaan, desert-bred from Saudi Arabia, presented by Sheik Fawzan el-Sabek.

Kuhaylan Rabdan–Kuhaylan Ajuz: Rabdan, descending from original Abbas Pasha stock, from Prince Mohammed Ali.

A complete list of stallions and mares is found in the R.A.S. studbook, volume 1.

"INSHASS"—THE ROYAL STABLE OF KINGS FOUAD AND FAROUK

The kings' khassa, or royal stable of the late kings of Egypt, Fouad and Farouk, was located at Inshass, their palatial country estate some

thirty miles northeast of Cairo. King Fouad was an avid racing enthusiast and supporter of the Royal Agricultural Society. He enjoyed
watching his favorite racehorses, particularly El Deree, perform on the
track, but he was not happy when his horses lost. Eventually he donated
El Deree to the society for use as a breeding stallion.

*A group of visitors to Inshass admire Hamdan, king of the
Inshass Stud.*

When King Fouad died in 1936, his sixteen-year-old son who had
been attending school in England was installed as sovereign. A connoisseur of precious things, Farouk became a collector of fine Arabians, and
in 1939 as a coronation gift from the Royal Agricultural Society he
received the famous white stallion Hamdan and three choice mares:
Hagir by El Deree x Fayza, Yasmeena by Awad x Bint Dalal, and Yaqota
by Balance x Bint Rissala. Dignitaries from around the world often paid
the king's khassa a visit and admired the gardens and orchards as well
as the royal stables. The red chestnut stallion Antar, as well as the grey

Sameh, with contrasting black mane and tail, never failed to draw admiring oohs and aahs from the visitors. But the crown of Inshass belonged to Hamdan, a magnificent white stallion who regally displayed himself as the spirited monarch of the herd.

The khassa was under the supervision of a most capable veterinarian, Dr. Mohammed Rasheed. Brilliant in his field, an author of studious works on breeding and nutrition, he saw to it that the king's horses were maintained in proper fitness, and he kept detailed and accurate records in the Inshass herdbook of the stock. All Arab horses were entered, though some of them were gifts which were not up to standard. Farouk of course could not refuse to accept a gift horse, but Rasheed saw to it they had a way of disappearing or being discarded after a discreet period of time had passed. Most of the entries were of old line Arab horses, however, the majority of them from Prince Kemal el-Dine, Prince Mohammed Ali, and the Royal Agricultural Society. There was a marked preference for the Saklawi Jedran strain, particularly stock tracing to the mares Roga, Ghazieh, *Ghazala, and Ghadia in the female line. There are also lines to this strain through the Dalal branch.

Among the entries in the Inshass herdbook one finds a number of gifts to Kings Fouad and Farouk from King Ibn Saud of Arabia, among them the mares:

Kuhaylah Krush: El Kahila
Saklawiyah: Hind, by Abeyyan as-Saifi; Mabrouka
Kuhaylah: Nafa'a, by Abeyyan as-Saifi
Abeyyah al-Masri: Rizqiya, by El SBayli of Hahan ibn-Muhayd
Saada El Diab: Doora, by Abeyyan as-Saifi
Other foundation mares of non-R.A.S. breeding were:
El Abeyyah Om Jurays: El Shahbaa, by El Hamdani El Naseri from
    El Haj Mohammed Ibrahim
(Strain unknown): El Samraa (by Hab El Rih x Bint El Sheikh) from
    Sheikh Omar Abd el-Hafiz.

A duplication in names of horses bred by the R.A.S., Inshass, and the princes is noted in the herdbooks, and when researching pedigrees of all Egyptian horses one must be absolutely sure to check each horse out thoroughly. Many novices and experts alike fall into the bottomless pit of pedigree duplicity and emerge grasping errors for their pains.

The studfarm at Inshass contained some one hundred fifty horses, more or less, depending on the foal crop and what was retained for the herd. There were a number of truly outstanding stallions and mares. The mares of the foundation of the stud are listed below:

Saklawiyah Jedraniyah Ibn Sudan: Bint Zareefa (Hadban x Zareefa), tracing to Bint Helwa, obtained from Prince Kemal el-Dine; Saada "Bint Ghazala" tracing to Roga.

Dahmah Shahwaniyah: Bint Bint Dalal "Wedad," by Ibn Rabdan x Bint Dalal from the R.A.S., tracing to Bint El Bahreyn.

Kuhaylah Jellabiyah: Radia (Gamil Manial x Aroussa) and Zahra

Ibn Fayda (by Ibn Rabdan x Fayda), a brown Saklawi Jedran, was foaled January 17, 1927, and purchased by the khassa from his breeder, Prince Kemal el-Dine.

PHOTOGRAPH COURTESY OF MRS. MOHAMMED RASHEED

(Gamil Manial x Negma) from Prince Mohammed Ali.
Kuhaylah Rodaniyah: Yakota (Balance x Bint Rissala) from the R.A.S.
Haddah Enzahiyah: Hagir (El Deree x Fayza) from the R.A.S.

The main breeding stallions used were of straight Egyptian stock, with the exception of El Deree, who was used extensively prior to being given to the R.A.S. The stallions are listed below:

Saklawi Jedran Ibn Sudan: Ibn Fayda (Ibn Rabdan x Fayda) tracing to Ghazieh "Bint Bint Horra" of Lady Anne Blunt; Rashid (Jamil [Blunt] x Zareifa—tracing to Bint Helwa) from Prince Kemal el-Dine; El Moez (Ibn Fayda x Bint Zareefa)
Dahman Shahwan: tracing to Bint El Bahreyn—El Belbesi (El Zafer x Bint Bint Dalal "Wedad"); Mekdam (Rustem x Bint Bint Dalal "Wedad"); El Zafer (Awad x Bint Dalal) from Prince Kemal el-Dine.
Kuhaylan Jellabi: Adham (Ibn Fayda x Zahra) tracing to Negma of Prince Mohammed Ali.

Among the horses exported abroad from Inshass were the stallions Nader (from the R.A.S.), El Moez, and Zaher—all sold to the government of the Union of South Africa in 1945. They were excellent individuals but unfortunately were not appreciated at that time and consequently did not contribute to the Arabian scene in that country as they could have, given the opportunity. The loss has been greatly regretted by the South African Arabian breeders who are now avidly seeking Egyptian-Arabian blood.

A change was in the making early in 1952, however, and revolution swept Farouk out of power. The Revolutionary Government took over the administration of royal properties, and with the new socialistic trend and the antiroyal attitude, the horses of Inshass went to the auction block. Gradually they were sold, and as few records were kept, they and other descendants have been irrestrievably lost. Not all the horses were sold, however. The army continued to breed the remaining ones while they were in military charge, for Inshass became and remains an Army base. Eventually the balance of Inshass horses remaining were transferred to the E.A.O. where they were kept at the stables of Mohammed Sultan. Some individuals were culled out and sold and then the re-

El Moez (by Ibn Fayda x Bint Zareefa [Azza]), a Saklawi Jedran, was foaled December 30, 1934, at Inshass and sold to the Union of South Africa November 11, 1945.

PHOTOGRAPH COURTESY OF DR. V. NOLI-MARAIS

Zaher (by Fayda x Zahra), a black Kuhaylan Jellabi, was foaled in 1939 and exported to the Union of South Africa together with El Moez in 1945.

PHOTOGRAPH COURTESY OF DR. V. NOLI-MARAIS

mainder were brought to El Zahraa. The stallions Antar and Sameh were then incorporated into the E.A.O. breeding program, as were such lovely broodmares as Rooda, Ghorra, Ameena, Ghazala I, Hafiza, Yasmeena, Shahbaa, among others.

Sameh (by El Moez x Samira—Inshass) was foaled April 4, 1945.

The first impression my husband and I received of the Inshass mares at Mohammed Sultan's stable, and later at El Zahraa in 1960, was a favorable one, but it was obvious that they were less classic in type than the E.A.O. mares. They were somewhat taller, bigger boned, rougher coupled, and considerably less beautiful in the heads. Their eyes were placed higher, their heads were not as wedge shaped, and their foreheads were narrower, giving them less refinement between the ears, which were also a bit longer and squarer in comparison. Perhaps it was the desert breeding or less intense linebreeding carried out at Inshass, but the difference was there and the E.A.O. management also knew it. Now through the use of Mansour blood, through his sons Sheikh El Arab and Nazeer, as well as through using lines that trace to Shahloul, the quality of the Inshass-derived stock has greatly improved.

The Farouk stallion Sameh[3] contributed a good deal to the E.A.O.

Ibn Hafiza (by Sameh x Hafiza), a bay Abeyan om-Jurays, romps in the stallion paddock at El Zahraa prior to his importation to America.

breeding program. He was a particularly striking individual, powerful in overall appearance, and he passed on extreme trotting action to his

3. Sameh is said by Raswan to trace in tail female to the Saklawi Jedran Ibn Sudan as-Subayah strain, and that this was in note he made while in Egypt. No strain is listed in the Inshass Herdbook, however, for Bint El Sheikh is noted only as "a gift from Sheikh Omar Hafiz."

get, as well as particularly smooth conformation. His head was clean and breedy, but with very little dish. His fillies were particularly lovely, and he was a better female sire than a male sire by far. His most outstanding son is *Ibn Hafiza,[4] imported to America by Gleannloch, Hafiza being a double-Hamdan mare. This stallion provides an excellent outcross to intense Nazeer breeding, possessing commendable size, long neck, overall smoothness, and refinement, and belongs to the relatively rare strain of Abeyan Om Jurays. One of the most beautiful stallions ever produced by the E.A.O. was El Araby, a superb bay stallion by *Morafic x Hafiza.

*El Araby (by *Morafic x Hafiza), a half brother to *Ibn Hafiza, met with an untimely death. He was one of the most handsome stallions bred by the E.A.O.*

Tall, elegant, long-necked, and very extreme of head, he had naturally brilliant park-horse action and carried himself as a mount of kings. Unfortunately he was killed before he had much chance in the stud. It is understandable why *Ibn Hafiza, his half-brother, should be so valuable in combining with the *Morafic bloodline in America. The Sameh blood will also make its mark in Europe, for several of his daughters

4. The asterisk before a horse's name, e.g., *Ansata Ibn Halima, denotes the horse was imported. A plus sign after it, as in *Ansata Ibn Halima+, denotes that the horse has won the Legion of Merit award sponsored by the International Arabian Horse Association.

were exported to the continent after his death.

Antar was also successfully incorporated into the E.A.O. program after 1959. He proved to be a popular horse with foreign visitors, although he had an aversion to anyone handling him other than his long-time groom, Ismaeen. Antar is known for producing outstanding females and nicked particularly well with Abla, a Dahmah Shahwaniyah Nazeer daughter. Antar and Abla were the two most famous lovers in Arabic literature, and perhaps this mating was selected by the Egyptians for its romantic appeal. It did, in fact, prove to be a happy union for the horse

Antar (by Hamdan x Obeya), a chestnut Saklawi Jedran foaled September 21, 1946, was a leading sire for the Inshass Stud until its dispersal.

world and Antar and Abla have been married ever since. Four of these daughters have been exported to America where they are becoming influential broodmares. The Antar daughter *Nihal was a popular choice with spectators and judges in performance classes during 1970, 1971, and

1973, winning the title of U.S. National Champion Western Pleasure Horse and becoming one of the Top Ten in English Pleasure at the U.S. Nationals. Another winning Antar daughter is the beautiful chestnut mare *Dawlat, with numerous halter championships to her credit.

It is always disheartening when great breeding farms are disbanded, and Inshass was no exception to the rule. Fortunately the E.A.O. was in a position to obtain the best of the Inshass stock.

Nabiel (*Sakr x *Magida), grey Abeyan om-Jurays, bred in America of primarily Inshass with R.A.S. lines was U.S. National Futurity Champion colt in 1974.

PHOTOGRAPH BY POLLY KNOLL

15

ARABIAN STRAINS: THEIR ORIGIN
AND MODERN DESCENDANTS

〰〰〰〰〰〰〰〰〰〰〰〰〰〰〰〰〰〰〰〰〰〰〰〰〰〰〰〰〰〰〰

THE TERMS strains and families constantly crop up in literature as well as in discussions about the Arabian horse, and although it has often been said that too much weight is attached to them (or not enough, depending on one's viewpoint), this aspect of breeding is one of historical importance that should be given credence and explored further.

Although the R.A.S./E.A.O. studbooks categorize horses according to the strain of the dam, the Egyptians do not follow a specific strain theory. Dr. Zaher gave us his definition of "strain" by saying: "A strain is a family in the breed. Any inbred family in any breed would have certain characteristics that may distinguish it from other individuals of the breed. There may be more than one family and each one may have its own marks. This used to happen in the case of sticking to family breeding as Arabs used to do."

Carl Raswan, the well-known chronicler of early Egyptian Arabians who lived among the Arab tribes for more than a decade, expressed a similar opinion in the *Raswan Index* "Breeding Arabians is not so different genetically speaking from raising other breeds of horses, or for that matter, purebred cattle or dogs. Every breed has certain strains with predominant qualities and characteristics which breeders seek to unite in a single individual. Whenever a perfect (distinctive) specimen was created, incest-breeding was adapted to fix the type. The primitive man of the desert arrived at the same means for establishing distinctive types within certain strains as the civilized man in the creation of modern breeds."

Historically speaking, strain names came into being among the Arabs through various and peculiar circumstances, as we shall see. However, much confusion has arisen regarding strains because all horses take the strain name through the tail female line, as was the bedouin custom. For example, in studying a pedigree in the eight-line (i.e., the great-grandparents), one may find that six ancestors are of the Kuhaylan strain and two, including those in the tail female line, are of the Saklawi strain. Thus the pedigree would be predominantly Kuhaylan in breeding, yet the horse would be considered a Saklawi because of its tail female line. The horse may or may not resemble the type Raswan attributed to the Saklawi family. Raswan divided the Arabian breed into three main strains, based on his observation that the Arabs by linebreeding or inbreeding within these strains had "fixed" certain characteristics which remained dominant for generations. Saklawi[1] was representative of feminine elegance, grace, and refinement, while Kuhaylan[2] signified masculinity, strength, boldness, and power. The Muniqi strain was of a racier build, usually more developed in the forehand and lighter behind. Numerous other strains related in type to these three primary strains, and thus by adding up the sum total of each strain within a pedigree, the breeder could (supposedly) arrive at the correct distinctive type his horse should resemble in the flesh.

In the sample pedigree presented here, seven out of eight great-grandparents are of the Kuhaylan or Kuhaylan-related strains, and only one is of the Saklawi strain. Quite possibly the horse belonging to this pedigree would resemble the type attributed to the Kuhaylan strain (particularly if he were of straight-Egyptian bloodlines): masculine, bold, and powerful, among other characteristics. If the reverse were true and seven out of eight great-grandparents were of the Saklawi strain, or even five out of eight, the horse could resemble the type attributed to the Saklawi strain: elegant, refined, longer-lined, very graceful, and so on. Again, the combination of bloodlines, i.e., bloodlines developed by different studs, has relevance. If the horse's pedigree was comprised of bloodlines bred by Crabbet, Marbach, Davenport, the E.A.O., and Babolna, one would find this method of evaluation far less reliable. In theory, and sometimes in practice, the Raswan method works. However, space does not permit our going into extreme detail here.

1. A classic example of this strain is Moniet El Nefous.
2. A classic example of this strain was Mansour.

Other authorities, such as Dr. Edward Skorkowski of Poland, also adhere to a strain theory, but disagree with Raswan's categorization. Lady Wentworth, in her *World's Best Horse*, disagreed with both, stating that exclusive "strain breeding" had no foundation, that it was impossible to segregate any strain, and that all pure strains could be bred together with equal success provided type is preserved. She rightly believed that if a horse departs from the proper type it is not a good Arab. Yet, when she tried to buy certain horses from Egypt, the Egyptians recalled, she wanted them from a particular strain or strains! In fact, the Blunts were staunch admirers of certain strains for certain qualities.

Probably the most useful statement to bear in mind when making one's way through the maze of opinions and seeming contradictions is

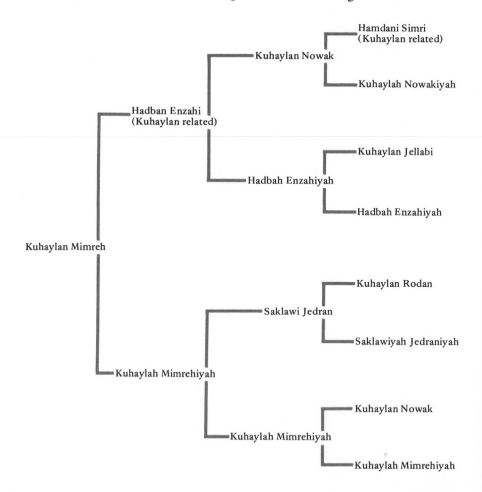

that offered by Dr. Pesi Gazder, a leading geneticist who has applied his research to Arabian horses and has written many knowledgeable papers about breeding and families. He told us he felt that "the confusion was caused in the usage of the words 'strain' and 'type.' All too often Raswan, et al., said 'strain' when they meant 'type,' and 'type' when they meant 'strain.' "

Ideally, strain names should be carried in pedigrees because in some cases type and strain (as defined by Raswan) do relate, and furthermore the family names are of interest from a strictly historical point of view.

Generally speaking, all members of a breed which are descended from relatively few ancestors are related to each other in some way, but as the common ancestors become more remote, their genetic influence upon their descendants must become less and less, and may be almost insignificant when three or four generations have passed. Only through linebreeding or inbreeding, which keep genetic relationship high, can the genetic influence of an ancestor be maintained in a significant degree. There is, however, a fairly widespread belief that some of these families possess special qualities that are carried forward to an unusual extent from generation to generation—that is, that these families are prepotent. Therefore, even though scientists generally consider that prepotency is the property of individuals and not of families, *the persistence of family characteristics over long periods cannot be overlooked.*

Although the modern Egyptian breeders in Egypt are reluctant to inbreed in the closest sense of the word (father to daughter, full brother to full sister, son to mother), yet some of the soundest and most beautiful animals of Egyptian breeding have come through intensifying the blood of certain individuals: examples are the doubling of Nazeer (Nazeer sons to Nazeer daughters), close crosses to Mansour (Nazeer to Sheikh El Arab daughters), the doubling of Shahloul (Alaa El Din to El Sareei daughters, El Sareei to Moniet El Nefous), the doubling of Hamdan (Hamdan to his daughter, Mahfouza, got Hafiza), and so forth. The great value of Egyptian Arabians to the world today is that they have a heritage of inbreeding[3] for elegance and refinement. The value

3. Inbreeding may be defined as the mating of closely related individuals, and implies a closer relationship between the two animals mated than the average of the breed. Generally speaking, this implies that the ancestor common to both parents is duplicated within the first four or five generations of the offspring of the mating. But there are varying degrees of inbreeding.

Doubling of Nazeer produced this beautiful filly, Ansata Sherifa (by *Ansata Ibn Halima *Ansata Bint Bukra). The sire and dam are also from the same tail female strain—Dahmah Shahwaniyah.

Feminine type and strain are correlated in the Moniet El Nefous family (Salawiyah Jedraniyah). Left to right: Mabrouka, Mona, Ibtsam, Fayrooz, and Moniet El Nefous. Type also relates to color in this family of chestnuts.

of inbreeding of course is that it increases uniformity within the inbred stock, and this stock in turn transmits its inherited characters to the next generation with greater regularity—which also is most important in out-crossing,[4] where the genes of a dominant individual are introduced to correct certain defects. After all, some degree of uniformity is essential to enable breeders to plan their matings at all, and indeed the creation of any distinct breed of animals with the capacity of breeding true to type depends on inbreeding for the purpose of stamping the desired characters firmly in the stock.

While it is true that inbreeding may also have the paradoxical effect of producing a certain number of individuals who are completely unlike the rest, and are worthless as breeding stock, this fact should never give rise to allegations that inbreeding causes degeneracy. Inbreeding as such does not cause degeneracy; it lays bare faults which have been hidden in the parent stock in the form of recessive genes. If the bad individuals are weeded out and inbreeding is continued with the sound progeny in each succeeding generation, the line gradually will be purified of the un-desirable recessives and will breed true for the valuable characters. When selection is made for vigor and fertility as well as for other attributes, there will be less talk about the evils of inbreeding.

Linebreeding is merely a less intensive form of inbreeding, and the frontier between the two is not well defined. It is less effective than in-breeding in that extraneous genes are introduced at each generation and therefore progress toward genetic purity, i.e., toward having all important genes in double strength, is slower.

Dr. Ameen Zaher, writing in his book *Arabian Horse Breeding,* makes several good points. "The saying 'There is more difference within breeds than there is between breeds' is sometimes true. Among different breeds of livestock one can find some individuals from a certain breed which closely resemble other individuals from another breed." He cites as an example the Arabian horse, Haleb, who took first place in the Morgan class in 1906. Regarding contrasting types of Arabian horses, he goes on to say, "Some call them families, others call them strains, but I would only call them different types within the breed.

---

4. Outcrossing is done where it may be desirable to bring into the breed as a whole, or into the breeder's strain, some outside blood. An "outcross" stallion or mare is usually unrelated or very distantly related to the mate for which it is selected.

"Is any Arabian horse a good Arabian horse as some people believe? The answer is no. Any Arabian horse should be judged according to the rules and standards that Arabs used to breed for. The existence of many types of Arabian horse does not mean that they are all good Arabs. A pure Arab is not always a good Arab. The word pure means only that he is closely related to the breed and that he got all his genes from Arabian horses that were bred in Arabia, but this does *not* mean that the genes which he got were the favorite genes for an Arabian breeder."

It is not possible to criticize accurately the early foundation stock of Egypt, for much information must be based on hearsay and photos, both unreliable sources, not to mention the bias of personal preferences (in the case of most English breeders years ago, the tendency was to like the more "Thoroughbred" types of Arabians). Many pictures of early Egyptian Arabians were photographic catastrophies, not only in terms of posing and composition, but also because the horses were depicted in old age or in poor condition. While a few photographs published here for historical value show individuals to be somewhat plain by modern comparison, the fact remains that most of them have become progenitors of highly celebrated classic stock today, proving that "blood will tell."

It must be remembered that all horses, regardless of which country they come from, are subject to certain defects in balance, beauty, general conformation, and bone structure; that is, these defects do not occur in just one strain or group of individuals. While some Egyptian horses have been unfairly criticized in print for leg problems, particularly sickle hocks, those countries touted for good legs, particularly Poland, produce their fair share of cow-hocked, crooked-legged animals nonetheless highly publicized as champions or brood stock. And while some breeders consider "sickle hocks" or the tendency to "stand under" a defect, others prefer it to the absolutely straight hind leg, which they feel lacks flexibility. Every country produces its exceptions, its averages, and its discards, no matter how great its breeders.

Many strains are listed in the Abbas manuscript, and all are of interest historically to breeders around the world today, no matter what bloodlines they have (and it is difficult to find many Arabian horses in Europe, Australia, South Africa, South America, or North America who do not have some measure of Egyptian breeding in their pedigrees). The strains mentioned here were chosen because they represent the primary strains of the E.A.O. today and are influential in other world studs. No attempt has been made to include all the strains still existing in Egypt, or to list every noteworthy horse within the strains mentioned. Space does not allow such an exhaustive discussion, and the study of the Egyptian studbooks as well as those of other countries, together with Arabian horse magazines, will provide much of the information. Further, it should be re-emphasized that the individual comments on the qualities and types within the strains are strictly generalizations and that there are exceptions to every rule.

Ghalion, now in Germany, is by *Morafic (by Nazeer x Mabrouka) and out of Lubna, Mabrouka's full sister.

No chapter on strains would be complete, however, without a comment on the Muniqi family, which has received such a muddled name through Raswan and his copiers. Linebreeding on inbreeding, as we have already seen, can fix a type which may or may not be desirable when compared to the standard of the breed. Linebreeding or inbreeding created a racy type in some areas of the Arab world which was desirable to its breeders for speed over short distances. These horses were characterized by long straight necks, long hips, and somewhat low croups; they were high-legged and usually plain in head. Similar to the English Thoroughbred in type, to a degree, they were favored in the establishment of the English Thoroughbred breed. Representatives of this type can be seen today in Upper Syria, where the Muniqi and Jilfan and related families were linebred. But there are also many individuals of the Kuhaylan and Saqlawi strains which are equally plain, or coarse, and have the same racy characteristics as the Muniqi. (Raswan also considered the Rodan, bred by the Ruwala, as contributing coarseness.) Selection can make or break any strain, and any strain or individual which departs from the standard of the breed is an off type.

Most knowledgeable authorities who have had experience with breeders in the Arab countries disagree with Raswan's Turkoman theory —that Turkoman blood was introduced into the Arabians bred by the Salqa tribe, and thus spread through the horses of the Arab tribes in the shape of the Muniqi strain. The Muniqi was and still is prized among the few remaining honorable bedouin breeders, and mentions of the strain in the Abbas Pasha manuscript reveal no comment against it. It was obviously not a collector's item, however, as far as Abbas Pasha was concerned. Furthermore, an "Anazeh racing type" existed long before the Muniqi theory.

The khamsa, or the celebrated five original strains of Al Sahaba, the followers of the Prophet, provided the subject for many discussions and tales. But interestingly enough, no matter who told the story, the Muniqi strain was always among the Five.

Khamsa means "five," but whether it was symbolical or actually five is open to conjecture, so fabled has it become. It is interesting to note that "al-khamsa" also refers to "the five phantoms or five ghosts, or the five elements which are the *primum mobile*, the intelligence, or *mens* which constitute the soul of the world." That it was attached to the Prophet there is no doubt, and as he was a spiritual leader who also spoke and preached in parables, it is possible there is some relationship to this interpretation.

While one account in the Abbas manuscript says that there is no "khamsa," another chapter is devoted to the subject. It explains: "The men of Al Ruwala were asked, and one of the whitehaired men spoke up saying that 'one of them is Muniqiyah Hadrajiyah, and one of them Jilfah Sitam Baludiyah, and one is Al Saklawiyah." The other two he

Similarity in type is achieved through linebreeding. Three linebred fillies at the E.A.O. observe Honeybear, the author's poodle.

did not know. At Beni Sakhr a gathering was held and it was related that "one of them is Muniqiyah Hadrajiyah, and one of them is Jilfah Sitam Baludiyah, and one of them is Mukhaladiyah, and one of them Howaytiyah, and one is Saklawiyah. That is what we heard from our grandfathers, and we do not know anything else." Yet another account from Ibn Dalmaz of the Arabs of Al Sardiya said that Saklawiyah was among the horses of Al Sahaba. "And they say that the horses of Al Khamsa, one of them is Muniqiyah Hadrajiyah, and one of them is Jilfah Sitam Baludiyah, and one of them is Saklawiyah, and one is Mukhaladiyah, and one we do not know."

Lady Anne Blunt also mentions accounts from various sources she talked with in the desert of Arabia, and lists Hamdani, Saklawi, Abeyan, Jilfan, and Muniqi, while yet another account lists Kubeyshan, Saklawi, Mukhaladi, Jaythani, and Treyfi. But without exception, the strains held in disrepute by a certain few today were without question most esteemed by the bedouins themselves. Lady Anne further mentioned that the strain of Muniqi was very desirable in the 1800s, noting however, that Pharaoh's sire, Managhy, accounted "for a certain coarseness difficult to define but otherwise always in the present fashionable strain of Managhys." There was no prejudice against this strain, however, *as regards purity*, and indeed many of the most famous Arab tribes in Arabia, Syria, and Egypt had this strain.

One of the dangers of an obsession with family or strain as opposed to type, is that it may lead to a serious undervaluation of the other elements of a pedigree, or an inaccurate mental picture of a given strain may be developed. That some horses of the Muniqi strain considered undesirable by Raswan, et al. were off types cannot be denied. Equally, it cannot be denied there are off types among *all* the strains, and that all were equally subject to "defilement" through carelessness or calculated human intervention. The main point that Raswan did drive home was that an off type is not desirable in the breeding herd, and that to breed away from it is wisdom. Indeed one cannot quarrel with his concept of the classic Arabian or with his desire to see it preserved. Unfortunately the Muniqi strain has suffered by comparison with other strains.

The Egyptian Arabians have won universal acclaim because people once again long to bring natural beauty into their lives at a time when machinery, modernization, and pollution surround us. These Egyptian horses have the special inherent grace and haughty elegance that all independent creatures of the desert inherit: an indescribable intelligence, a free spirit, a regal bearing and a loving and willing heart to do their master's bidding if treated with dignity.

The following chapters present the historical background of certain strains and families which have been preserved and play an important role in all Egyptian-Arabian pedigrees, and in the pedigrees of most Arabian horses around the world. The reader is encouraged to examine the photographs in this book thoroughly and to compare the resemblances among them, noting the characteristics that are handed down from early generations to the present day through tail female lines. In studying the prepotency of certain families, one picture may indeed be worth a thousand words.

The most accurate records to date regarding strains are those of the bedouins themselves: their own words as transcribed by Aly Gamal Shamashirgi for his master, Abbas Pasha. The foreword to the Abbas Pasha manuscript sets the stage:

Notice about the classification of horses: I say about classifying the lineage of Arabian horses, the first to take precedence is Dahman Shahwan of the Kunayhir strain, and Duhaym al-Najib. Secondly is Kuhaylan Mimreh. After that Saklawi Jedran, which is divided into three sections: the dearest and most precious is the family of Al Samniyat, then the family of Al Sudaniyat, and third the family of Al 'Abd. And after that is Saklawi al-Obeyri and Marighi—both from the same family.

And after that Hadban al-Nazhi, which includes six families in the following order: Hadbah al-Munseriqah, Hadbah Mushaytib, Hadbah Jawlan, Hadbah al-Fard, Hadbah al-Mahdi and lastly Hadbah al-Bardawil, which is not to be mated.

And after these Kuhaylan al-Tameri; then Shueyman al-Sabbah, Hamdani Simri al-Khales, Abeyan Sherrak, Rabdan Khoshaybi, Kuhaylan om Arqub Shuwayhah and then Kuhaylan om-Janoub.

And I say yes, although the Saklawi is the most preferred, I prefer Dahman Shahwan of the family of Kunayhir and Duhaym al-Najib, and Kuhaylan al-Mimreh. And therefore I have arranged the classification in the order of what I consider best.

The quotations in the following chapters are taken from the Abbas Pasha manuscript. A generalized description of some modern-day descendants of each strain follows each history. Like the morning stars of creation, pedigrees too have their useful pattern. To help make that pattern clearer, a chart of Arabian strains and substrains follows. The strains are listed alphabetically; main strains are in caps, substrains in upper and lowercase. Confusion exists over the spelling of strain names, and therefore some of the various spellings are noted.

1) ABEYAN (EBEYAN, OBEYAN, ABAYAN, UBEYAN)

Afdahi
Dahwa
Dasim
Durayjiye
Fehada
Hadr al-Bashir
Hartsh
Honaydis
Howayna
Hufre
Hurmah
Jalam
Jurays (Om or Abu)
Kharish (Harriesh)
Khodayr (Heddr)
Libdi
Lomaylimi
Obeidah
Samh
Sharabdama
Sherrak
Showayiri
Suhayni
Tamhur
Ubayd
Ulian
Urujiye
Wudayhi (Oudeha)
Zahein

2) ARQUB [OM or ABU] (URQUB, ARGUB)

Al Hadeb
Shuwayhe
Suwayriye
Usheyki

3) DAHMAN (DAKHMAN, DEHMAN)

Amayer (Amir)
Khumayis (Humeys)
Kunayhir
Mujalli (Meadjil)

Najib (Nejib)
Om Amr
Shahwan

4) HADBAN (HEDBAN)

Ahdab
Ahmut
Al Fard
Al Mahdi
Al Munseriqa
Bardawil
Bunud
Dahiri
Enzahi
Ghafil
Hamidi
Haqshe
Jadallah
Jawlan
Katil
Mushaytib
Terhi
Uayli
Zahmul
Zayti (Zaydi)

5) HAMDANI (HEMDANI)

Ibn Ghurrab
Simri (al-Khales)
Ghayam
Jafil
Qasil

6) JILFAN (JELFON)

Ajeymi
Dahwe (Dahwah)
Furayjan
Futaymi
Jadallah
Jarullah
Kuziyyi
Stam (Sitam) el-Boulad

7) KUBAYSHAN (KUBEYSHAN, KUBAISHAN)

Al Omeyr (Al Amayer)

8) KUHAYLAN (KOHEILAN, KUHEILAN, KEHILAN)

Abbud	Harqan	Milhan
Abeysa	Hashe	Mindal
Abhul	He Uawi	Mindil
Absan	Heyfi (Hayfi)	Mimreh (Memreh)
Abu Jenub	Humah (Homat)	Mohssen (Musinne)
Adiat	Hunaynan	Muabhali
Adub	Ishr	Muradi
Afas (Afess)	Inzelhi	Musaddaqe (Musadik)
Ajuz	Jalala	Naij (Nayej)
Akhras	Jallabi (Jellabi)	Naofali (Naufali)
Amayir	Jaribe (Jereban)	Nasif
Amradi	Jarshan	Nauwaq (Nowwak)
Anazah	Jawish	Nuume
Ans (ad-Darwish)	Jazi	Qaqa
Armushan	Jeitni (Jeytani)	Qarde
Arnabi	Jenneh ed Tayr	Qauwali
Arslan	Jimayze	Qaysi
Atheer	Johara (Jahiri)	Qinyan
Awaj	Juwayhi	Quli
Aurif	Kashiniye	Radwan
Ayelan	Kenan (Kinian)	Raqwah
Azbari	Khabite	Ras al-Abayad
Bayari	Khadali (Hidli)	Ras al-Fadawi
Berk	Khars	Raudat
Botieh	Khamise	Rawa
Buraysan	Khamisi	Roaha
Dair (Dahara)	Kray (Cray)	Rodan (Rudan)
Edjani	Krush	Ruba
Dhubyan (Dabian)	Lazaziye	Samne
Dukhi	Libdi	Sareer (Om or Abu)
Dunays	Madani	Saur
Durayb	Mahure	Sekti
Essheyr	Majnun	Shair
Fajri	Manfuhe	Shalliaa
Furayja	Marafa	Shanin
Gaga	Marsukhe (Marzuki)	Sharif (Sherif)
Ghandour	Maryum	Shat
Gharbi	Masnah	Shawaf (Shauaf)
Ghazali	Maysan	Sheikh (Shaykh)
Goulli	Mehayet (Mahid)	Shilu
Hakkakiya	Mendikh (Mindakhi)	Shiyah (Sheyha)
Halawi	Merreh	Shuayla
Hallouj (Haluj)	Meyel	Shueynan

Shunayna
Sueyti (Suwayti)
Sukni
Summune
Surah (Om or Abu)
Suwayrihe
Tahiran
Tamiri

Tariki (Tariqi)
Treyfi
Treyshi (Turayshi)
Umayri
Umsays
Urf (Om Maarif)
Wabera
Wati

Zabili
Zandai
Zahqab
Zibberi
Ziyade (Ziada)
Zoayr (Zuayr)

9) MUNIQI (MANEGHI, MANAKI, MAANAGI)

Ashiye
Ekra
Hedruj
Humeys
Hurjuli
Saluqi
Shaddahi
Shumayte (Shumait)
Sidli (Sadlah)
Sishri

10) MELEKHAN (MALIKHAN)

11) MILWAH (MELWEH)

Sharban
Tabur

12) MLOLESH

13) MUWAJ (MAWAJ)

14) QURAYE

15) RABDAN

Al Shahb
Khoshaybi
Mashajid (Mashejed)
Razni
Sulaysili
Zalla (Zeliah)

16) RISHAN (RESHAN)

Arjasi

Hejrisetta
Sehiki
Sherabi

17) SAADAN (SADAN)

Haub
Tawkan (Tauqan, Togan)

18) SAMHAN (SEMHAN)

Al Gomeaa (Qumiye)
Hafi

19) SAKLAWI, SAQLAWI (SEGLAWI, SAKLAOUI)

Al Abd
Ali Gurri
Al Saqt
Anjemi
Araj
Arjebi
Arkabi
Asef
Ashbe
Ayyuq
Bahiman
Daalan
Daghir
Daliye
Duwaybe (Duwaybi)
Ejrife
Ghayyush
Hodayri
Imriye
Jedran (Ibn Sudan, Ibn ed Derri, and Ibn Zobeyni)

Jirbiye
Kamisa
Khalyaui
Malih
Marighi
Masad
Meshui
Nejmet as-Subh
Obeyri
Ramali
Samni
Sheyfi (Shiefe)

20) SHUEYMAN (SHUWAYMAN)

Al Wadaj
Amiriye
Sabbah (Sbah)
Shame
Zahi

21) TUWAISAN (TUWAYSAN, TUWEYSAN)

Qami (Al Gami)
Qiyad

22) WADNAN (OUADNAN)

Khursan

16

THE STRAIN OF DAHMAN SHAHWAN

THE FOLLOWING HISTORY is from the Abbas Pasha manuscript:

Mohammed ibn-Qarmalah, Sheik of Qahtan, was asked about the history of Al Dahmah.

He replied: "Al Dahmah belongs to Shahwan, and she is from the horses which belonged to our Lord Suleiman [King Solomon], peace be upon him! And the Kuhaylah was called Al Dahmah[1] because of her dark color. And the eyes of the Kuhaylah were as if rimmed with kohl.[2] And all the present day pure horses existing are descended from the tail female line of the afore-mentioned.

"As for the stories related to you which say that the Kuhaylat are five (Al Khamsa), they are lies. As for Al Dahmah of Abu Shahwan and Jey, she is known among us, O Qahtan, to be from Obeida, and Shahwan is of Obeida. And from Shahwan til now she is maintained. And from Shahwan and Jey there are seventeen grandfathers.[3] And Al Dahmah is the one who is famous.

"And when she went to Kunayhir from the Ajman, the strain was cut from us, O Qahtan.

"And from Kunayhir a strain passed to Hashr ibn-Wareek of Qahtan, then it was cut off from Hashr.

"And from Kunayhir another strain passed to Abdullah al-Khalifa, Ra'i of Al Bahreyn, and was blessed at his place until now.

"And the strain was cut off from Kunayhir and us, O Qahtan, and we take Allah as our witness that she is Dahmah Shahwan, the most pure of the horses that exist. This is what we know."

A small portion of a poem which Shahwan wrote about his mare after

---

1. Dahmah (the feminine form) means dark or black; Dahman is the masculine form.
2. Black powder—often soot or antimony—used by Oriental women for darkening the eyelids.
3. "Grandfathers" is used by the Arabs to mean "generations."

she was stolen from him poignantly illustrates his devotion to her:

> I love you, O Dahmah
> As if you were part of me
> And my family
> And though there may be horses many
> You are more to me
> Than all the others.

Abbas Pasha particularly valued the Dahman strain and went to great lengths to ascertain its history. The above is only a very short synopsis of the whole intriguing tale. Ali Pasha Sherif valued it as highly as did Abbas, and it is said that he remarked: "If I had only one strain to choose from in maintaining my stud, I would choose Al Dahman." Perhaps these connoisseurs were drawn to this family because it is said this strain was known to have the most beautiful heads of all, both in the past and in the present. Indeed they represent the most harmonious blending of masculine and feminine qualities.

It is not without significance, therefore, that the first Egyptian-Arabian imported to America, and to receive registration papers, was of this Dahman Shahwan strain. Few people realize that the Ali Pasha Sherif horse, *Shahwan, was a true pioneer on the Arabian horse show trail. As a "white" foreigner from a "red" land, he encountered hostility in the new world.

It all began with a well-known businessman of Hemlock Glen, New York, J. A. P. Ramsdell. Mr. Ramsdell had called on the Blunts at Sheykh Obeyd near Cairo in the late 1890s, and was shown the horses of the stud by Judith Blunt. Although he missed seeing Lady Anne and Wilfrid, on July 3, 1895 he wrote to them in England and told them of his great interest in the Arab breed; "I want a fine horse, a handsome individual, with beautiful action and fine carriage of head and tail, a good big soft eye and plenty of spirit, one that I can take pleasure in breeding to and take pride in showing."

In reply to his inquiry, Wilfred Blunt offered him Shahwan, who was one of the most outstanding individuals in the stud. He was entered in the Crabbet Arabian herdbook by Lady Anne as "Shahwan, a Dahman Shahwan. An imported grey horse foaled in 1887, Jan. 12, a Dahman Shahwan of the strain of Ibn Khalifeh, Sheykh of Bahreyn. Dam: a grey Dahma Shahwaniya: Dam's granddam the mare of Ibn Khalifeh. Sire:

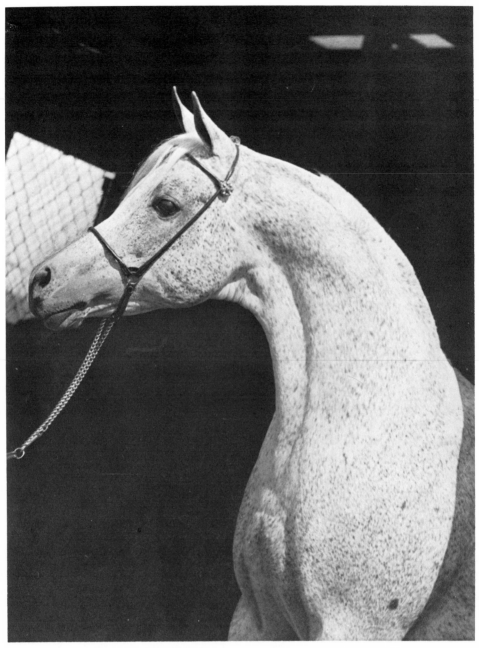

The most famous Dahman Shahwan stallion of our time—
**Ansata Ibn Halima. A perfect Dahman type.*

PHOTOGRAPH BY SPARAGOWSKI

Wazir, the celebrated white Saklawi Jedran bred by Ali Pasha Sherif. Bred by Ali Pasha Sherif but foaled in possession of Mohammed Sadyk Pasha, to whom Ali Pasha Sherif gave the dam in foal. Purchased from M. Saadyk Pasha Jan. 1892, imported to England 1892. White with black hoofs. Fine style, a surprising carriage of tail, great strength of back and quarters and free shoulder action. Height 14.1, girth 64½, 7″ below knee."

Shahwan (by Wazir x a Dahmah Shahwaniyah of Ibn Khalifa's strain) was bred by Ali Pasha Sherif and foaled in 1887 in the possession of Mohammed Sadyk Pasha. Purchased by the Blunts and shipped to England in 1892, he was sold to J. A. P. Ramsdell in 1895 and was the first Ali Pasha Sherif horse to be registered in America.

Mr. Ramsdell was interested, but somewhat hesitant because he had a preference for chestnuts. He wrote to the Blunts on August 20, 1895: "If Shahwan were only chestnut or bay I would be only too glad to take him. . . . I will put the matter entirely in your hands and take any horse you send as I think you know much more about Arabs than I do." It was Ramsdell's ambition to "keep my little stud small and make it the best in America."

Even though Ramsdell thought that "it is too bad Shahwan is white," the Blunts believed Shahwan would suit him and shipped the horse to America in September of 1895, with the stipulation that if he won at shows another 50 guineas would be owed; if not, the sale was complete at 250 guineas.

On December 1, 1895, Mr. Ramsdell wrote: "We took him to the county fairs till they were all over and were disappointed at not showing him in Madison Square Garden, but there was no class for Arabs and they would not take extra stock. It was rather slow showing our horses alone, but I intend to keep it up until Arabs are recognized and classes made for them. Then I hope for some competition, but nothing can beat Shahwan, he is perfection. Mrs. Ramsdell and I are both very proud of him."

Ramsdell had a rough show road to travel, however, and jealousy prompted malicious reports from abroad that Shahwan's get were not good and that the Blunts had sold him on that account (not true), the gossips going so far as to say that "the pink spots on Shahwan's skin and the curly hair in his mane and tail are evidences of 'cold blood' "! Ramsdell went on to say, "Please do not think I am finding fault with the little fellow. I appreciate him and am very fond of him, only mention these facts to show that his enemies do him all the harm they can." The Blunts later regretted not having kept more of Shahwan's progeny themselves.

In April, 1896, Ramsdell happily informed Wilfrid Scawen Blunt: "Shahwan was in the Arab Stallion Class where he took first prize against the Arab 'Bedr,' a very pretty horse but had not the bone and substance Shahwan has."

Shahwan went on to place in open shows, but not as well as he should have, Mr. Ramsdell felt. Spencer Borden, one of the early importers and breeders of Arabian horses in America, thought Ramsdell foolish to enter the horse in open hackney classes, and told the Blunts so.

Despite his appreciation of Shahwan, Ramsdell still wanted a chestnut, for he wrote to the Blunts: "He [Shahwan] is all you said he was and has a deal of magnetism. We are all very fond of him, he has such a good disposition, but there is a prejudice in this country against grays;

he has had but one mare outside of my own. The others have all taken Ras Aloula (on account of his color), although he is not half as good a horse. . . ."

It is amusing to consider that less than a century ago the "fortunate color of the East," as Lady Anne called the white horses, was the less fortunate color of the West. One of the great horses of that era went begging for mares because of his color!

In spite of his color, however, Shahwan created much interest in the Egyptian Arabians, and it was only a few years later that another celebrated Ali Pasha Sherif Arab, this time the white Saklawiyah Jedraniah, *Ghazala El Beida, voyaged West and founded in America one of the great families of history.

THE DAHMAN SHAHWAN FAMILY
SINCE 1900

The famous foundation mare of Ali Pasha Sherif, El Dahma, was a Dahmah Shahwaniyah and the ancestress of a prolific line of the highest quality and most classic type. Dr. Pesi Gazder remarked when discussing Egyptian-Arabians that if he had to choose the most important foundation mare of all time, he would have to choose El Dahma. The choice was well founded.

Two branches of her family exist through the mares Sabah and Farida. The Sabah branch came into prominence in America through the Babson importation of 1932, which brought the fine mare *Bint Bint Sabbah into the Babson breeding program. An article in *The Arab Horse* of May 1937 said of her: "The third prize winner, the Arab mare, *Bint Bint Sabbah, emerged a heroine. Weighing little more than 800 pounds she carried 189 pounds finishing the half distance in one hour 16 minutes in the mud, and walking the second lap so as not to finish ahead of the three hour minimum. Her head and tail were always up and she never took a deep breath." She became a prolific producer for Babson, and many exceptionally beautiful mares and stallions trace to her, among them FaHabba, FaAbba, Habba, Aana, Khebir, and Fabah.

Bint Sabah (spelled Sabbah in the U.S.) was a superior broodmare for the R.A.S., also producing Layla, dam of the celebrated Nabeeh "Sid Abouhom," as well as the beautiful mares Nour and Sabbouha and the exquisite Bukra. Bukra was considered by the late General von Szandtner as a *prima Stute*—a first-class Saklawi (type) mare. She was extremely elegant with a chiseled tapered foreface and a teacup muzzle. When bred to Nazeer she produced some of the most classic Arabians of the time. Her lovely grey daughter "Hosnia," imported to America as *Ansata Bint Bukra, is equally breathtaking and a replica of her elegant mother. She became the first Nazeer daughter in America to produce two champions. Her full brother Gazal in Germany was sought after as a sculptor's model and outstanding sire until his death in 1972. Another full brother, dazzling white, was presented to the king of Yemen, and yet another full sister remains in Egypt. On the track, Yeslam, also by Nazeer, raced a hole in the wind but unfortunately succumbed to colic before he could make a truly memorable record. All the Bukra children have supremely beautiful heads, the females standing about 15 hands in height, the stallions 15 hands or over. In fact, Bukra ranks as one of the most beautiful Egyptian mares of any age.

The Sabah line has yielded equally good stallions and mares, and is

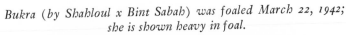

Bukra (by Shahloul x Bint Sabah) was foaled March 22, 1942; she is shown heavy in foal.

an invaluable foundation line. Bint Sabah's son Sheikh El Arab, by Mansour, was one of the most prepotent stallions ever produced by the R.A.S., as well as one of the handsomest. An iron grey with silver mane and tail until he finally went white, he appears to have been responsible for some of the dark greys of like coloring in modern Egyptian pedigrees. The members of the Sabah family are generally characterized by

The grand matriarch, Bukra, in old age. She was considered by General von Szandtner to be the "prima stute"—first-class elegant feminine type.

compact conformation, short backs, well-shaped average necks, strong straight legs and sufficient bone, excellent overall balance, prominent withers, deep girth, and very good slope of shoulder. Their croups are relatively flat and their hips are very long, which tends to make the croups look shorter than they really are. In America the stallions by *Fadl x *Bint Bint Sabbah tended to have much longer necks and backs than their full sisters, and they appeared somewhat taller or larger because of it—likewise the sons of Bukra in Egypt. The family is char-

*Ansata El Sherif (by * Ansata Ibn Halima x * Ansata Bint Bukra)*
is a young champion.

Sheikh El Arab (Mansour x Bint Sabah), foaled January 17, 1933.
A top stallion in the 30's. Sire of El Bataa, Halima, Kamla, Rouda,
Wanisa, Yashmak, Yosreia.

acterized by excellent tail carriage and extremely brilliant action, often making them fine performers in the park class. Their heads are generally beautiful, and they have a slightly longer foreface and longer ears than the Farida line.

The Farida branch of the El Dahma family represents the ultimate in this strain with regard to classic type. Farida was a broodmare par excellence. She was the dam of the beautiful Shahloul daughter Futna,

Ghazal (by Nazeer x Bukra) was exported to Germany in 1955,
where he became a superb breeding stallion.

PHOTOGRAPH BY CARL HEINZ DOMKEN

who is represented in several important American imports; she also produced the fine bay mare Ragia, dam of the celebrated mare Halima, by Sheikh El Arab. General von Szandtner thought highly of this mare and selected her lovely daughter by Sid Abouhom for the Marbach Stud in Germany. When bred to Nazeer, Halima produced the exceptionally handsome stallion Ibn Halima. Imported to America as *Ansata Ibn Halima, this horse went on to win the coveted U.S. Top Ten award at the U.S. Nationals in 1966, 1967, and 1969, and helped to popularize the Egyptian-Arabian in America in the mid-sixties because of his ex-

*Ansata Nile Queen (by Ansata Ibn Sudan x Falima) is double
*Ansata Ibn Halima and traces in tail female to *Bint Bint Sabbah.
She represents an ideal blending of Saklawi and Dahman strains.*

*Bint Farida, by Mansour, was foaled May 3, 1931; she was an
outstanding broodmare.*

treme classic type and naturally brilliant park action. Few would disagree that he has one of the most beautiful Arabian heads in the breed
and consequently has become world famous for "that Halima look."

In keeping with the tradition that the Dahman family has the most
exquisite heads, one may also point to the truly exceptional mare,
*Ghazalahh, a daughter of Bint Farida and a great favorite of all who
see her at Gleannloch Farms in Texas. Abla is another superior broodmare tracing to the Farida line, and three of her daughters by Antar are
now in the U.S. Farida was also the producer of the greatest racehorse
ever bred by the R.A.S: her son Balance outran everything in his day
and still holds the track record for a mile of 1.46 carrying 132 pounds.

*Amaal (by *Morafic x *Bint Maisa El Saghira). A handsome
representative of the Durra tail female line; and he is "double
Nazeer."*

PHOTOGRAPH BY JOHNNY JOHNSTON

Halima (by Sheikh El Arab x Ragia) was the dam of *Ansata Ibn Halima (U.S.A.) and Moheba (Germany). She is shown here at age sixteen.

*Bint Nefisaa (by Nazeer x Nefisa) is a typically beautiful mare of this family.

*El Hilal (by *Ansata Ibn Halima x *Bint Nefisaa) was linebred on the sire and dam's side to Farida; he is a dominant young sire.*

*Ramses Fayek (by Nazeer x Faysa II), shown in his paddock prior to importation to America in 1970.

El Sareei (by Shahloul x Zareefa), left, poses with Sameh (by El Moez x Samira—Inshass). El Sareei was one of the most beautiful stallions ever bred in Egypt.

The Farida line, and also the Sabah line, crossed with Mansour and Nazeer is responsible for some of the most supremely beautiful Arabians of the era, and they are usually very uniform in type. A study of the mares Abla, *Bint Nefisaa, *Ghazalahh, Halima, Helwa, and so forth, as well as the stallions of that family, proves their common uniformity in balance, good legs, magnificent heads, and brilliant action.

The Dahman Shahwan family through Durra, tracing in tail female to Bint El Bahreyn, provides a totally different branch of this strain, different in type from the El Dahma family, even though it is most likely that she or her dam came from the Al Khalifahs. The Khalifahs have been the preservers of this strain for some two centuries, and still breed it to this day. Lady Anne Blunt described Bint El Bahreyn as a bright bay with four white feet. She was bred by Aissa ibn-Khalifah, sheik of Bahreyn (Eastern Arabia) in 1898, who brought her as a gift to Abbas Pasha Hilmi II, Khedive of Egypt in 1903. Lady Anne purchased her from the Khedive on December 26, 1907, for £60. She noted, however, that "this mare has one defect, ears like *bats'* ears, but they need not be transmitted; her filly did not have them and otherwise she is very fine. The Khedive no longer cares for Arabs. I saw the mare in 1903." Among her foals were Dalal, by Jamil [Blunt], "a very beautiful filly with gazelle-like head," influential in the Inshass herd.

The Durra descendants of Bint El Bahreyn were tall of leg and some-what larger in overall structure than the El Dahma family. Extremely elegant creatures with long heads and an appreciable dish, they include Bint Durra and *Bint Bint Durra, imported by Babson, and the lovely broodmare Zareefa. Zareefa produced by Shahloul the exquisite mares Assila and Maisa and the truly magnificent copper bay stallion El Sareei, one of the most ideal Arabians one would ever hope to see. El Sareei never sired his equal, but his daughters are producing well and his son *Tuhotmos represents a doubling of the Shahloul blood which is very desirable as an outcross for Nazeer.

*Bint Bint Durra unfortunately produced only a few straight Egyptians in America, notably Fay Dalla, who produced the handsome chestnut stallion Daaldan. *Bint Bint Durra was shown in endurance, finishing the 1937 Vermont trail ride in perfect condition. Mr. George Cason, manager for the Babson farm in those early years, wrote that "in 1936 and 1937 the Arab horses were competing in open competition. Mr.

Descendants of the original Ali Pasha Sherif mare, EL DAHMA, which are straight Egyptian. Mares are in full caps, stallions in lowercase. This is only a partial list of horses descending from this mare, but it gives an impression of her world-wide influence. Horses remaining in Egypt are not listed. They can be found in the Egyptian studbooks. An asterisk denotes imported to the U.S.

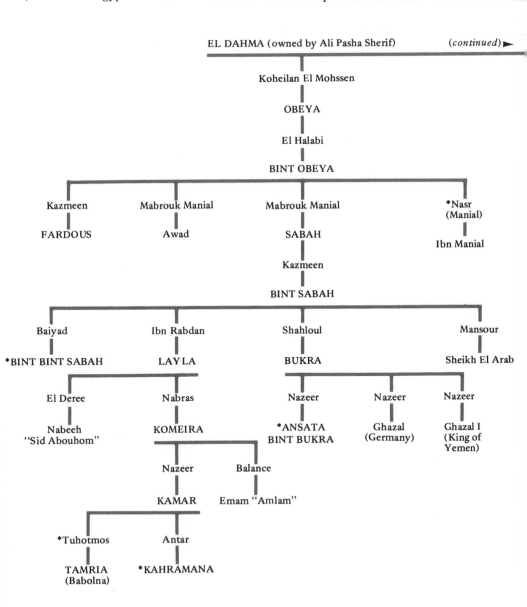

EL DAHMA (owned by Ali Pasha Sherif)   *(continued)* ▶

Koheilan El Mohssen

OBEYA

El Halabi

BINT OBEYA

Kazmeen	Mabrouk Manial	Mabrouk Manial	*Nasr (Manial)
FARDOUS	Awad	SABAH	Ibn Manial

Kazmeen

BINT SABAH

Baiyad	Ibn Rabdan	Shahloul		Mansour
*BINT BINT SABAH	LAYLA	BUKRA		Sheikh El Arab

El Deree	Nabras	Nazeer	Nazeer	Nazeer
Nabeeh "Sid Abouhom"	KOMEIRA	*ANSATA BINT BUKRA	Ghazal (Germany)	Ghazal I (King of Yemen)

Nazeer   Balance

KAMAR   Emam "Amlam"

*Tuhotmos   Antar

TAMRIA (Babolna)   *KAHRAMANA

Descendants of EL DAHMA (continued)

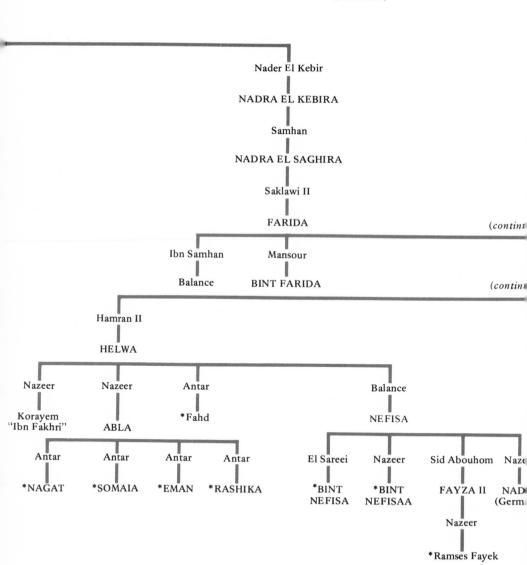

Nader El Kebir

NADRA EL KEBIRA

Samhan

NADRA EL SAGHIRA

Saklawi II

FARIDA   (*contin*

Ibn Samhan   Mansour

Balance   BINT FARIDA   (*contin*

Hamran II

HELWA

Nazeer   Nazeer   Antar   Balance

Korayem
"Ibn Fakhri"   ABLA   *Fahd   NEFISA

Antar   Antar   Antar   Antar   El Sareei   Nazeer   Sid Abouhom   Naze

*NAGAT   *SOMAIA   *EMAN   *RASHIKA   *BINT   *BINT   FAYZA II   NAD
                                            NEFISA   NEFISAA   (Germ

                                                                   Nazeer

                                                                   *Ramses Fayek

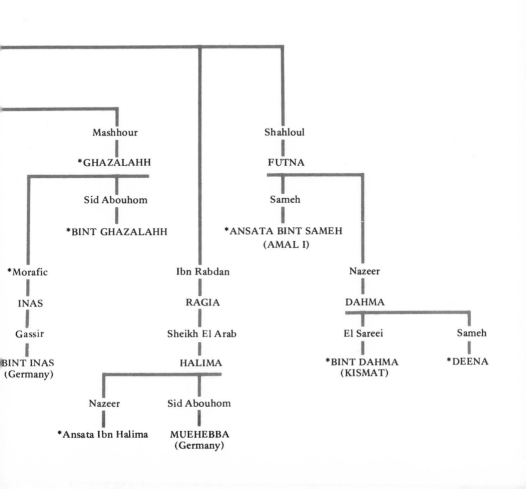

Mashhour

*GHAZALAHH

Sid Abouhom

*BINT GHAZALAHH

*Morafic

INAS

Gassir

BINT INAS
(Germany)

Ibn Rabdan

RAGIA

Sheikh El Arab

HALIMA

Nazeer

*Ansata Ibn Halima

Sid Abouhom

MUEHEBBA
(Germany)

Shahloul

FUTNA

Sameh

*ANSATA BINT SAMEH
(AMAL I)

Nazeer

DAHMA

El Sareei

*BINT DAHMA
(KISMAT)

Sameh

*DEENA

Babson's stable did more for the promotion of the breed at this time than any other stable. There were less than 1000 registered Arab horses living at this time in the U.S." Even the British lauded these plucky mares, for it was written in England's periodical *The Arab Horse* (May 1937) that "Mr. Babson's *Bint Bint Durra, the mare class winner, a dark chestnut with straight hard legs, was of rarely symmetrical proportions and strength, as well as grace of body. Her stable mate, *Bint Saada, was very similar, but less compactly coupled. Their expression was that of the ideal Arab, gentle and generous, as if they would give all they had to a good master."

Gassir (by Kheir x Badia), foaled March 23, 1941. He is shown with his groom in 1959.

The Durra line again came into the spotlight with the importation of *Bint Maisa El Saghira by Gleannloch Farms. A classic bay mare of excellent size and substance, she went on to win many championships at halter and performance in the mid-sixties, including U.S. Top Ten awards in halter, English pleasure, and park. She was very influential in making new friends for Egyptian Arabians and has been a broodmare par excellence since her retirement to the broodmare band. Another mare of this family also made Arabian history when she brought the highest price ever paid for an Arabian broodmare at the U.S. National Arabian sale in October, 1972. *Ansata Bint Elwya, imported from Egypt, sold for $40,000. Her colt, Ansata El Hakim, by *Ansata Ibn Halima, subsequently sold to the P.S. James Arabian Stud in Australia and became the first straight-Egyptian import to that country.

*Daaldan (by Fadaan x Fay Dalla), descended from *Bint Bint Durra.*

Considering the record, there is no doubt that the strain of Dahman Shahwan was rightfully placed first in Abbas Pasha's manuscript as well as in esteem by the two most famous Arabian horse-breeding pashas of Egypt. A chart showing some of the Dahman Shahwan horses is provided on pages 307–309.

17

THE STRAIN OF
SAKLAWI JEDRAN IBN SUDAN

ALY BEY SHAMASHIRGI wrote the following in the Abbas Pasha
manuscript:

In the presence of the majless of the sheiks of Shammar, and in the presence of Nasr al-Sohaymi, the Sheik of 'Onayzah of the people of Al Qasim, and in the presence of a large number of people, Talal ibn-Rashid and Obeid ibn-Rashid questioned Talal ibn-Ramal about Al-Saklawiyat, his horses. And Talal ibn-Ramal is an old man, well advanced in years. And he replied to the people mentioned:

"The strain of Al Saklawiyat belonged to my father, and our first white-haired men of the tribe told me about the history. And I, O Talal ibn-Ramal, my hair has become white, and I will tell you like the first ones told me. . . ."

And Talal ibn-Ramal was asked: "How did Al Jedraniyah pass to Ibn Jedran; from where did Al Jedraniyah originally pass to Ibn Jedran?"

And Talal ibn-Ramal answered at the gathering: "These are mubti sayings—from the old times—but we heard from our first grandfathers that the origin of Al Jedraniyah is Kuhaylah Ajuz from among Al Khamsa, from the time of Al Sahaba.[1] And the Kuhaylah was 'awdah, a saqla mare.[2] And the Saklawi strain was named after her, saqla Kuhaylah mare. And Saklawi is a name.

"And the Saklawiyah originally passed to Ibn Jedran from one of two tribes; either from Al Dafeer or from Al 'Issa. This is what we have heard from the first ones."

1. Al Sahaba means the friends and first followers of the Prophet Mohammed.
2. 'Awdah means an old or aged broodmare while "saqla" means "kick," meaning here that she was a kicker. Saqlawi has subsequently been written with a kaf instead of the qaf due to variation in pronunciation throughout the Arab world.

And the assembly took place in the presence of the Emir of Al Muwalli, Aref Bey, of the descendants of Ibn al-Zarba; Abdurahman, Sheik of Beni Khaled, Dabbi ibn-Shutaywi, and Hayzoum, the son of the brother of Dabbi from Al Sabaa, and Butr ibn-Adnayan of Al Jasim, and Hamad al-Abeetah, who was an hundred years old and ten.

And when questioned, Hamad al-Abeetah replied: "Ay, by Allah, O Ali Bey, I have in my possession many histories, and I, O Hamad al-Abeetah, will relate to you the histories that happened some 400 years ago.

"The origin of the Saklawiyah stud goes back to Hatem Emir Tai [Ti, Tay, Tye, Tayi]. And Hatem died and his paternal cousin, Mahanna al-Faris, Emir Tai, was his heir. And at that time there were no Anazeh or anyone else, for the only ones who were present at that time were Emir Tai and Emir al-Muwalli. And there was a battle between Emir Tai and Emir al-Muwalli.

"And it happened that Ibn al-Zarba, Emir al-Muwalli, unhorsed Mahanna al-Faris, Emir Tai, from his mare and made off with her. And she was a hamra [bay] mare who was pregnant. And she produced a filly at Fayad ibn-Zarba's place."

Hamdan ibn-Hulayl, from the people of the North, testified on the testimony of Suleyman abu-Hamayil, that the Saklawiyah's origin is from Ibn Zarba of Al Muwalli. And when he raided Jauf, on his way back he fell upon Al Sardiyah and ran off with some of their camels. So Al Sardiyah pursued him and asked that they be returned. And Ibn Dalmaz had captured from one of them a Saklawiyah, but he did not know it was a Saklawiyah. And he gave her as a present to his guest, a Badrani. And when he discovered she was a Saklawiyah, he was afraid the news might reach the Emir of Al Sardiyah, who would want to recover her knowing her value. So he took her and fled in the direction of Al Karak. And he encamped with Al 'Amr where he remained some time with Abu al-Hamayil, and left the mare with his family. Later on he left the mare in the charge of his wife, having impressed upon her to take good care of the mare while he went on his holy pilgrimmage to Mecca. And Abu Hamayil wanted to make a ghazu [raid], so he beguiled the wife of Al Badrani into allowing him to take the mare. And he went on his raid and plundered twelve female camels. And he gave six of them to the mistress of the mare.

And after some time he borrowed the mare again and made another ghazu on Beni Sakr, who were living in the land of Al Hejaz. But when he attacked they turned upon him and Tahhan, from the clan of Ibn Zohayr, unhorsed him, and he gave the mare to Ibn Bakr, one of his men.

And Ibn Bakr mounted the mare and went on a razzia. But in the course of the raid they became afflicted with great thirst, and the mare was almost exhausted. So he left the mare by herself and went in search of water. When he returned she had disappeared. So he asked people about her and finally traced her to Al Jauf, where he learned that people from Shammar had found her and given her water to drink and took her along with them. And on their way Ibn Jedran, who was well known for his raids, happened to fall upon them. And he plundered them and took the Saklawiyah.

Dabbi ibn-Shutaywi and Ali ibn-Sudan were questioned in the house of Dabbi Shutaywi, in the presence of Hussein ibn-Shalhoub and Zaydan ibn-Turki and Saud ibn-Said, the paternal uncle of Neyf ibn-Murshid, and Haizum, the son of the brother of Dabbi, and in the presence of the old and young people of Al Qamsah.

"Swear to us by your honor, good fortune, your religion and faith. And tell us the positive truth about that which you have heard from your grand-fathers' grandfathers concerning the history of the horses of Ibn Sudan."

They replied: "By Allah, O Ali Bey, we will tell you the history we have heard from our grandfathers and our elders and the white-haired men of the tribe, that she originated from Hadhud ibn-Jedran. And she passed to Beni Khaled. On the day of Al Arban, when Abdul Azziz abu-Saud ruled Nejd, a shaqra [chestnut] 'awdah mare belonging to Hadhud Ibn Jedran became disabled."

And on the day in which water was sold [the men continued], Hadhud ibn-Jedran with his sick shaqra mare passed by Al Khaledi, a shepherd of Shuwai of Beni Khaled, who was tending his sheep. And Hadhud ibn-Jedran went to him with the mare and implored him: "Look at this mare, Al 'awdah; she is disabled. You can see she is a Saklawiyah.[3] Save her, and as you save her I will sell her to you for the price of your saving her life."

And so the shepherd brought her a gourd of water and he began to let her drink and refreshed her by dampening her nostrils with cool water. And Hadhud went back to his people.

And when the mare had drunk the water she revived and pulled herself together. And she again became beautiful.

And an Arab of Beni Hussein bought her from Al Khaledi, who had given her water to drink. And the mare went to Beni Hussein. And Al Hus-seini went as a guest to the house of Hadhud ibn-Jedran. And Al Husseini said to Ibn Jedran:

"O Hadhud, the shaqra mare which had been disabled and was separated from you, O Hadhud, in the region of Beni Khaled. From which stud is she?"

And Hadhud ibn-Jedran replied: "By Allah, O Husseini, she is my mare, Saqlawiyah Jedraniyah."

And when Hadhud told him, Al Husseini returned to his people. And he covered the mare by one of the horses of his people, and she produced a hamra [bay] filly. And the day the filly became two years old, Al Husseini

3. Apparently Ibn Jedran refers to her distinguishing type. If so this is most indicative that certain strains were of a distinctive type in the desert at that time.

took her and sold her to Al Sabaa, of the Arabs of Al Qamsah. And Salim, the paternal cousin of Shutaywi, saw her and bought her from Al Husseini for eight camels. And on the day he bought her he asked, "What is the filly's origin, O Husseini?"

And Husseini replied: "She is a Saklawiyah Jedraniyah, and if she is not a Saklawiyah Jedraniyah, then I, O Husseini, have no methani[4] from you."

And the filly went to Salim. And they say that her mother died at Al Husseini's. And she had not produced any color [i.e., any foals] at his place but the hamra filly which went to Salim.

And Salim covered her by Al Buhaym, the Saklawi horse of Saud. And she produced a beautiful shaqra filly. And he gave the mare back to Al Husseini in exchange for the methani.

So Mansour ibn-Sudan bought the hamra mare, the mother of Salim's filly, for ten camels, through the intermediary who acted for Al Husseini.

As for the hamra that Mansour ibn-Sudan had taken, she was blessed and proved productive at his place, and the horses that died, and the horses that reached the High Stud [of Abbas Pasha] are all descended from the hamra mare. And we testify by Allah, on the testimony of our grandfathers and the old men of the tribe, that this is the history that we know. And that the Saklawiyah is originally from Hadhud ibn-Jedran; that was passed on to Beni Khaled, and from Beni Khaled to Beni Hussein, and from Beni Hussein to us, Al Sabaa.

Abbas Pasha was not alone in his quest for the Saklawiyat, for this had also been a favored strain among the Arabs. Fortunately for the Egyptians Abbas Pasha acquired the largest and best collection ever assembled under one roof, and today we have many descendants of these original horses to work with.

Prince Mohammed Ali remarked in his books *Breeding Purebred Arab Horses:* "I have found as a result of my many experiments that horses of the strain of Saklawi Jedran were the most courageous. A Saklawi will fight for his master, and in charging nothing will frighten him; he will charge a gun, a lion, and even a locomotive if put to it." The prince's comments are not without foundation, for those who have owned horses of this strain would undoubtedly bear him out. The Egyptian pedigrees of the late 1800s are filled with names of Saklawi Jedran stallions. Prince Ahmed Kemal Pasha had several superb old Saklawi

---

4. Methani is the term used for a lease agreement on a mare whereby the lessee is able to obtain produce from the mare, or may elect to keep the mare and return her produce to her owner in exchange for her.

stallions who, along with the Ali Pasha and Abbas Pasha horses such as Wazir and Zobeyni, were responsible for the high quality of the studs. The stallion which is counted most often in modern pedigrees, however, is Mesaoud, whose influence at the Crabbet Stud was profound. More than any other stallion, he is responsible for the fame of Crabbet throughout the world, and he is probably the most influential stallion in the world in Arabian pedigrees, if one were to pick a single individual.

Mesaoud was bred by Ali Pasha Sherif and purchased from him by the Blunts in 1889. He was actually Judith Blunt's horse. On the auspicious occasion of his arrival all the necessary precautions were taken by Zeyd, the Blunts' Muteyr bedouin assistant, to see that the evil eye was averted from the horse. Avoiding well-traveled routes, Zeyd brought Mesaoud, Khatila, and Merzuk through the desert to Sheykh Obeyd and sacrificed a lamb on the threshold of the garden, completing the ceremony by sprinkling blood on the foreheads of the three horses.

Before being exported to England Mesaoud spent his years in Egypt with the Blunts as Judith's favorite riding horse and the subject for her artistic talents. The Blunts decided to try him on the racetrack, and so they placed him in partial training at their own farm and worked him as best they could, for they had nothing to gallop with him and were unable to judge his speed.

Mesaoud worked handily, and carrying the yellow and green colors of the Blunts made his debut at Gezira Racetrack on September 1, 1890, in the Cairo Eclipse Stakes for Arab maidens. The distance was one and a half miles and he carried 8.9 stone (121 lbs.). Mesaoud took the track proudly with the Blunts in attendance and Judith fully expecting her horse to win. Unfortunately Mesaoud got off to a very bad start in the nine-horse field, yards behind the other horses, and although he lessened the distance and left three horses far behind, he was not able to come up within the mile-and-a-half distance of the race. Had there been another half mile, the jockey thought that Mesaoud would have come up, for he was gaining. But the jockey also felt that three miles would suit the horse better than two.

Wilfrid Scawen Blunt commented that Mesaoud's dam, the grey Yemameh, was "a very splendid mare with the finest head in the world," and of course his sire was the celebrated Dahman Shahwan, Aziz, whom Lady Anne at first disliked, though she later revalued his merits. Mesaoud was shipped to England along with the other lot of horses in

1891, and written up in the Crabbet Arabian herdbook as "a bright chestnut with four white feet and blaze, a mark of white under the chin, also group of white specks under jowl. Beautiful head and ears, very fine shoulder, great depth in front of girth, powerful quarter, large hocks and knees, and remarkably deep cut sinews. Very fine mover, fast walker, and trotter. Tail set on very high and carried magnificently. Dark line along back. Ht. 14.2½, girth 69″, below knee 7¾″."

As a show horse Mesaoud won first prize at the Crystal Palace in 1896, 1897, and 1898, and fourth prize at the International Horse Show in Paris in 1900. He was sold in June, 1903, to Wladislas Klinewski, "a Niezdow pres Opole Royaume de Pologne de Russie," for 240 guineas, and taken to Russia in July, a few days after the sale of July 4, 1904.

It has become customary in America to add up the number of lines to Mesaoud in a pedigree, and these numbers have become unbelievably high. He is given credit, or discredit, by most breeders for being responsible for the increase in white markings and the changing of the balance in the Crabbet herd from bay to chestnut. However, one finds that the majority of horses that are inbred to Mesaoud are also inbred to Rodania —an original Blunt mare who was chestnut and who we know carried a white factor, for *all* her foals had white markings to some degree. Nothing is known of her ancestors' colors, but it is obvious from the pedigrees that it was the combination of Mesaoud and Rodania (chestnut with white combined with chestnut with white) that was primarily responsible for the flashy chestnut and high white patterns such as those of the mare Rose of Sharon.

As a sire Mesaoud was sensational, and his reputation and influence is unmatched by any other Arab stallion in the world, including the celebrated Skowronek, for most of the Skowronek progeny bred by Crabbet carried strong lines to Mesaoud. The English have never objected to "high white," and Lady Anne Lytton, Lady Wentworth's daughter, mentioned that "both my grandfather and my mother favoured the white because it almost always went with the best of types. In fact my mother lost the bays altogether and I think this was because she went for the best conformation and this was almost always found in the chestnuts.[5]

One of the most elegant, graceful, and valued lines for producing ex-

5. Lady Wentworth told her mother that in her opinion grey was not worth preserving (at Crabbet), for all the best strains in style and quality were chestnut, bay, or brown.

treme "elite" refinement is the line to Horra, a beautiful white Ali Pasha Sherif mare and own sister to the celebrated Wazir. Her dam, Ghazieh, also white, was an original Abbas Pasha mare. Lady Anne Blunt was particularly attracted to this family and tried to buy the fabulous white stallion Amir (by Aziz) from the pasha, but she would not pay the pasha's price. So taken was she by this magnificent horse that she described him as "*the* white Seglawi Jedran of Ibn Sudan. . . . his head is perfection. . . . his pedigree is the very best of the best, and he is really lovely . . . *perfect* except light of bone." The latter she did not believe would be inherited by his progeny, it being a consequence of the conditions under which the horses were reared, and she had proven it easily correctable.

The two most outstanding female descendants of Horra were the "very fine" Bint Horra (dam of the Inshass mare Ghazieh Bint Bint Horra), and Helwa. Helwa produced the influential chestnut mare Johara, and the very special Bint Helwa, better known as "the broken-legged mare," whom Lady Anne placed first in the Sheykh Obeyd herd-book. Colonel Spencer Borden wrote of her that "were it not for her injury she would be a beauty; pure white, with a head such as Schreyer would seek as a model." A priceless individual, she was foaled in 1887 and purchased from Ali Pasha Sherif on December 14, 1896, for £80 with her filly foal about six months old by Ibn Sherara (Ghazala "Bint Bint Helwa," later known as *Ghazala El Beida). Bint Helwa was sired by the chestnut Dahman Shahwan, Aziz, whom Lady Anne described in 1897 as "looking glorious" when he was ridden out before her. Her dam was Helwa, whose sire was the celebrated Shueyman by Jerboa. Thus her pedigree was straight Abbas Pasha stock. A true Saklawiyah, she

---

The fact that the Blunts selected for those colors over the years is probably responsible for this opinion, yet the statement is quite incredible. Apparently Lady Wentworth changed her tune when Skowronek came along.

It is obvious that many of the best pedigreed Arabians have had some of the "brightest" markings, including roaning and flecking. Wilfrid Blunt perhaps summed up the situation best in his notes written in 1904: "In the matter of white markings, again tastes and prejudices differ much. Three white legs (the off fore dark) with a star are handsome in chestnut and are the fortunate combination in the Mohammedan taste. But there is a practical objection to all white markings. White affects the colour of the skin so that in many countries these are liable more than where the skin is dark to mud fever and the sore heels caused by insect plagues. I therefore recommend their gradual elimination from the Crabbet Stud. A dark chestnut with no white but a star would be probably perfection."

proved to have the courage, strength and will to survive that have endeared this strain to all breeders and that were singled out for praise by Prince Mohammed Ali.

Bint Helwa's test came ironically on a Friday the 13th in 1897. She had been turned out with Fulana and Johara, her full sister, in the small meadow opposite Newbuildings entrance gate. The entry in the Crabbet

Bint Helwa (by Aziz x Helwa), foaled 1887—"the broken-legged mare."

COURTESY OF LADY ANNE LYTTON

herdbook mentions that the three mares appeared perfectly quiet when turned out, but when left to themselves they decided they wanted to come home. "They got through the thicket and hedge and over the bank and ditch onto the road where Bint Helwa was found with her leg broken standing waiting for someone to come for her, which they did after the other mares came home alone. She had hobbled almost to Newbuildings gate and there she stopped." The vet and Webb, the Blunt's overseer, were for shooting her, "but to this WSB would not consent. With great difficulty she was got up the hill into the yard and under the roof of the shed where an admirable sling was arranged by Webb. There were splints made of elm bark. . . . By September she was gradually improving. . . . In the course of the spring she was gradually deprived of the sling and on April 18 she foaled, no one being present, and she and the foal were found together in the morning, all well. She is able to limp about and even go at a game trot lamely, but the leg is frightfully misshapen." Despite her handicap she managed to have eight foals for the Blunts before her death in 1907.[6]

Col. Spencer Borden purchased *Ghazala El Beida for £200 direct from Sheykh Obeyd in Egypt. Before her departure, however, this mare provided Egypt with a true gem, the filly Ghadia, foaled March 3, 1904, and sired by the Jellabi stallion Feysul, of Ali Pasha Sherif. The filly was noted as "a first-class foal" by Lady Anne, who retained her and her half-sister by Jamil, named Jemla. Ghadia was later known as Radia "Ghadia," and became a celebrated mare for the Royal Agricultural Society as did her daughter Zarifa (Zareefa), by Sahab, foaled in 1911—"a very beautiful filly—the most lovely in the world." She was to become influential in the Inshass herd of King Fouad and King Farouk.

The Ghadia line was to become one of the most treasured producers for the R.A.S., for when Ghadia was bred to the handsome Mabrouk Manial, Bint Radia resulted, and she when crossed with Ibn Rabdan produced the Fabulous Four: Shahloul, the spectacular white stallion who stood as head stallion at the R.A.S. for many years and was responsible for some of the most beautiful heads produced in his era; his full brother, Hamdan, senior stallion for Inshass; Radwan who went to the Agricultural Department of Cairo University; and Samira, who was judged the most beautiful Arabian mare in Egypt during an annual agricultural show in Cairo. *Ghazala's descendants generally raced well and

6. An interesting footnote to the entry reads: "Foal's front legs sometimes held exactly in the position of the dam's broken limb, bent inwards and as if weak, but it seems able to do this at will. Sometimes the off leg is thus held, at other times the near one, at other times again both, as if the mare having a strong impression had transmitted it to the mind of the foal. Sept. 1898—foal has entirely lost all traces of this mental impression."

many had an excellent way of going and good trotting action, and appreciable size, height, and substance, as well as overall elegance, long necks, and very extreme heads.

Sámira when bred to Balance produced Zaafarana, a mare of exceptional quality and action whose brilliant trot and ceremonial presence were a pleasure to behold. She became the dam of such winning racehorses as "Amralla," Farfour, Farfoura, and the American import *Talal (who raced as Johnny Boy), a spirited and regal white stallion with a spectacular trot. *Talal is a crowd pleaser wherever shown and achieved U.S. National Top Ten status in halter at the U.S. National Champion-

Samira (by Ibn Rabdan x Bint Radia), foaled January 30, 1935, the dam of Zaafarana.

ships in 1969. *Talal's full sister, the very elegant *Ansata Bint Zaafarana, was imported by the Ansata Arabian Stud as a yearling and remained unshown until she was fifteen years old. Already a mother of note, she

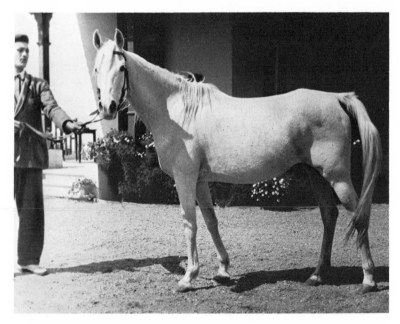

Zaafarana (by Balance x Samira), foaled February 14, 1946; the dam of *Talal, *Ansata Bint Zaafarana, and Amralla "Ziada."

*Ansata Bint Zaafarana (by Nazeer x Zaafarana), imported in 1959 as a yearling. She was first shown at age fifteen and won champion mare and most classic Arabian.

made her debut in the ring prancing like a young mare and handily won Champion Mare and Most Classic Arabian of the show.

Another line to this strain is preserved through the Babson import of the thirties. *Bint Serra, dam of the white monarch Fay El Dine, one of the late great stallions of the breed. He exemplified the Saklawi type as defined by Raswan, and even in old age he brought to mind Prince Mohammed Ali's description of the Saklawi. His huge black luminous

*FaSerr (by *Fadl x *Bint Serra) was responsible for many black Arabians.*

eyes were set in an exquisite head; indeed, he exemplified the strain in refinement and quality. His full brother, the "Black Beauty," FaSerr, was the exact opposite in type, however, taking more after his sire, *Fadl (a Jellabi), than his dam. Of imposing masculine appearance, but not lacking in elegance, FaSerr won the Chicago International Grand Championship at halter in 1955, then one of the largest shows in the country. Mr. Babson was the first American Egyptian breeder to experiment with breeding full brother to full sister, which he did in mating FaSerr to FaDeene. The result was the striking, very prepotent grey stallion Ibn FaSerr, a real credit to the breed as an individual and sire, and a testimony to Mr. Babson's foresight.

A particularly beautiful mare of the Saklawi strain was *Maamouna, imported by J. M. Dickinson, but unfortunately she left no straight Egyptian descendants to carry on. In Egypt the line descends through Zaafarana's progeny and the mare Saklawia and her progeny. In America it is preserved through *Ansata Bint Zaafarana, *Hayam, and some female descendants of *Bint Serra. There are also numerous lines through Gulnare and Guemara, but very few if any of these can be classified as straight Egyptian.

Medallela (by Awad x Khafifa), foaled March 17, 1935, is pictured here as a young mare; she was the dam of El Bataa and WANISA.

Another branch of this Saklawi family comes through Roga El Beda, a celebrated mare of Ali Pasha Sherif, and daughter of Bint Horra. From Roga have descended the mares Saada and Dalal. *Bint Saada came to America in the Babson importation and contributed in America the stallion Fadaan, by *Fadl, but unfortunately she died without leaving any female progeny to carry on, and nothing from Saada remains in Egypt. Dalal, however, has left the most notable mark of all through her progeny in the Inshass herd, and in the R.A.S./E.A.O. through Khafifa, dam of Medallela. Medallela was bred to Sheikh El Arab and got the excellent mares El Bataa and Wanisa. The bay El Bataa, who bore a striking resemblance to Halima (both by the same sire, although the latter was better-bodied), produced three superb fillies by Nazeer; the black *Bint El Bataa, imported by Richard Pritzlaff; and the two greys *Bint El Bataa, imported by Gleannloch, and *Ansata Bint Nazeer (Fulla), imported by Ansata Arabian Stud. Wanisa went on to produce the elegant matriarch of the Nile Valley, Moniet El Nefous, whose bloodlines figure prominently throughout the world today.

El Bataa (by Sheikh El Arab x Medallela), foaled March 17, 1944, was the dam of three full sisters by Nazeer in the U.S.

A bright chestnut with a faint star and a few tiny white hairs on the face, Moniet's soul is exposed through her kindly eyes. To those who know her, she is living proof that "the beauty of the universe is unfolding, as it should." Her loveliness transcends time. A true Queen of Egypt, she is the Bride of the Nile; the Beauty of the Past, the Joy of the

Present, and the Hope of the Future. One can especially love her for a failing common to all mortal horses: she cannot withstand the temptation of an outstretched hand bearing sugar. Old age has not dimmed her eyesight, and the thought of sugar brings her joyfully trotting from any section of her domain. Woe to the tantalizer if no sugar is in hand, for the royal wrath descends and queenly outrage at the trick is promptly displayed.

Moniet's three daughters, Mabrouka, Mona, and Lubna, all by Sid Abouhom, have admirably carried on her line in Egypt. She was also bred to Alaa El Din in her later years, producing two chestnut fillies, neither of which was in a class with the former, and one of which was stunted. Her colt by the same stallion was imported to America and despite a slow start due to his emaciated condition as a youngster, he progressed handsomely to proper maturity.

Two of her most beautiful daughters were by Nazeer: Maya, an exquisite grey filly, died young, but the incomparable *Bint Moniet El Nefous was imported to America by Richard Pritzlaff, where she graces his picturesque New Mexico ranch. She has been a prolific producer for him, and is without a doubt the most like her dam of all Moniet's daughters.

Four sons of Moniet were also imported to America: *Fakher El Din by Nazeer, *Soufian by Alaa El Din, *Tuhotmos by El Sareei, and *Ibn Moniet El Nefous by *Morafic, the latter winning U.S. Top Ten at Halter in 1971. Moniet's blood now permeates the European breeding programs through her grandchildren, and without question she is one of the greatest broodmares. The chestnut mares Mabrouka and Mona possess their mother's unmistakable head, and they in turn have passed it on to their offspring. Mabrouka began her career as a broodmare with a colt which, had she done no more than produce him, would have assured her equine immortality. Her first son, *Morafic, hit the ground literally at the run and made every attempt to live up to the traits ascribed to the strain. A spectacular white horse of extremely elegant type, he was especially spirited and so powerful that he easily bluffed the jockeys at the racetrack. They were incapable of controlling him, nor would anybody discipline him, and after he blemished his neck by running through a fence, the E.A.O. withdrew him from the track and returned him to the stud. Since then he has made history as an outstanding sire. His blood is now found in choice European studs as well as in

America, where he was later imported by Douglas Marshall to head the Gleannloch breeding program. *Morafic was shown to a championship at halter and park performance, where he developed a decidedly pleasant manner after being placed in the capable hands of trainer Tom McNair. Unfortunately, however, like many horses who have been transplanted from the desert, *Morafic suffered from loss of weight and worried constantly over his harem of mares. After several years he

*Bint Moniet El Nefous (by Nazeer x Moniet El Nefous) closely resembles her dam. She is shown here with her foal by *Rashad Ibn Nazeer.

finally adjusted to his new life, but by that time had become so valuable as a sire that it was foolish to haul him around the country. Sons and daughters of *Morafic have been winning championships and U.S. National awards with amazing regularity and they are in demand as breeding stock the world over. Indeed he was a very special horse.

Mabrouka, not satisfied with a spectacular son to bring her acclaim, produced an equally beautiful daughter who was imported by the An-

*Maya (by Nazeer x Moniet El Nefous), an outstanding young
filly who met with an untimely death.*

**Bint Mona (by Nazeer x Mona), imported to America in 1964,
has an exquisite head typical of this family.*

*Mabrouka (by Nabeeh "Sid Abouhom" x Moniet El Nefous)
was the dam of *Morafic and *Ansata Bint Mabrouka.*

*Morafic (by Nazeer x Mabrouka). World famous!

PHOTOGRAPH BY SPARAGOWSKI

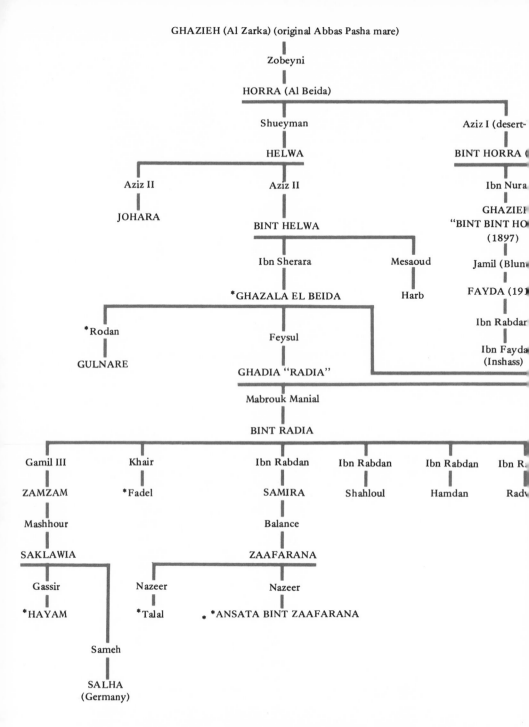

Descendants of the original Abbas Pasha mare, Ghazieh (al zarka, meaning "the grey,") which are straight Egyptian. Mares are in full caps, stallions in lowercase. This is only a partial list of horses descending from this mare, but it is to give an idea of the worldwide scope of her influence. Horses remaining in Egypt are not listed. They can be found in the Egyptian studbooks. An asterisk denotes imported to the U.S.

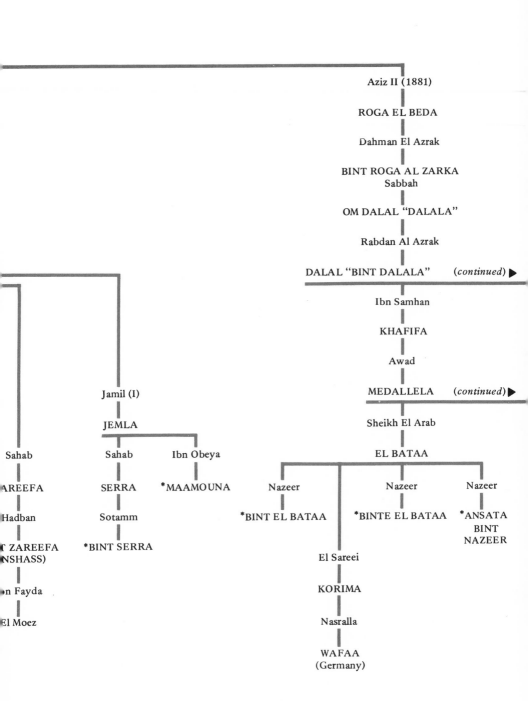

Aziz II (1881)

ROGA EL BEDA

Dahman El Azrak

BINT ROGA AL ZARKA
Sabbah

OM DALAL "DALALA"

Rabdan Al Azrak

DALAL "BINT DALALA" (*continued*) ▶

Ibn Samhan

KHAFIFA

Awad

MEDALLELA (*continued*) ▶

Sheikh El Arab

EL BATAA

Jamil (I)

JEMLA

Sahab   Sahab   Ibn Obeya

AREEFA   SERRA   *MAAMOUNA

Hadban   Sotamm

T ZAREEFA   *BINT SERRA
NSHASS)

n Fayda

El Moez

Nazeer   Nazeer   Nazeer

*BINT EL BATAA   *BINTE EL BATAA   *ANSATA
                                    BINT
                                    NAZEER

El Sareei

KORIMA

Nasralla

WAFAA
(Germany)

Descendants of GHAZIEH (*continued*)

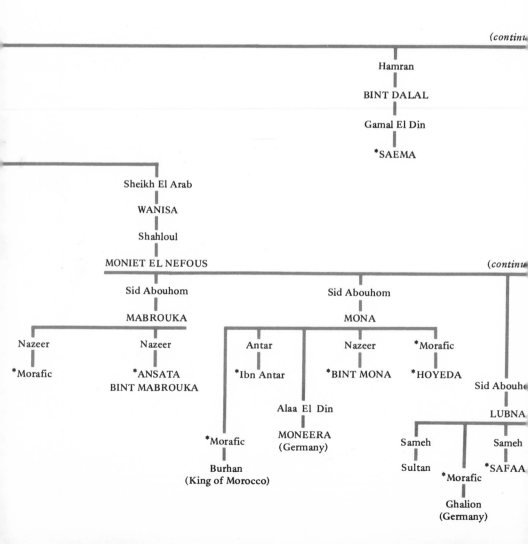

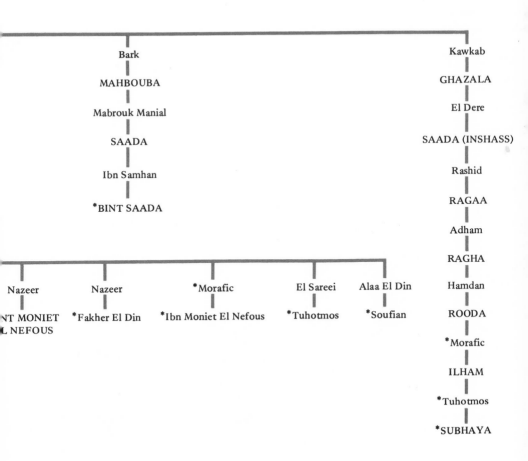

Bark

MAHBOUBA

Mabrouk Manial

SAADA

Ibn Samhan

*BINT SAADA

Kawkab

GHAZALA

El Dere

SAADA (INSHASS)

Rashid

RAGAA

Adham

RAGHA

Hamdan

ROODA

*Morafic

ILHAM

*Tuhotmos

*SUBHAYA

Nazeer

NT MONIET
L NEFOUS

Nazeer

*Fakher El Din

*Morafic

*Ibn Moniet El Nefous

El Sareei

*Tuhotmos

Alaa El Din

*Soufian

Ansata Bint Mabrouka (by Nazeer x Mabrouka) was one of the great broodmares of all times.

*Ansata Ibn Sudan (by *Ansata Ibn Halima x *Ansata Bint Mabrouka) is the first (and only, to date) straight-Egyptian-bred stallion to win a U.S. National Champion Stallion at Halter award (1971).*

PHOTOGRAPH BY SPARAGOWSKI

ANSATA BINT MABROUKA

sata Stud as a yearling. An ultra-classic grey filly with a long neck and great black "apple" eyes, she surpassed her mother in quality and beauty. As elegantly feminine as *Morafic was handsome, she too became a champion when shown. Her first colt, a champion white stallion, was by her stablemate *Ansata Ibn Halima and was named in honor of Abbas Pasha. He was brought to the Babson farm to introduce the newly imported blood. Today he is the pride of Homer Watson, the late Mr. Babson's dedicated and able manager, who carries on the administration of the Babson Stud for Mr. and Mrs. Theodore Tieken.

Bint Mabrouka's second son, Ansata Ibn Sudan, was named for the famous bedouin breeder, Ibn Sudan, whose strain name he bears. An exceptional individual from the beginning, not only in pedigree, "Sudan" caused much talk around the country and was much in demand as a breeding stallion even before he won acclaim. Shown to championships early in his career, he became U.S. National Top Ten at Halter as a four-year-old, together with his famous father in 1969, a rare event in the Arabian show world. When shown at the Nationals again in 1971 under the toughest competition of eighty-three champion stallions, Sudan became the first U.S. National Champion Stallion of straight Egyptian bloodlines. Thus he combined the best of the past: the Dahman strain through his father, *Ansata Ibn Halima, and the Saklawi through his mother, *Ansata Bint Mabrouka—the very strains beloved by Abbas Pasha remaining, in fact, just as precious to this day.

Because of the desirability of inbreeding to fix type, it seemed worthwhile to try it with two such outstanding individuals as *Morafic and his full sister, *Ansata Bint Mabrouka. The result was Ansata Shah Zaman, aptly translated "king of the age." A fiery, elegant white stallion, Shah Zaman is a champion and has proved to be a spectacular producer—just as was hoped for in the mating. He is living proof that inbreeding can be safe and desirable when the choicest and most robust stock is used.

Another closely bred stallion of this line is *Ibn Moniet El Nefous, bred in Egypt and imported to the U.S. as a yearling. A truly stunning white horse, he stands taller than any of this family to date, and is proving to be an excellent sire for his owner, Jarrell McCracken, who paid a record price of $200,000 for him as a mature sire.

This Saklawi group can be characterized by its extreme refinement

Ansata Shah Zaman (*Morafic x *Ansata Bint Mabrouka*), a popular young sire, is the product of inbreeding full brother to full sister.

Ibn Moniet El Nefous (*Morafic x Moniet El Nefous*) has an intensified pedigree of Moniet blood. He was U.S. National Top Ten stallion at halter and is a popular sire.

PHOTOGRAPH BY SPARAGOWSKI

and graceful qualities; the mares generally stand 14 hands 2 inches to 15 hands high, but it is not unusual if they are over or under this norm. *Morafic stands over 15 hands and has put height into most of his get, as well as length. *Ibn Moniet El Nefous is over 15 hands, and Sudan stands at 15 hands as does Shah Zaman. Excellent trotting action has been common in this family; they are well proportioned and substantially boned, and have a tremendous depth of girth, pronounced withers, well laid back shoulders with long scapula, and relatively long forefaces with tapering teacup muzzles and an extreme concavity below the eyes. They have what the bedouins would describe as a "camel head"—a longer and finer foreface than the "gazelle head," which is much shorter and appears broader between the eyes. This family does not seem to have enjoyed success on the track comparable to that of the Helwa line, but it is also possible that they have not been given equal opportunity to race. Chestnuts predominate, then greys, lastly bays.

A chart of the strain is shown on pages 330–333.

18

THE STRAIN OF HADBAN ENZAHI

WHEN ALI BEY SHAMASHIRGI investigated the Hadban Enzahi strain, he learned the following:

Shabat Al Mani' of Al Suwayt, and he is advanced in age, and Ali Mani', the son of the brother of Shabat, attended the gathering and were questioned in the presence of Sultan ibn-Suwayt and a large number of people.

"Tell us about their origin and what was their strain, and from where they came."

The above-mentioned replied that: Mani' was at the time of Beni Lam, who is from our grandfathers. And we don't know how she passed to Mani'. But we have heard and know from our old people that there is no Hadbah but the horses of Mani'. And she is Kuhaylah om-Maarif. And the reason for calling her Hadbah at Mani' was because he had a mare with a profusely long mane which covered her forehand completely (Hadbah salifa). And for that reason she was called Hadbah. And she passed from Mani' to Nazhi of Al Fudul the day they forced them at the hillside of Massel.

"And she was blessed at Al Nazhi and she became Hadbah Nazhi from Al Nazhi. And from Al Nazhi her blood spread through the tribes."

The Hadbah al-Nazhi, or as it is now written, Hadbah Enzahi, descend in Egypt from the root mare Venus "Shekra Zefra" (she was also known by other names), who was bred by the Shammar tribe and imported into Egypt by Hassan abu-Amin's Agha in 1895. Her daughter Hadba produced the two mares Bint Hadba El Saghira and Gamila, from which are descended two families or branches of the strain. From the former came the outstanding broodmare Samiha (by Samhan), which produced Bint Samiha by Kazmeen. Bint Samiha bred to Mansour gave Nazeer, the stallion that undoubtedly has had more influence on

Ibn Rabdan (by Rabdan x Bint Gamila), foaled May 17, 1917.
"A world champion type," Raswan called him.

Samiha (by Samhan x Bint Hadba El Saghira), born
October 4, 1918.

the Egyptian line within the past twenty years than any other single individual.

It was an unforgettable sight to see Nazeer prance out of his shaded box stall into the bright October sun, quite unmindful of his twenty-five years. Majestically scanning the palm-fringed blue horizon before trumpeting a love call to his mares, he posed beneath an arched trellis of bright pink bougainvillea, a vision in white elegance, the classic Arabian personified: a model to have delighted Vernet, Delacroix, Adam, or Schreyer. One knows he understood that "beauty is its own excuse for being."

Bint Samiha (by Kazmeen x Samiha), foaled July 13, 1925, was the dam of Nazeer and Shams.

Nazeer put that special nobility in the heads of his get that marked his stock as if they had been stamped from the same mold. It was easy to pick out Nazeer foals in comparison to those sired by other stallions on the farm, for they had that "extra spark," a look of eagles, as it were, or more appropriately, the wide-eyed look of the desert, some-how native to all creatures of the sands. Nazeer's blood not only improved legs in general (the credit is due to his sire Mansour and probably to the Mimreh blood), but also produced good conformation, strong toplines, tremendous shoulders and depth of girth, and appreciable substance and size; although he stood about 14 hands 3 inches him-

Nazeer (by Mansour x Bint Samiha), foaled August 9, 1934. A successful racehorse, he was one of the great breeding stallions of all time.

self, he appeared larger. Sheik Abd el-Aziz el-Sabek, Nazeer's trainer and one of the great Arabian racehorse trainers of his era, thought of Nazeer as "almost perfect." He remembered him as being "very alive and alert—a magnificent horse" when he trained him for the track. Indeed he too had been well named: "observer or director of all he oversees."

Hadban Enzahi (by Nazeer x Kamla), head stallion at the Marbach Stud in Germany.

PHOTOGRAPH BY E. SCHIELE

"Double Nazeer" has become a byword in Arabian circles, and not without good reason. As one gets farther from this Nazeer blood a vast change in type is noted, and that special something he contributed could well be lost if inbreeding is not kept at a high level within some breeders' stocks. The Mansour blood was invaluable as a sire line, and the Mimreh blood cannot be retrieved through a tail female line in

Egypt. Today Nazeer sons and daughters and grandchildren are famous the world over. They enhance the stables of the king of Morocco; the king of Yemen; the historical Marbach Stud, among others in Germany; the Babolna Stud in Hungary; and the Tersk Stud in Russia. They are also found in Syria, Nigeria, Australia, Canada, Britain, Bahreyn, and Arabia, and in the most select studs throughout America. They are more than ably prancing in their handsome father's footsteps, carrying on the true classic tradition of the breed as established in ancient as well as modern-day Egypt.

The value of Nazeer blood cannot be overemphasized, and its worth should never be underestimated. The United States is fortunate to have more Nazeer children than any other country, even more than all other countries combined including Egypt, and the American stock far surpasses the Nazeer get left behind. Indeed there is nothing remaining in the homeland that can measure up to the following group:

Stallions: *United States*—*Rashad Ibn Nazeer, *Ansata Ibn Halima, *Ghalii (deceased), *Morafic (deceased), *Talal, *Fakher El Din, *Ramses Fayek.
   Germany—Hadban Enzahi, Ghazal (deceased).
   Russia—Aswan; *Canada*—Lateef. (SF IBN NAZEER) deceased

Mares: *United States*—*Bint Moniet El Nefous, *Bint El Bataa, *Ansata Bint Mabrouka, (deceased), *Ansata Bint Zaafarana, *Bint Maisa El Saghira, *Bint Maisa El Kebira (deceased), *Bint Nefisaa, *Bint Mona, *Ansata Bint Bukra, *Ansata Bint Misuna, *Ansata Bint Nazeer, *Bint El Bataa, *Lamia (deceased).
   Canada—*Bint Hemmat (deceased).

There is no mistake about it. It was the "Nazeer look" that lit the torch and brought the Egyptian Arabians into the world's limelight once again.

Bint Hadba also produced Bint Rustem by Rustem, who in turn produced the mares Kahila, Salwa, and Hind, by Ibn Rabdan, and the stallions *El Akhrani and Mashhour, by Nabras and Shahloul, respectively. Hind when mated to Sheikh El Arab produced the beautiful Yosreia, who became influential in the broodband through her Nazeer daughter Shahrzada, and through Farasha (Frashah) by "Sid Abouhom"

*Ansata Bint Misuna (called Bint Maysouna in Egypt), by Na-
zeer x Maysouna, shows the exceptional beauty of this line
despite a disfigured nostril.*

PHOTOGRAPH BY POLLY KNOLL

*Hassan (by Nazeer x Hemmat), an exceptionally
beautiful stallion.*

and Mohga by El Sareei. The last-named was dam of the U.S. Reserve National Champion Mare, *Nahlah.

Bint Samiha was the dam of such beautiful mares as Shams, Samha, and Kamla, the latter the dam of Hadban Enzahi at Marbach. Both Shams and Kamla are very influential to this day in the Egyptian, European, and American studs through their progeny.

Another branch was that through Bint Gamila, dam of Ibn Rabdan, the most important sire of his day. Ibn Rabdan was a very elegant dark chestnut stallion who, Dr. Zaher said, "had great finesse," while Carl Raswan described the horse as "a world champion type." In addition to siring the Fabulous Four mentioned in the Saklawi group, he was influential in the studs of Prince Kemal el-Dine, Prince Mohammed Ali, Inshass, and the Royal Agricultural Society. A very commanding stallion of good size and having a beautiful long supple neck, he passed these qualities to his offspring with consistent regularity. The Egyptians are now returning to Ibn Rabdan blood by making close-up crosses to him in their pedigrees, particularly through Shahloul and Hamdan.

Prince Mohammed Ali remarked in his book that Ibn Rabdan always sired foals of his own chestnut color, and would continue to do so until bred to a mare "who produces the form and type of her own strain. If she is the better bred she will dominate in the formation and coloring of the foal." It is interesting to recollect, therefore, that all the foals he sired when bred to the magnificent Mahroussa were grey, and resembled their dam to a great extent; the Fabulous Four from the beautiful Bint Radia were likewise grey, although they seemed to take almost equal qualities from their sire and dam. He also got the black mare, Salwa, when bred back into his own Hadban strain. Her black grandson, Gharib (by Antar, and who is linebred to Ibn Rabdan), is now at the Marbach Stud in Germany and was chosen admittedly for his color to combat a pigmentation problem in the herd.

Another son of Bint Gamila's was Baiyyad, by Mabrouk Manial, who was overshadowed by Ibn Rabdan in the stud. He was the sire of *Bint Bint Sabbah. No female descendants of the Gamila branch survive in tail female; thus the strain carries on through the other branch.

The Hadban Enzahi family has been prolific in the stud, producing both beautiful horses and good racing stock. They generally have substantial bone; average to long necks; and good to superior heads,

Bint Yosreia (by Nazeer x Yosreia) at Hamdan Stables.

Rafaat "Aswan" (by Nazeer x Yosreia) was presented to the U.S.S.R. in 1964.

Shaarawi (by *Morafic x Bint Kamla), a young breeding stallion in Egypt.

Mohga (by El Sareei x Yosreia), a striking black mare.

*Nahlah (by *Morafic x Mohga), the first imported Egyptian
mare to win Reserve National Champion mare at halter (in 1967).

Bint El Nil (by Antar x Shahrzada), full sister to *Dawlat.

*Gharib (by Antar x Souhair), a black stallion sold to Marbach
Stud in Germany.*

Ayda (by Nazeer x Lateefa), a beautiful Nazeer daughter.

usually having considerable width between the eyes, medium length of foreface, and a somewhat squarish muzzle by comparison to the Saklawi group. They moved well, but in general the Bint Rustem derivatives have not had extreme front action as compared to some individuals of other strains, or of the other branch of this strain. The family overall have good height, ample withers, and are of overall pleasing symmetry. Those having crosses to Mansour appear to have more masculine qualities. Both outstanding sires and outstanding broodmares have come from this family, as we see in examining breeding records over the years in Egypt. A very large number of this strain is now represented in America through importations made since 1960, and in Europe also. It is a great "blending" family, nicking well with all strains.

19

AL KUHAYL: THE STRAINS OF
KUHAYLAN MIMREH, KUHAYLAN JELLABI,
AND KUHAYLAN RODAN

KUHAYLAN MIMREH

THE ABBAS PASHA manuscript relates:

At the gathering Sultan Ibn Suwayt, sheik of Al Dafeer, was asked about Kuhaylah al-Maryum, the Kuhaylah al-Mimreh, as it is said she belongs to you, O Dafeer. And Sultan ibn-Suwayt and Dahsh al-Khashm, the paternal cousin of Diyyab al-Maryum of Al Suwayt replied:

"Al Maryum belongs to us, O Dafeer. But she is called Mimreh in the north. And Al Mimreh is the brother of Al Maryum [that is, they are both Mimreh]. And the horses of Al Mimreh are from Al Maryum. And Al Maryum is a Kuhaylat Ajuz of the oldest horses. And therefore she doesn't need any explanation."

And the exact origin of her strain [they continued] is from Al Mugheerah, of the first tribes. And from what we have heard and are positive of, she passed from Al Mugheerah on the day that 'Ijl ibn-Hulaytem fell upon Qahtan early one morning. And she went to Qahtan, and she has remained with Qahtan since that day.

And one day Al Maryum made a ghazu on Qahtan, at a time which we have no recollection thereof, and he took her from Qahtan. This was during the time of our grandfathers. And she was called at his place after his name, Al Maryum. Otherwise she is a Kuhaylat Ajuz from the most precious and ancient strain of horses.

And she passed from Al Maryum al-Dafeeri to Al Maryum of Al Sabaa mubti—in the old times—which we who are present don't recollect. And the strain was cut off from Al Dafeer. And she produced foals at Al Sabaa.

And this testimony [the narrator resumes] was corroborated by Nahar ibn-Muwayni, one of the sheiks of Al Sabaa, who also possessed Kuhaylah al-Mimreh.

This very important strain has unfortunately been allowed to die out in Egypt, an indescribable blunder. The old and lovely R.A.S.-bred Baraka at the age of thirty is currently alive in South Africa and still bearing foals for her owner, Dr. Noli Marais. She is the last known remnant of this strain bred by the Egyptians.

The Mimreh strain was characterized by strong build and conformation of masculine type, with good bone and substance, a classic type, but not generally having the extreme heads of the Dahman or Saklawi strains. They appeared well balanced overall, without any extremes in height; that is, they did not have a great amount of daylight under them. They also proved themselves on the racetrack. It is an especially valuable strain and has been too little considered by most strain enthusiasts. From the Mimreh family have come both outstanding sires and outstanding dams.

The best known horse of this line was Mansour, whose dam was Nafaa El Saghira, a Kuhaylah Mimrehiyah descending from the stock of Ibn Muwayni of the Sabaa bedouins. Mansour was most prepotent in the stud and a very handsome masculine stallion of wonderful proportion and great vigor and strength. He was especially noted for his fine, strong bone structure and excellent topline, magnificent powerful hindquarters, and straight strong legs. Had he done no more than sire Nazeer, Bint Farida, Sheikh El Arab and *Roda, he would' have rendered the breed an incalculable service; but he sired many other impressive get as well. His half-brother Ibn Samhan was also successful as a sire and got the well-known stallion *Zarife and the lovely mare *Bint Saada.

Mabrouk Manial, bred by Prince Mohammed Ali, was especially influential in the royal studs and sired some of the most celebrated Arabians in his day, among them the superior broodmares Saada, Sabah, Bint Radia, and Mahroussa, as well as the stallions Awad and Baiyyad. His influence in the twenties was probably greater than that of any other stallion. Another good stallion was Hadban, half-brother to Mabrouk Manial and also a fine sire, but not as prominent in modern pedigrees.

The very handsome Zad El Rakab was also a successful racehorse, proving that handsome is as handsome does, but he was sold to South Africa where his value was not recognized until too late.

Mansour (by Gamil Manial x Nafaa El Saghira) was foaled April 19, 1921. A prepotent sire, his progeny included Nazeer, Sheikh El Arab, and *Roda.

The percentage of Mimreh blood up until three generations ago was of considerable significance, but now since there is no longer any tail female line to reintroduce it or to use in inbreeding, it is lost to the Egyptian breeders as far as straight-Egyptian bloodlines are concerned unless Baraka should produce a foal to a straight-Egyptian stallion. That possibility is remote, and thus the only other recourse is inbreeding to Mansour in the hope of preserving the desirable balance and harmonious characters afforded by this particular strain.

Fayda (by Ibn Rabdan x Mofida), a handsome mare of the Kuhaylah Mimrehiyah strain.

Baraka (by Ibn Manial x Gamalat), foaled December 25, 1942, died in South Africa in 1972.

PASTEL BY C. DOMKEN

THE STRAIN OF KUHAYLAN JELLABI

The history of this strain has been related in a previous chapter. Most of the stock tracing to this female line were bred by Prince Mohammed Ali, and except for *Nasr have been quite masculine in appearance, though not without refinement. They are broad and short in head and foreface (gazelle heads), strong through the chest, powerfully built, and move well. Usually they are between 14 and 15 hands tall. They are best known in America through *Fadl and *Maaroufa, full brother and sister sired by Ibn Rabdan, both exemplifying the Kuhaylan Jellabi type. *Zarife and *Roda were also similar in overall picture and when mated they produced Hallanny Mistanny, the black stallion who has contributed much to American breeding programs. He was a very masculine individual and prepotent in this respect, not only because he was "double Jellabi" or, as some would say, "pure in the strain" because his sire and dam were of the same tail female line, but because *Roda was by Mansour, a very masculine type, and *Zarife was by Mansour's half brother, Ibn Samhan. Thus, both the Kuhaylan Mimreh and the Kuhaylan Jellabi lines were "doubled," and their strength or masculine characters were intensified.

*Nasr, on the other hand, was more refined and elegant, and one could say he had more grace and "stretch" or eliteness than the others of this line.

Today the Jellabi strain in America survives in straight-Egyptian stock primarily through *Maaroufa. The other imported mares such as *Aziza, *Roda, *H. H. Mohammed Ali's Hamama, and *H. H. Mohammed Ali's Hamida were crossed with desert-bred, imported, and domestic lines and were very influential in creating outstanding American-bred Arabians. It is only unfortunate some of these mares did not leave behind straight-Egyptian progeny with which future breeders could work. One of the loveliest mares of the Inshass Herd was Ghazala I; she bore the stamp of the desert and was the last mare of the Jellabi strain retained by the Egyptian Agricultural Organization. All her foals were sold off the farm, and then she died.

THE STRAIN OF KUHAYLAN RODAN

Nasser ibn-Funaykh of Al Shaalan, the Ra'i of the Stud, was asked: "O Nasser, from where did Kuhaylah Rodaniyah pass to you? Do you or do you not know any history about her?"

And Nasser ibn-Funaykh replied: "Aye, by Allah, I have knowledge. We have heard from our grandfathers that her origin is mubti—from the old times. And some time ago she passed from Beni Khaled, on the day of Al Arban at Nejd, to Al Sayah of Shammar, and from Sayah al-Shammari she passed to Funaykh, my grandfathers, I, O Nasser. And my grandfathers said about the aforementioned mare: She is Kuhaylat Al Ajuz, and she is to be mated. And she is the most cherished one of the stud, and the height of the stud. And she is mubti—of the old stud.

"And I, O Nasser, testify by my grandfather's testimony, and by Allah on my honor and good fortune, that she is of the aforementioned stud and is to be mated and is nadir—the height of the stud. And this is the history which I know.

"And Funaykh, my grandfather, gave a mare to Rodan of the people of the stud, and Rodan is one of us, being a relative from Shaalan. And Rodan sold the chestnut 'awdah mare who had no more teeth and was unable to eat barley, to Al Wezwez of Al Sabaa of Al Masaribah. And the stud was cut off from us, O Ruwala. And she was blessed at Al Wezwez of Al Sabaa. And there was a battle between Bishr and Al Ruwala, and we captured many horses from them, and among them a safra [white] Kuhaylah mare of Rodan whose father is Al Araj. And also a shaqra [chestnut] mare whose father is Al Aswad. And they are from the stud of Kuhaylah Rodaniyah."

*   *   *   *

The saying of Sheik Faysal [Shaalan]: "The safra Kuhaylah mare of Rodan, her father is Al Araj, and the father of the shaqra mare is Al Aswad, and they were sent with Ali Bey to the High Stud. And Abu Darib, the sheik of Beni Sakhr bought from this stud a safra Kuhaylah Rodaniyah mare of Al Mowayijah of Al Sabaa, and she is at the High Stud [of Abbas Pasha]."

Abbas Pasha, as we note from the story above, obtained some mares of the Kuhaylah Rodaniyah strain, but those which Egypt employed in the establishment of the R.A.S. descended from the Rodaniyah mare imported by the Blunts from Arabia to England. As she is one of the most influential mares in Crabbet pedigrees, and a great influence in Egypt and America as well as Europe and wherever Crabbet horses were sold, it is of interest to note her background.

According to the Blunts' records, Rodania was foaled about 1869, a

Kuhaylat Ajuz of the strain of Ibn Rodan, or Kuhaylah Rodaniyah. She stood 14 hands 2 inches high and was chestnut, with the near hind leg white to above the fetlock, and a blaze to the mouth (with pink on the upper lip). She had been wounded on the quarter belly and chest—perhaps a wound sustained on a razzia. She was deep of jowl and her eyes showed a white oval like human eyes. She had extraordinary strength and style of going up to any weight, but had a somewhat uncertain temper, perhaps due to ill treatment. She was a celebrated mare in the desert, the Blunts stated, and they purchased her for £124 in the desert near the wells of Abu Fayal on April 12, 1882, from her owner, Tais ibn-Sharban of the Gomussa branch of the Sebaa Anazeh tribe, who had taken her the previous summer from the Ruwala.

The Blunts prized this strain greatly, probably because it more resembled the English thoroughbred in type, and they wrote:

We had heard of this mare two years before we saw her on our journey through the Nefud to Nejd at the well of Shaqig where we met a son of Beneyeh ibn-Shalaan. We were then told that Beneyeh had quarreled with his cousin, Sotamm ibn-Shalaan, on account of his chestnut mare which Sotamm insisted on having and managed to take by force, failing to get her by fair means. Beneyeh then had left Sotamm to fight his own battles with the Sebaa in the course of which, last summer, Sotamm lost this mare for whose possession he had sacrificed a valuable alliance, who was taken from him by Tais ibn-Sharban of the Gomussa tribe of Sebaa. We saw this mare April 10, as Tais ibn-Sharban rode past while we were talking to Afret Misrab and Abtan ibn-ed-Derri about his Managhyeh half sister to Meshura, and then asked what she was—the answer "oh that, that is Beneyeh ibn-Shaalan's mare." Two days afterwards we bought her deciding as one always must in the desert in a few minutes, and having had no opportunity of discovering what seems to be her only defect (except age), her temper. She is the only one in all the stud that must be described as bad tempered; that is she is not safe to go near, she strikes with her forefeet and now and then kicks. This may, however, be only from rough treatment as she already (Oct. 1881) appears to be rather less savagely suspicious than 6 mos. ago.

Wilfrid Scawen Blunt consigned Rodania to Class 2 of the Crabbet horses (though Lady Anne apparently considered her Class 1), and wrote, "She may give sires to Class 2. She is to be covered by Seglawi's only." Indeed he was right, for this had been the best "nick" over the years, providing the extra refinement needed by the strain.

*Rashad Ibn Nazeer (by Nazeer x Yashmak) being schooled by
the late Col. Hans Handler, director of the Spanish Riding
School, during his visit to Rancho San Ignacio in 1964.

When the Egyptians purchased the group of horses from Crabbet, the two mares Bint Rissala and Bint Riyala were acquired and placed in the broodband. However, the progeny of the two mares differed considerably in type.

Lady Wentworth noted that the postmortem on Rissla indicated seventeen ribs and seven lumbar vertabrae, a count unique in horse breeds, while her dam, Risala, had seventeen and six as compared to the usual five. Bint Rissala "Razieh" was a tall, relatively long-bodied mare with short croup and straight stifle; her shoulder was rather straight though she had ample withers and a very long elegant neck. Her most

Yashmak (by Sheikh El Arab x Bint Rissala), foaled January 24, 1941, was the dam of *Rashad Ibn Nazeer and *Sanaaa, among others.

noteworthy contributions to the Egyptian program were the mare Yaqota by Balance, later in King Farouk's herd, Yashmak by Sheikh El Arab, and Kateefa by Shahloul. Yashmak was a big, tall, graceful bay mare with long supple neck, longish head well shaped with huge black eyes, and much improved in type over her dam. The Saudi Arabian princes during their visit to El Zahraa continually remarked over her size in comparison to many of their desert-bred mares in Arabia. She produced by Nazeer the American import, *Rashad Ibn Nazeer, who has become an influential sire; the tall grey mare Om El Saad by Shahloul; the fine-boned bay mare Rahma by Mashhour; the very elegant bay mare Rashida by El Sareei; and the pretty-headed *Sanaaa by Sid Abouhom. Om El Saad produced by Nazeer Bint Om El Saad who, when bred to the Farouk stallion, Sameh, produced the liver chestnut *Serenity Sonbolah, a brilliant mare in the show ring and U.S. National Champion Mare in 1971. Another stallion of this line is *Refky, a U.S. Top Ten winner in 1971 by *Morafic x Refica, who was by Nazeer x Om El Saad. Another noteworthy champion at halter and performance is Hossny, an iron-grey stallion with white mane and tail who has stamped this deep black-grey color on most of his foals.

*Om El Saad (by Shahloul x Yashmak), born December 1, 1945,
is shown here in old age.*

The mare Kateefa also produced noteworthy individuals, particularly her daughter Bint Kateefa, a striking chestnut by Sid Abouhom, and when bred to Nazeer she produced the exceptionally beautiful white stallion Kaisoon, now in Germany. Kateefa also produced the grand old

Hossny (by *Ansata Ibn Halima x *Sanaaa), a champion halter and performance horse, is noted for siring iron greys with white manes and tails.

PHOTOGRAPH BY SPARAGOWSKI

Mosry (by *Morafic x *Sanaaa) struts his stuff in Texas before moving to Colorado.

*Serenity Sonbolah (by Sameh x Bint Om El Saad), the first imported Egyptian mare to win U.S. National Champion at halter (in 1971).

*Shamah (by Sameh x Rafica), a champion mare of exceptional balance and quality.

*Kateefa (by Shahloul x Bint Rissala), foaled September 9, 1938,
was a broodmare of outstanding merit.*

*Bint Kateefa (by Naheeh "Sir Abouhom" x Kateefa) was the
dam of Kaisoon and *Bint Bint Kateefa.*

Alaa El Din (by Nazeer x Kateefa) raced well in Egypt and has been successful in the stud.

*Moftakhar (by Enzahi x Kateefa) raced well in Egypt and sired many fine performance horses in America.

*Moftakhar, who sired excellent performance horses in America, and Alaa El Din by Nazeer, a striking dark chestnut who raced well on the track and has sired race winners. Alaa El Din is by a grey and out of a grey, but the strong chestnut recessive in the Rodania line manifests itself in his color and that of his offspring. Although he has hardly any white markings, other than star and strip, he has been responsible for an unusual amount of white in the Egyptian program within the past few years. The Egyptians have used him consistently on the chestnut Moniet line resulting in more height but less beautiful heads, in comparison to other strain crosses. He has gotten much roaning and high white, including body spots and in one case a spot the size of a basketball on the side of one filly which was sold to Hungary. In the past Mesaoud has been given the undesirable credit for all the high white in Crabbet horses, but as he was so frequently mated with the Rodania line one is inclined to believe that she was responsible in good measure. It is indeed strange that after all these generations the high white should crop up in Egypt only through this *particular* female line. True, it is more often found where chestnut is bred to chestnut, but even though the Egyptians have bred chestnut to chestnut in the past, this excessive amount of white had not resulted. Nor have they ever used Rodan stallions to any extent in the breeding program.

The Rodania line through Bint Rissala has been characterized by a very distinct type: long, well-shaped necks, relatively long forefaces, and long heads, which have been much improved through Shahloul, Sheikh El Arab, and Nazeer. They are quite elegant individuals, relatively long in body, substantial in bone and substance, and stand high off the ground. They tend to be somewhat short yet flat in the croup and could be stronger over the loins. They usually have good tail carriage. Action has been a laudable part of their makeup, and they make excellent show horses. Many of the modern Crabbet horses carrying a high percentage of Rodania blood through Rissala are tall, bold-moving horses. The Egyptian import *Sakr has been brilliant in park classes, electrifying crowds with his presence and power and recently winning Reserve National Champion Park Horse at the U.S. National Championships. As a rule, both stallions and mares of this family stand fifteen hands or over.

The other branch of the Rodania line is that of Bint Riyala, which is maintained through her granddaughter Malaka's progeny. This family is

Kaisoon (by Nazeer x Bint Kateefa), a leading sire in Germany.

PHOTOGRAPH BY E. SCHIELE

*Omnia (by Alaa El Din x Ameena) is "double Rodania," sire and dam being of the same tail female strain.

Riyala (by *Astraled x Ridaa), bred by Crabbet, was the dam of *Bint Bint Riyala.

COURTESY OF C. COVEY

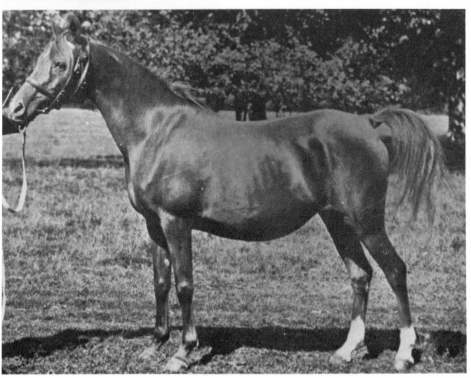

Mabdouha (by El Deree x Malaka), performing one of his tricks.

Waseem (by Nazeer x Malaka), a bold masculine stallion.

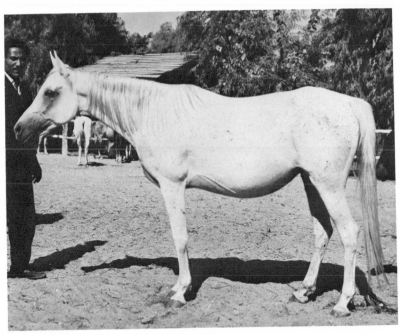

*Nazeera (by Nazeer x Malaka), dam of *Omayma, *Romanaa II,
*Manzoura, and *Serenity Luftia.*

*Dalia (by *Morafic x *Romanaa II), champion mare and a U.S.
Top Ten English pleasure winner.*

well represented in America through the Marshall imports, two of which were U.S. National Top Ten Mares: *Fawkia by Sameh and *Romanaa II by Sameh, as well as *Sabaa El Zahraa, who was U.S. Top Ten Stallion. Other notables are *Salomey, *Omayma, and the Serenity imports *Luftia, *Sagda, and *Bint Mamlouka. Members of this family are generally not as tall as Bint Rissala's progeny; they are broader in the chest, much shorter in the neck, more compact in conformation, and somewhat more masculine overall. Their heads are shorter—that is, the foreface is shorter—and they are just slightly broader between the eyes. When the sire and dam are both of this strain, however, particularly where the Rissala line is bred back into the Riyala line, the resulting progeny are usually taller and frequently take after the Rissala family.

In studying the pedigrees of influential Egyptian horses one finds the Rodan stallions entirely in a minority except for the use of Alaa El Din, whereas the mares have been prolific and the Rodania family, in fact, is one of the largest in Egypt today. But in England the Rodan stallions have been incorporated heavily into the breeding programs, so that this line has become a dominant factor.

20

HORSE RACING IN EGYPT

〰〰〰〰〰〰〰〰〰〰〰〰〰〰〰〰〰〰〰〰〰〰〰〰〰〰〰〰〰〰〰〰〰〰〰〰〰〰

ARABIAN HORSE RACING is and has been for countless centuries a favourite pastime among inhabitants of the Nile Valley. In ancient times the pharaohs enjoyed racing in their light swift chariots drawn by the finest steeds of the day. It is said that such luminaries as Amenophis II "could not be overtaken in the races," and early records allude to the speed attained in various exploits. Thus from Pharaoh to Farouk, and even in modern socialist Egypt, horse racing continues to draw many enthusiastic spectators and to flourish as a national sport, although it survives in far less opulent surroundings and far more austere circumstances than in bygone days.

Racing on horseback came to the fore among the Arabs during the days of the Prophet Mohammed, who encouraged the breeding and training of the most select horses among his followers. He himself maintained a racing stable, overseeing the training of his animals and even betting on his own mares. Moreover, he attended races and frequently awarded the prizes to the winners. Although his teachings forbade gambling, he said: "He who races his mare with another horse, unknown to him, and the winner is a matter of chance, it is not gambling; but if he bears in his mind that his mare will win—this is gambling."

The first races were held in the year 4 of the Hegira (A.D. 626). Horses were not raced until they reached the age of five, for the distances were long and the Arabs were fearful of breaking down young foals. At least ten horses were required before a race could be held, and a committee was appointed to examine the age and condition of the entrants, and to control the races in general. In those days the Arabs were concerned with the selection and breeding of horses more than the actual sport of racing. Caliph Abu Bakr, the first of the caliphs, is said to have carried off the honors that first historical day of racing under Islam, the distance being over six miles and run from Kafiat to Saniat il-Woudaa. Horse racing gained in popularity throughout the Moslem world, stimulating caliphs and sultans to build those magnificent hippodromes throughout the Middle East in which to pursue their favorite sport and house their superb Arabian horses. Indeed it was appropriately named "the sport of kings."

The splendid Heliopolis racetrack, now a public park.
PHOTOGRAPH BY CARL RASWAN, 1932

In past years Egypt boasted some of the most luxurious stables and racecourses ever built. The costly and historic Arabesque pink stucco buildings of the splendid Heliopolis racetrack were among the most beautiful the Arab world possessed, and many a classic race was run over its course with royalty in attendance. Today races are held on two courses in Cairo during the winter, Gezira and the new Heliopolis track, and in summer at the two courses in Alexandria, Smouha and Alexandria Sporting Club, both remnants of royalty's pleasures. The stately Gezira Sporting Club on Gezira Island in the midst of the Nile, once part of Mohammed Ali's estates, has been a landmark for decades and is still a reminder of the grandeur of yesteryear. Yet one wonders how much longer it can survive against the rapid expansion and modernization of Cairo. The modern racecourse at Heliopolis was recently constructed in the desert beyond the city to take the place of the old Heliopolis course which was, to the displeasure of many, torn down and turned into a public park for the people of Nasser's United Arab Republic.

In 1936, Prince Mohammed Ali wrote in *Breeding Purebred Arab Horses:*

And now everywhere you chance to look the old order is passing and giving place to the new. . . . This is my lament as I look upon our present world. There are pictures of ancient sportsmen around me. I know the legends of their exploits and the meaning of sport in those days.

Lords and great men and even amateurs owned stables in the olden days in order to protect their country in times of war. Later the officers took up racing, sincerely and honestly, because they loved horses. Racing became the sport of honourable men.

Glance at the champions of the past. Carle Vernet represents all their strength and loveliness. Now look at the modern winner of races in the Arab world; look at his ears, the size of his head, the coarseness and vulgarity. Forget perfection and ideals of beauty, but win the race.

Tragedy always sells well.

They always say that races are held for the encouragement of breeding. If it is so, why do they look at the speed of the horse and not at his endurance? Speed in life is not always necessary, but endurance there must be.

In the early 1900s the Royal Agricultural Society supported racing when it was under the patronage of the king of Egypt, and there were many of the wealthy pashas and members of the society in the Jockey Club. These were the glamorous days when such famous horses as *Nasr, *King John, Nabras, El Deree, and other renowned horses trod the Egyptian turf, and the races were rigidly controlled by the Jockey Club. Racehorses were then classified into four categories,[1] but this is

1. (1) Any horses except country-breds and Arabs; (2) any horse got, foaled, and kept in Egypt, the Levant, or India who has less than 50% Arab blood or none at all; (3) any horse of mixed breed (same as 2) who has 50% or more Arab blood; (4) Arab

Ibn Rabdan and Balance, two classically bred E.A.O. stallions. Ibn Rabdan won five races while Balance garnered fourteen wins and became the Man O' War of Egypt.

no longer the case today. At that time some four hundred horses made up the total entry for the year, whereas in the past decade as many as a thousand horses may complete the racing calendar.

Racing ability is not a prime requisite for the purebred Arabs of the E.A.O.'s classic breeding program, and never has been. The E.A.O.

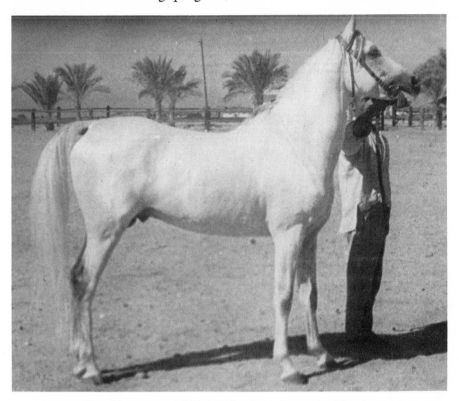

Enzahi, a successful E.A.O.-bred racehorse sired by the desert-bred Nabras and out of Fardous.

does not believe in sacrificing classic beauty for the racier lines generally found on the mixed-breed "Arabs" of the Middle East tracks. It does not, as a practice, race its future broodmares, but prospective breeding stallions as well as particularly well qualified fillies are sometimes leased to private individuals who meet very strict requirements as to proper

horses. Horses took their age from September 1, e.g., a horse born in August became a yearling on the next following September 1. Measurement of a horse six years of age held good at all future meetings and was final. The assigned weights were: three years, 126 lbs.; five years, 145 lbs.; 6 years and up, 147 lbs. Size (height) was also a consideration in assigning weights. Unfortunately no times were kept in the very early 1900s.

care and treatment, and at the close of the colt's or filly's racing career he or she is recalled to the stud. Many E.A.O. horses are sold outright to private breeders and racing owners at an annual local auction. Some are of very high quality, and particularly up to the mid 1960s, when no export market of any consequence existed, many excellent animals were sold off the farm in order to keep it financially solvent and to make way, of course, for the increase in stock the following year. Some were sold to the police as mounts for officers, and for use as breeding stock in supplying future mounts.[2] In recent years, however, the export demand has far exceeded the supply and the horses sold at local auctions are generally the culls of the farm. When the E.A.O. and the Ministry of Agriculture saw there was an increased demand for racehorses in Egypt, at the request of the local Egyptian racing breeders they developed a racing strain for local sales into which they incorporated the Trouncer stallion Sharkasi, a good racehorse who came from Upper Egypt. His get raced exceptionally well and he was available to any breeder for servicing mares.

While the primary function of this book has been to depict the pure Arabian horse at his best in Egypt, it is unfortunate that not all so-called Arab horses are entitled to bear the name, for crossbreeding to obtain faster horses has been introduced into the desert and the Arab countries since English intervention there. Dr. Ameen Zaher despaired of this problem and mentioned in one of his newsletters in 1959 that the Arabian horse in Saudi Arabia was far from the distinguished breed it once had been, and that "English Thoroughbreds—as we lately heard—are introduced to the country to improve (?) the original stock."

He went on to relate that "in Iraq . . . the English Thoroughbred blood was introduced to the country through the British cavalry. Crosses were therefore abundant and it could be considered that the majority of Iraqian Arabs today are the offspring of these crosses."

"In Egypt and some other Arabian countries where the Arabs are raced there is a difficulty of some crosses being introduced to classification committees as pure Arabs. These usually when passed as Arabs are faster and mostly winners. This condition is very troublesome to racing

2. The police maintained excellent breeding farms and accurate records, producing some outstanding Arabs and Arab crosses to mount their officers. Eventually, however, they capitulated to the country's economic need for foreign exchange in time of war, and sold most of their Arabs to America and some to Germany.

clubs." The havoc raised by the infusion of Thoroughbred blood into Arab stock in Arabian countries is not to be overlooked by those who seek the true Arab steed. The Thoroughbred horse Tabib, among others, is given credit for much of the wreckage in the breeding of Arab race horses, for he was used extensively at stud and his blood is now incorporated in many so-called Arabians racing in Egypt, Iraq, Lebanon, and Jordan today. With the sudden increase of interest in the West in

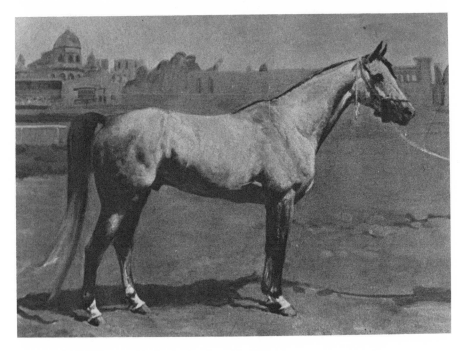

Balance (Ibn Samhan x Farida), Egypt's most outstanding racehorse of all time.

Arabian horses from desert countries, many town Arabs have hastened to clean up on paper the pedigrees of their fine coursers who are winning races and are pretty Arabs in appearance, but whose blood is contaminated. Not only are Americans and Europeans showing renewed interest in the Arabian horses bred in the Middle East today, but the Arab princes and the well-to-do-sheiks of the oil-rich domains have suddenly realized the added prestige of owning what is rightfully their heritage, and are paying all sorts of prices for anything that resembles a noble steed. This is not to intimate that some of the emirs of Arabia and rulers of other countries, as well as a few principled bedouins, have thrown their studs open; indeed, some still have well-bred pure Arabians and have redoubled their zeal to protect them.

Emam "Amlam" (by Balance x Komeira), bred by the E.A.O.
and a head sire for Hamdan Stables.

In Egypt it is very educational to spend a day with the Jockey Club's Classification Committee, which reviews all horses before they are allowed to race. These men are to be given due credit for a strong attempt to see that Arab type is a prime consideration in passing the horses, but the early method of classifying in four categories no longer exists; it has been replaced with a single category so that anything resembling closely a good Arabian is passed to race.

In examining the horses the committee requests that each horse be walked before it for judgment; next, if the committee deems it necessary, the horse is galloped by a jockey. The schooled eye can readily judge when watching them run which horses have Thoroughbred blood and in what degree, even though when standing still many are handsome indeed and within the standard of Arabian type. Those horses showing the most Thoroughbred blood run closer to the ground as they increase in speed. The short back of the Arab horse, however, never flattens out toward the ground in comparison with the Thoroughbred's longer back and lower, longer, stretchier gallop. It seems that the sloping haunch, not so much the lower croup, is the dead giveaway for foreign blood. In other words, the point of hip to buttock line is far more angular in the mixed-blood horse than in the pure Arab, enabling the animal to get a stronger drive off the rear quarters and consequently a longer reach. Extremely high withers are another sign of foreign blood as well as extra substance and height. It does not appear that poor or coarse heads are penalized nearly as much as the above points.

Classification of the horses may take a full morning and part of the afternoon, depending on the number in the lineup, which may reach seventy-five or more, and the time of the year. Some humorous incidents break the general monotony, and it is refreshing to note that Americans and Europeans are not the only ones who "ginger" tails on occasion in an effort to make their horses show proper high Arab tail carriage. The committee members are not fooled by this ruse, however, and horses so treated are disqualified.

The classifications are arranged in the following manner: The first classification is for three-year-old horses, known as beginners. If the horse passes, it receives a beginners' rating. After winning one race, it receives a third-class rating. It is returned for reclassification after winning three races, which then gives it second-class status if it passes. It is not reclassified again until it has won a total of five races, when it must be reclassified, and after reaching the age of five years or having won five races, it is classified for a permanent Arab horse racing certificate and if passed, receives admission to the General Stud Book of Egypt.

Despite attempts to retain Arab type, there are no real pedigree criteria or inspection of stud farms by the Jockey Club. The General Stud Book of Egypt is really then just a register, containing the names of many pure Arabs such as those from the E.A.O., as well as of many that are bred privately, many of which are known to be impure. Recognition of this book as a pure Arab register would be folly; however, it is a sincere attempt by the Egyptians to formulate an Egyptian breeding program for Arab-type racehorses based on a nucleus of registered horses. They had to start somewhere, and this is a good beginning of its kind.

A day at the racing stables proves a memorable and educational experience for any horse lover. When the night's curtain has barely lifted

above the desert, life has already quickened round the barns as the grooms get their charges fed, groomed, and satin shiny before the morning workout. Soon the clatter of iron-shod hooves rings out through Heliopolis, the "city of the sun," heralding the morning advance of the coursers to the racetrack for practice. Although many of the horses are stabled at the track itself, facilities are insufficient to house all horses racing, and many of the old-time trainers still prefer to use their own stables which are scattered throughout the area. Therefore many horses are ridden as many as two or three miles over varied terrain, to and from their workouts. Most have arrived between six and eight o'clock, and are walked round the track with a boy up. After the workout, which

Zaafarana (by Balançe x Samira), a beautiful mare, was the dam of the E.A.O.'s finest racing stock.

the trainer oversees, the horses are ridden back to the stables and cooled out. At mid-morning they are watered, and a half hour later receive their first grain ration. They are rested until mid-afternoon, when they are groomed and then ridden at a walk for about an hour. By 5 P.M. they are fed again. One day a week they are rested.

Horses await the call for classification at the new Heliopolis racing club.

The Classification Committee, sitting under umbrellas, observes a young horse for proper Arab type and action.

On the big tracks barley is the main feed; oats and corn are rarely given. In Egypt, *berseem,* a fresh succulent green forage similar to lucerne or alfalfa, is fed in place of hay and serves to keep the bowels well regulated. When dried, this forage also makes excellent hay. On days of heavy workouts or races anywhere in the Middle East, the evening meal is usually cut in half and no forage is fed the night before or on the morning of the race.

Since the saliva test has practically prevented unscrupulous trainers and owners from getting away with doping on the major tracks, many have taken to using vitamin shots of B and C two or three hours before the race. This is not considered a dope, but administered in correct amounts supposedly acts as a quick energy booster. It is also a common practice to give racehorses a mixture of sugar and water to restore energy after a severe day's work.

Leg problems are naturally encountered with racehorses in all countries, but a large percentage of the trouble in Egypt is caused by poor practice tracks and the abominable way in which the horses are shod. These daily workout courses, to which all horses are restricted in training, have a heavy sand footing and are rarely graded or rolled. The actual races, however, are run on the turf which is in relatively good condition by comparison. Aluminum shoes are used when obtainable, but due to foreign-exchange problems and the economic plight of Egypt in recent years, few can afford this luxury. Thus the local blacksmiths fashion iron shoes as light as possible. Medicines and good tack are also very expensive if imported, and unfortunately many of the local products are not yet up to European standards. Another great factor in leg problems is that the hooves are always cold shod. Extreme care is never taken, even with the finest racing animals or at the best stables, to insure an excellent shoe fit. The blacksmiths, most of them left over from British Army days, never look at a foot properly before placing the shoe on it, and use a chisel and knife instead of nippers and rasp to shape the foot. Almost every horse is either high or low on the inside or outside, and one can rarely pick up a perfectly shod hoof. Consequently the horses break down more readily and their toes are turned in or out all too frequently, thus throwing undue stress on the tendons. If as much emphasis were placed on proper farriery as is placed on grooming, the

Ziada (race name Amralla), by Sid Abouhom x Zaafarana, won many races for owner Aziz Ezzet. He was later used at stud by the E.A.O.

Jockeys up at the paddock of the Gezira Track.

racing careers of many horses would be considerably prolonged.

The distances raced in Egypt varied from 4½ furlongs to 2 miles up until 1962, when length measurements were changed to meters, weight measurements to kilos. Distances now range from 900 meters to 3350 meters, and horses carry from 98 pounds to 153 pounds. Two-mile racing was reinstated in 1961 and the Jockey Club had hopes of gradually lengthening some races in due time. Several prominent Egyptian authorities have stated that they feel the true test of the Arab is in long-distance racing. Under heavy weights the pure Arabs will show superiority in staying power over the mixed-breed Arabs.

Training programs are somewhat similar to those of Thoroughbreds, as short distances are the order of the era. The big heavier-boned crossbreds invariably develop the worst leg troubles, particularly bucked shins and strained tendons. Blistering is sometimes resorted to, but firing is used when other remedies fail to work. While on the subject of bone, we may note that the words "dense" and "fine" are used to describe the characteristic Arabian bone structure. Fine bone is more common to the desert-bred horses which have been raised under desert conditions. Horses having been bred for generations away from the desert under stable or farm supervision, in climates and environments in which the Arabian breed is not indigenous, appear to retain the fine bone structure, but dryness or tautness of tendon seems, to the naked eye, less pronounced. One may see someone walk up to a horse and calculate the measurement by putting his or her hand around the shin bone and remarking that the horse "has very good bone." Such a measurement has no relation to the quality or quantity of bone, however. One cannot tell "good bone" unless one can see a section of the shin bone, which of course can only be obtained from the skeleton. A section of the common bone will show a number of sponge-like cells. The larger the cells, the weaker the bone; the smaller the cells, the stronger and more ivory-like the bone. A poorly bred horse of baser type will have cells almost as large as a small pea; the better bred horse will have cells no bigger than the head of a common pin.

Selection and training in this day and age does not differ too much from years past. Abdulla Abal Kheil and his father-in-law, Abd-el-Aziz el-Sabek, were two of the leading trainers in Egypt for many years and

Gulsun Sherif receives trophy for winning from Mrs. Douglas B. Marshall of Gleannloch Farms during the Marshalls' visit to Cairo in 1969. Her father, Ahmed Sherif (far right), looks on.

*Talal (racing name Johnny Boy), by Nazeer x Zaafarana, participated in forty-three races in Egypt and retired sound. Exported to the U.S., he won U.S. Top Ten at halter—proving that racehorses can (and should) be beautiful.

under their tutelage were usually eighty or more Arabians from all corners of the Middle East, including those of Egypt and a few select individuals from the E.A.O. Their primary objectives in selecting a race-horse rested on the following points: long scapula and well-sloped shoulder; normal length of neck; strong short back; good length from point of hip to point of buttock; good barrel and depth of chest; short cannon and short tendon, clean and clear with no knots on the legs or tendons; moderate pasterns, not too long or too sloped, not too short; sound feet; legs when viewed from behind or front turning neither in nor out; thick bones a poor risk for long racing future. This was very evident among the Syrian and Iraqi horses they were training, several of which had been fired in both front legs in order to prolong their career.

Looking back on racing in his book, *Training and Horse Management in India*, written more than eighty years ago, M. Horace Hayes recorded certain maxims that remain true of Arab horses throughout the Middle East today, and particularly Egypt: "The subject of pure blood and high caste in the Arab is one on which I have never been able to gain any exact information; nor do I think that any distinct rules as to external appearance can be laid down that would not equally apply to any other breed of horses intended to gallop fast, and 'stay' with a fair weight up. Many Arabs, which are most unlikely shaped, to our eyes, often turned out the best. These horses take a long time to mature, while their powers rarely become fully developed before they are eight or nine years old, and until they have been raced for two or three seasons. On this account, one should not lose heart because a likely-looking son of the Desert does not answer one's expectations at any early date. I may mention that Arabs can stand more work in India than any other class, and that their forte is undoubtedly distance."

Although it is well known that most Arabian racing people in the East today care little for "classic beauty" in a racehorse, many of the classic Egyptian Arabians did in fact have excellent racing records. Horses bred by the royal families, the R.A.S./E.A.O., and private breeders of repute have long competed against Arabians from other countries, no matter what their classification, and done quite well. In order to give a better picture of them as racehorses, following are a few racing records of well-known Egyptian horses selected as a partial his-torical reference. Most are influential in modern American pedigrees.

RACING RECORDS OF EGYPTIAN-ARABIAN
HORSES BRED BY THE R.A.S./E.A.O., AND
ROYAL FAMILY, AS WELL AS SOME
ARABIAN DESERT-BRED IMPORTS TO EGYPT

(*Wins only* are noted. F = furlongs, M = miles.)

NAME	DATE	DISTANCE	WEIGHT	No. HORSES COM- PETING	TIME
DAHMAN SHAHWAN STRAIN					
Farida Branch					
BALANCE, foaled June 10, 1928	5-22-32	5F	114	5	1.08
(Ibn Samhan x Farida)	6-5-32	5F	106	9	1.07
	8-21-32	6F	111	7	1.19
From 1932 to 1934 Balance	1-15-33	9F	112	8	2.03
won 14 races, placed second	2-12-33	7F	119	3	1.35
in 2, and was third in 1. He	3-26-33	7F	126	3	1.35
was Egypt's leading race-	5-20-33	1M	132	3	1.46
horse of his era.	7-1-33	1M	124	3	1.47
	1-21-34	1M	124	22	1.53
	3-3-34	1M	130	4	1.53
	3-10-34	9F	133	13	2.02
	4-21-34	6F	127	—	not taken
	7-1-34	1M	136	4	1.47
	7-7-34	7F	140	8	1.37
KORAYEM, foaled	3-2-57	7F	121	13	1.32.4
April 14, 1952	3-29-57	7F	117	11	1.33.8
"Ibn Fakhri"	8-4-57	1M	116	15	1.49
(Nazeer x Helwa)	9-20-57	1M	131	6	1.51.6
Sabah Branch					
NABEEH, foaled March 2, 1936	8-26-39	5F	92	9	1.09.8
	3-17-40	6F	116	—	not taken
"Sid Abouhom"	4-14-40	6F	119	7	1.20
(El Deree x Layla)	4-28-40	6F	109	7	1.20
From 1939 to 1945, won 14,	3-15-41	6F	126	8	1.20
placed second in 9, and was	3-29-41	6F	133	8	1.19.6
third in 6.	11-2-41	7F	109	8	1.35.2
	11-22-41	1M	113	7	1.53.2
	12-27-41	1M, 1½F	113	5	2.08.2
	Missing	1M	112	13	1.46.8
	1-18-43	1M	123	15	1.50.6
	8-8-43	6F	115	12	1.18
	11-8-44	7F	126	14	1.35.6
	3-10-45	7F	130	10	1.33.4

Name	Date	Distance	Weight	No. Horses Competing	Time

Sabah Branch (*continued*)

Name	Date	Distance	Weight	No. Horses Competing	Time
ENZAHI, foaled	5-21-39	5F	118	5	1.10
November 25, 1935	10-29-39	1M	107	9	1.51.6
(Nabras x Fardous)	11-26-39	1M	112	13	1.53
	2-4-40	1M, 1F	102	11	2.05
KOMEIRA, foaled Septem-	7-27-41	6F	115	6	1.24.2
ber 17, 1937	1-18-42	7F	109	9	1.39
"Modallah"	2-18-42	6F	115	9	1.22.6
(Nabras x Layla)					
SAYYAD, foaled March 2,	1-11-42	6F	120	9	1.23.4
1938	2-28-42	6F	114	5	1.20.4
(Michaan x El Dahma)	4-6-42	1M	117	7	1.49.2
From 1941 to 1944, won 7,	12-19-42	1M	109	5	1.49.2
and was second in 11, third	1-2-43	1M, 1½F	112	9	2.09.4
in 5.	5-2-43	1M	116	7	1.47.6
	12-24-43	1M, 1½F	101	15	2.04.4
EMAM, foaled	5-7-49	5F	118	20	1.04.8
December 27, 1945	8-30-50	6F	118	8	1.19.8
"Amlam"	9-3-50	5F	129	7	not taken
(Balance x Komeira)					
IBN BUKRA, foaled	3-10-62	1200Met.	124	11	1.22.4
May 5, 1958	4-21-62[a]	1400	117	6	1.34
"Yeslam'"	4-22-62[a]	1900	116	5	2.10
From Nov. 1961 to Apr.					
1962, ran 12, won 3, and was					
in second 1, third in 3. Died					
of colic, 1962.					

Bint El Bahreyn Branch

Name	Date	Distance	Weight	No. Horses Competing	Time
HAMRAN II	11-3-34	6F	119	11	1.22
foaled March 30, 1930	12-1-34	4½F	119	7	1.02
(Hamran x Durra)					
From 1934 to 1935, won 2,					
and was second in 3, third					
in 1.					

[a]Won both races in two consecutive days.

NAME	DATE	DISTANCE	WEIGHT	No. HORSES COM- PETING	TIME

SAKLAWI JEDRAN IBN SUDAN STRAIN

Radia Branch

NAME	DATE	DISTANCE	WEIGHT	No. HORSES COMPETING	TIME
RADI	3-5-33	7F	120	13	1.38
foaled August 23, 1928	3-18-33	6F	114	9	1.22
(Ibn Samhan x Bint Radia)	3-25-33	6F	118	9	1.21

In 1933, won 3, and was
second in 1, third in 1.

*FADEL	6-28-42	5F, 7yds.	108	11	1.07.8
foaled October 15, 1938	11-13-42	5F	114	6	not taken
(Kheir x Bint Radia)	12-13-42	5F	118	8	1.06.2
	11-6-43	7F	110	7	1.36.8
Total races, 41. Won 7, and	4-17-44	1M, 31yds.	108	8	1.48.2
was second in 6, third in 9.	4-23-44	7F	112	10	1.37
	7-2-44	7F	100	9	1.39.8

SAWRA	4-17-54	5F	119	12	1.06.2
foaled November 6, 1950	7-17-54	6F	116	8	1.21.4
(Sir Abouhom x Kawsar)	7-25-55	5F	123	8	1.07
	2-20-55	5F	125	8	1.03.6
	4-2-55	6F	121	7	1.19.8
	4-23-55	1M	123	7	1.52.6

EL BARRAK	3-16-57	6F	114	8	1.20.6
foaled January 21, 1954	4-27-57	4½F	125	5	0.58.7
"Farfour"	6-23-57	6F	113	7	1.23.6
(Sid Abouhom x Zaafarana)	7-6-57	5F	119	8	1.07.8
	11-3-57	6F	118	8	1.20.6
	12-7-57	7F	109	11	1.33.8
	3-15-58	6F	110	11	1.18.8
	3-28-59	7F	120	15	1.35.4
	5-17-59	6F	126	9	1.19

ZIADA	5-23-58	5F	122	6	1.08.2
foaled March 3, 1955	8-1-58	6F	113	10	1.19.4
"Amralla"	8-8-58	6F	117	10	1.21.4
(Sid Abouhom x Zaafarana)	9-27-58	1M	108	8	1.47
	1-1-59	1M, 2F	106	6	2.20.6
	4-25-59	7F	108	13	1.33.8

Saada Branch

DAHMAN	7-21-35	7F	108	10	1.33
foaled March 31, 1932					
(Ibn Rabdan x Saada)					

In 1935, won 1, and was
second in 1, third in 2.

NAME	DATE	DISTANCE	WEIGHT	No. HORSES COMPETING	TIME
KUHAYLAN MIMREH STRAIN					
ZAD EL RAKEB	8-24-40	6F	114	7	1.22
foaled March 13, 1937	11-24-40	1M	112	8	1.54.2
(Balance x Bint Gamila)	12-1-40	1M	117	7	1.51.8
In 1940–41, was third highest	5-4-41	1M, 4F	112	7	2.47.2
money winner: won 4, was					
second in 1, third in 7.					
KUHAYLAN JELLABI STRAIN					
*NASR	12-23-23	1M	124	11	1.57.6
foaled 1918	4-28-24	6F	117	7	1.20
(Rabdan x Yamama)					
Total races, 12. Won 2, and					
was second in 4, third in 2,					
fourth in 4.					
HADBAN ENZAHI STRAIN					
IBN RABDAN	12-11-20	6F	123	13	1.22.4
foaled May 17, 1917	1-2-21	5F	105	12	1.07.4
(Rabdan x Bint Gamila)	1-29-21	6F	130	7	1.27
Total races, 16. Won 5, was	3-26-21	IM	111	6	1.54.6
second in 2.	7-3-21	6F	120	11	1.20.2
NAZEER	12-18-37	4½F	114	9	0.59.6
foaled August 9, 1934	6-19-38	5F	124	7	1.07
(Mansour x Bint Samiha)	7-17-38	5F	121	6	1.08.2
Total races, 20. Won 4, and	2-4-39	6F	124	4	1.20.2
was second in 6, third in 1,					
fourth in 4.					
MAAROUF	8-13-44	1M, 1F	122	9	2.11.6
foaled September 26, 1937	9-9-45	1M	133	13	1.55.2
(Nabras x Bint Samiha)					
From 1944 to 1946, ran 17,					
won 2, and was second in 9,					
third in 6.					
MOZZAFFAR	7-20-49	6F	118	17	1.22.2
foaled December 26, 1945	1-29-50	1M	102	9	1.49.4
"Wanis"	3-5-50	7F	124	14	not taken
Balance x Hind	4-2-50	1½M	124	11	2.42.6

(Mozzaffar continued on next page)

NAME	DATE	DISTANCE	WEIGHT	No. HORSES COMPETING	TIME
(Mozzaffar continued) In 1949–50, won 5, and was second in 1, third in 1. Second highest money winner of that season.	9-15-50	1M, 1½F	131	21	2.06.8
EL MOUTANABBI foaled March 5, 1949 (El Nasser x Fasiha)	6-14-53	6F	118	13	1.20.4
	11-28-53	6F	124	5	1.20.8
	3-7-54	7F	121	7	1.35.6
	7-26-55	1M	114	5	1.49
	8-20-55	7F	119	8	1.34.6
	12-17-55	1M	103	12	1.51
NASRALLA foaled March 20, 1956 "Shahriar" (Balance x Sehr)	3-19-60	1M, 1F	114	8	2.07.4
	7-19-60	1M	113	7	1.49
	8-26-60	1M, 31yds.	121	4	1.49
	2-4-61	1M	113	10	1.49.4

KUHAYLAN RODAN STRAIN

Bint Riyala Branch

NAME	DATE	DISTANCE	WEIGHT	No. HORSES COMPETING	TIME
RIYAL foaled June 29, 1931 (Ibn Rabdan x Bint Riyala)	5-27-34	7F	116	8	1.30
	7-21-34	5F	111	8	1.10
	11-17-34	6F	112	6	1.22
In 1934–35, won 3, and was second in 5, third in 1.					
RABDAN II foaled June 24, 1930 (Bint Bint Riyala)	11-25-34	6F	123	14	1.22

Bint Rissala Branch

NAME	DATE	DISTANCE	WEIGHT	No. HORSES COMPETING	TIME
SHAHID foaled March 9, 1952 "Abou Soufian" (Sayyad x Kateefa)	6-19-55	5F	121	—	1.08.2
	7-17-55	7F	112	15	1.37.4
	7-31-55	1M	111	14	1.54.2
	7-8-56	1M	102	17	1.47
	9-29-56	1M, 3¼F	117	15	2.36.2
	7-6-58	1M, 3¼F	117	12	2.34.4
NAMIC foaled March 2, 1953 "Ibn Sid Abouhom" (Sid Abouhom x Om El Saad)	8-24-57	7F	124	11	1.36
	9-8-57	6F	120	8	1.20
	9-22-57	5F	125	9	1.06
	2-15-58	7F	111	7	1.31.8
	3-23-58	5F	120	9	1.05
	4-21-58	5F	124	10	1.04.6

(Namic continued on next page)

Name	Date	Distance	Weight	No. Horses Competing	Time
(Namic continued)					
	1-3-59	6F, 14yds.	105	13	1.20.4
	2-27-60	6F	110	10	1.18.4
	8-7-60	6F	129	11	1.21.4

DESERT-BRED HORSES
Imported to Egypt from Arabia or Bred in Egypt; Not R.A.S./E.A.O. Breeding

Name	Date	Distance	Weight	No. Horses Competing	Time
EL DEREE	12-6-24	6F	110	11	1.22.2
STRAIN: Saklawi Shiefi	7-18-25	6F	126	12	1.20
The Royal Khassa of	5-8-26	7F	121	10	1.35.2
King Fouad.	7-3-26	7F	126	9	1.37
Won a total of 14 races.	7-18-26	7F	101	11	1.33.2
*KING JOHN	12-16-28	1M, 1F	129	7	2.12.2
Imported to U.S. in 1929.	7-21-29	5F	133	5	1.08.2
	8-4-29	1⅛M	105	7	2.34
*MALOUMA	4-3-29	6F	125	10	1.23.8
STRAIN: Kuhayla Nowakiya					
(Maloum x Sheha)					
Imported to U.S. in 1929					
Ran 12, won 1, was second in 2, third in 1.					
MICHAAN	1929	6F	112	10	1.24
STRAIN: Kuhaylan Ajuz	1929	7F	126	11	1.36
	1929	6F	129	6	1.19
	1933	1½M	131	8	2.31
NABRAS	3-7-25	5F	113	16	1.08
STRAIN: Hadban Enzahi	5-3-25	round the course	107	6	2.33.8
At age 3, ran 5, won 2, was second in 3.	1-17-26	6F	116	11	1.24
at age 4, ran 4, won 3.	6-5-26	1M	121	7	1.54
	1928–29	1½M	126	6	2.45.2

Comparative racing-record table (all entries read from the rotated chart). Each group lists **Time · Weight · Year** unless noted. For the Egypt (General) and Turkey groups the third figure is **No. of Races**; in the Turkey columns the upper number in each square represents 1951 and the lower represents 1960.

Distance	Meters	≈ Fur.	TB Records (Worldwide)*	Arabs — India	Arabs (General) — Egypt	Arabs (Pure) — Egypt	Thoroughbreds — Turkey	Arabs — Turkey	Arabs — Poland
4½	—	—	0:51 · 117 · 1951	—	1:02 · 126 / 0:59 · 125 · 19	0:53.6 · 114 · 1957 / 0:58¾ · 125 · 1957	—	—	(1959)
5	1000	4.9	0:56.4 · 120 · 1959	—	1:04.8 · 129 / 1:03.4 · 128 · 32	1:04.6 · 125 · 1958 / 1:03 · 125 · 1955	1:00 · 129 · 46 / 1:01 · 124 · 47	1:05 · 128 · 57 / 1:06 · 123 · 75	(1960)
6	1200	5.9	1:08 · 115 · 1957	1:21 · 119 · 1847	1:18.6 · 126 / 1:18.4 · 118 · 75	1:21.4 · 129 · 1940 / 1:20 · 126 · 1925	1:10 · 120 · 43 / 1:12 · 128 · 43	1:16 · 132 · 79 / 1:17 · 123 · 78	1:21 · 123 · before 1939 / 1:21 · 120 · 1939
7	1400	6.9	1:20 · 115 · 1955	—	1:36.4 · 134 / 1:31 · 126 · 70	1:35.4 · 120 · 1959 / 1:31.8 · 109 · 1958	1:26 · 127 · 65 / 1:31 · 136 · 62	1:33 · 130 · 144 / 1:39 · 139 · 152	—
1M	1600	7.9	1:33.2 · 128 · 1956	1:52 · 145 · 1874 / 1:50.5 · 126 · 1877	1:51 · 135 / 1:47.4 · 104 · 45	1:51.6 · 131 · 1958 / 1:46 · 132 · 1933	1:39 · 128 · 66 / 1:37 · 124 · 73	1:50 · 145 · 130 / 1:48 · 120 · 162	1:47.5 · 136 · before 1939 / 1:56 · 123 · 1960
1M 1F	1800	8.9	1:46.4 · 113 · 1959	—	2:05.2 · 135 / 2:04.8 · 105 · 15	2:12.2 · 129 · 1928 / 2:02 · 133 · 1934	1:53 · 124 · 43 / 1:51.5 · 128 · 48	2:04 · 119 · 112 / 2:05 · 132 · 123	2:03.5 · 123 · before 1939 / 2:08.5 · 128 · 1960
1M 1½F	—	—	1:52.6 · 123 · 1953	—	2:08.8 · 138 / 2:07 · 133 · 23	2:09.4 · 112 · 1942 / 2:06.8 · 131 · 1950	—	—	—
1M 2F	2000	9.9	1:58.2 · 127 · 1950	2:18¾ · 142 · 1884	2:24 · 139 / 2:16.8 · 110 · 10	2:20.6 · 105 · 1959	2:05 · 128 · 36 / 2:08 · 128 · 49	2:14.5 · 134 · 57 / 2:19 · 131 · 63	2:14.5 · 136 · before 1939 / 2:29 · 139 · 1960
1M 3F	2200	10.9	2:14.2 · 126 · 1920	—	—	2:34 · 107 · 1929	2:23 · 124 · 9 / 2:27 · 128 · 8	2:35 · 134 · 9 / 2:37 · 129 · 9	2:36 · 128 · 1961 / 2:31.5 · 141 · 1961
1M 4F	2400	11.9	2:23 · 124 · 1929 (England)	2:48 · 106 · 1846 / 2:49.5 · 126 · 1883	2:48 · 117 / 2:43.6 · 118 · 9	2:47.2 · 112 · 1941 / 2:42.6 · 124 · 1950	2:31 · 123 · 15 / 2:48 · 154 · 12	2:52 · 134 · 17 / 2:48 · 129 · 17	2:52 · 128 · 1959 / 2:52 · 143 · 1959
1M 5F	2600	12.9	2:38.2 · 130 · 1956	—	—	—	3:01.5 · 123 · 2 / 2:52 · 116 · 3	3:10 · 129 · 1 / 3:16 · 123 · 1	3:10 · 143 · 1959 / 3:09 · 138 · 1961
1M 6F	2800	13.9	2:52.8 · 117 · 1950	—	—	—	3:05 · 124 · 2 / 3:10.5 · 128 · 2	3:18 · 128 · 2 / 3:31 · 130	3:19 · 130 · before 1939
1M 7F	3000	14.9	3:13.8 · 119 · 1947	—	—	—	3:22 · 122 · 2 / 3:27 · 128 · 2	3:43 · 132 · 8 / 3:40 · 128 · 8	3:49 · 132 · 1959 / 3:41 · 132 · 1961
2M	3200	15.9	3:15 · 142 · 1924 (England)	3:50 · 131 · 1847 / 3:49 · 142 · 1884	3:20.2 · 121 / 3:20 · 121 · 2	—	3:35 · 124 · 1 / 3:57 · 128	5:07 · 132 · 1 / 5:14 · 123 · 1	4:01 · 135 · before 1939 / 3:46 · 130 · 1939
2M 4F	4000	19.8	4:14.6 · 118 · 1948	—	—	—	—	—	—
3M	—	—	5:15 · 113 · 1941 (Mexico)	5:54 · 131 · 1845	—	—	—	—	—

Conversions: 8 FURLONGS = 1 MILE · 201.164 METERS = 1 FURLONG

*AMERICAN RECORDS UNLESS OTHERWISE NOTED.

TOTAL NO. OF HORSES RACED FROM 5 NOV. '60 TO 25 MAR. '61 – 7752, TOTAL NO. OF RACES ON CALENDAR – 300.

TOTAL NO. OF TB HORSES RACED IN 1951 (138), " IN 1960 (165). TOTAL NO. OF ARAB HORSES RACED IN 1951 (315) " IN 1960 (373). * IN BOTH SECTIONS OF TURKEY THE TOP NO'S IN EACH SQUARE REPRESENT 1951, THE BOTTOM NO'S 1960.

21

DANCING HORSES OF THE NILE VALLEY

〰〰〰〰〰〰〰〰〰〰〰〰〰〰〰〰〰〰〰〰〰〰〰〰〰〰〰〰〰〰〰〰〰〰〰〰

IT SEEMS FITTING that we take our leave of the Egyptians in the open air beneath the canopy of blue sky and the golden orb of the sun which have framed Egypt's horses and horsemen in all their beauty for centuries. In ancient times the Egyptian noblemen dashed towards the skyline in their blazing chariots, and superiority in equestrian skills warmed the hearts of Egypt's horse-loving populace. Today horse lovers still abound, and indeed no sight in the Nile Valley is quite so impressive to them as a group of gaily caparisoned "dancing horses" and their Arab riders performing at a festival or competition. A sport unique to Egypt, it has been highly developed in the past four or five decades. Most of the credit for its popularity goes to a most dedicated horseman, the late Abou Ali Gazia.

The dancing horses have also captured the imagination of Egypt's modern artists, among them Rifaat Ahmed, who is famed for his creative portrayals of these spirited steeds and their riders. When asked in an interview why he was so fond of this subject, he replied that he painted dancing horses "because of their intelligence and grace; because of their lively actions and spirit when they react to the pulsating music. If I were an animal, I'd want to be a dancing horse. I believe they even had dancing horses in pharaonic times, as evidenced by tomb paintings in Luxor and Gurna."

We know that from the time of the Hyksos the Egyptians employed the horse in war, and it appears that they got the idea of making horses dance from watching them prance with anticipation before a battle. When preparing for attacks or *razzias*, the Arabs of former times gath-

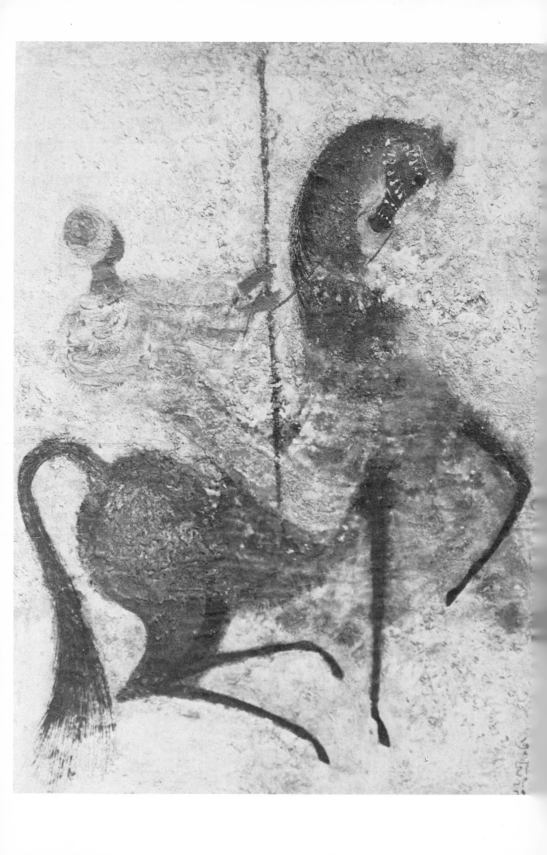

ered their horses to them by beating drums or playing musical instruments, and as the horses which had been haltered waited while the drums continued to roll, they became anxious to be off and join the fray of battle. They began prancing in place and "dancing" as horses will do when they become nervous. The Arabs of course noticed these movements and became attentive to the fact that the horses did this to the rhythm of the beating drums. After the razzias were over, there would be celebrations to the music around the campfire and the horses would be brought to join in the celebrations.

Eventually, as we have seen, the Arabs began migrating to Egypt where they settled into a sedentary life of sorts, but only about a hundred and fifty years ago did they actually begin to develop the war maneuvers and dancing movements of their horses into an art, adding musical instruments and fancy saddles in place of the primitive, simple accoutrements which they used on raids.

In the town of Luxor, whose rulers many centuries ago liberated the Nile Valley from the Hyksos, the festival of Amon is still held annually in January to commemorate the god Amon, king of the gods of ancient Egypt. The Karnak square echoes with thousands of visitors who throng to see the attractions of the festival, vibrating as it did long ago beneath the footsteps of the ancients on feast days when Amon, in the form of the god Min, left his divine palace and traveled up the Nile amid splendid ceremony to visit his temple at Luxor. The festival has helped revive ancient pastimes, such as fighting with the quarter staff, that are practiced alongside more modern sports.

Most popular of the games is the traditional horse tournament, dear to all the Egyptians. Hand-clapping and shouts ring out from all four corners of the square when the *tahtib* championship is to be held. *Tahtib* is a form of fencing with a cane, originating in very ancient days as is attested to by the paintings and hieroglyphic inscriptions that embellish certain tombs of the nobles at Gurna. As in the case of any custom inherited from early Egypt, *tahtib* has survived to present day because it has nothing irreverent or brutal about it.

The cup for equestrian *tahtib* is strongly disputed between the champions of Upper and Lower Egypt, and while watching their skillful

Dancing horses have captured the imagination of Egypt's modern artists.
PAINTING BY RIFAAT AHMED

Apollo, Egypt's champion of dancing horses, "dances," in place before the pyramids of Giza. His master, Zaki Ghoneim, guides him while dismounted.

thrusts and parries, one is reminded vividly of the battle scenes which must have taken place during the crusades. Observing scrupulously the rules of combat and showing chivalrous conduct towards the opponent, each combatant nevertheless uses his strength and skill to the full to gain all the points possible.

The rules of *tahtib* are simple. The contestants are generally about the same age and of equal strength. The stick used is long and stout and resembles the staffs carried by the Biblical elders we see in paintings. The thrusts may be aimed at any part of the body, but it is customary to aim only at the chest, the arms, and the head. As the contest is judged by points, all thrusts hitting the chest or arms are counted; any blow touching the head eliminates the contestant receiving the blow. Feinting is allowed and is often used by a contestant to fatigue his adversary. The competitor may, if he chooses, hold his staff in both hands as much for defense as offense.

Tahtib is practiced both on foot and on horseback. It goes without saying that, when played on horseback, the game demands of the player a good seat, a sense of balance, and a great deal of strength and suppleness. The horses used in this kind of tournament require special training, just as do those used for polo. They are chosen from among the strongest and most vigorous foals and are submitted to a strict training which demands much patience and skill on the part of the teacher. It is said that when a foal is suckling one should approach it and raise a long stick over its head and body. If the foal stops and inquisitively walks towards the stick, it should become a *tahtib* or a dancing horse, having displayed the proper curiosity and temperament. A docile horse is not desired; it must be robust, have abundant spirit and curiosity, and be able to accept discipline which is often harsh under Arab methods of teaching.

Another favorite exhibition at the festival of Amon is the *mirmah*, performed by the more reckless riders. The horseman, armed with a stout pole, sets off at a gallop and then, all at once, pulls up short, stopping his horse at full speed by thrusting his pole into the ground. It is a difficult test of strength, skill, and balance, for the stop is so abrupt that if the horse were to advance one more step with the pole embedded firmly in the ground, the horseman would without question be thrown clear of the saddle.

From time immemorial the horse has had a considerable place in

The tahtib *competition, a form of fencing with a cane, as interpreted by Rifaat Ahmed.*

Egyptian folklore and craftsmanship. Today in various towns through-out the Nile Valley, in the narrow streets of the *souk*, where the sun shines through dusty *mashrubaya* lattices in lacy golden patches, one finds tiny shops where harnessmakers work. Like most Oriental crafts-men, the harnessmaker often sits squatting on the floor of his shop. Around him hanging from the ceiling are skeins of colored wool and silk, and nearby one sees the work laid out for the day. Harness orna-ments abound, for the Egyptian cannot own a horse, whether it be cart horse, racehorse, or dancing horse, without some form of decoration, if only a blue bead and colorful tassle to ward off the evil eye. With bits and pieces of brightly colored wool or silk, the craftsman deftly makes rosettes and pompoms and combines them to form charming decorations. He buys only the natural cotton, wool, and silk, then dyes them himself in his modest house, jealousy guarding the secret of his dyes' composi-tion. Then, sitting all day in his shop, he ties, combs, cuts, and joins his bright skeins, holding the threads with his big toe. Here and there he sews large colorful beads of glass or small charms of shell, or bits of mirror, into intricate arabesque motifs. Pompoms of wool and cotton are used for ordinary occasions, but when the horse is prepared for a ceremony or a dance, rich silken tassels are considered in keeping with the auspiciousness of the occasion. Those that form the breastpiece are called *labba*, from the word *lebba*, the name of the wide gold necklace worn by bedouin women, while the whole harness is called *shaband*.

Horses destined to become dancers are said to be carefully chosen by an expert who selects only foals that show signs of being extremely sensitive to the slightest sound, which should predispose them to accept the movements and training required. It is only natural that a horse trained for dancing should be graceful of carriage and hold his head well, and it is possible to assume that he may develop some sort of ear for music out of pure habit. Those horses which have become adept at dancing often display keen interest and sometimes tremble and prance in place when they hear a captivating melody. However, while a horse may be somewhat predisposed towards dancing, it is unlikely that he would be found executing complex movements without any incentive from his master.

Training of the dancing horse begins when the animal reaches three years of age and if he is relatively adept, it takes the pupil about a year

Ansata Bint Zaafarana models a typical Egyptian wool halter designed by Egypt's finest halter craftswoman, Om Ezzet.

Abu Murrah, Egypt's leading dancing horse trainer, teaches his stallion Fadlallah how to salute.

The riders who have mastered this sport lay great stress on the presentation of their mounts. Here, Caesar Ghoneim practices with his famous chestnut stallion, Askari, a son of the E.A.O.-bred Wanis.

When the performance is ready to start, lively folk songs are played by the musicians.

Saddle and harness trappings of pure silver on velvet belonging to the late King Farouk. Note the royal crest worked in silver.

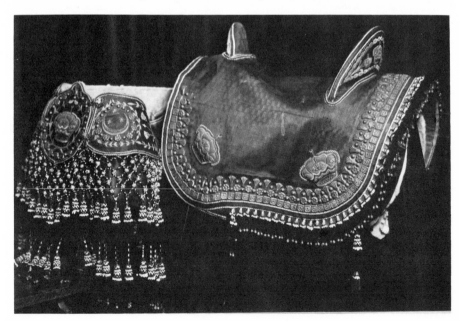

to learn the fundamentals. Usually the trainers attempt to give a young horse a sense of rhythm by working with spurs and leg pressures. A very severe bit is also used, which would hold even the most fractious charger. As bad habits or incorrect positions acquired by the animal at the start of its training may never be corrected, great patience and skill are required to inculcate the absolute obedience needed to control the carriage of the head, the suppleness of the back, proper balance, and the movement of the feet. It is not enough that the rider be adroit, but the horse itself must be extremely sensitive to the touch of the reins, and of the knees and feet of the rider.

A perfectly caparisoned dancing horse, and a great champion, owned and trained by Hussein Mahgoub.

The horse is first taught to "salute" by raising its front legs one at a time, the trainer catching the animal behind the knee with the crook of a cane and bringing the leg forward. Gradually the horse responds to a touch of the mounted rider's foot and will salute automatically or shake hands.

Executing the salute, Abu Murrah works with a Tahawiya mare prior to a competition at Gezira Island.

Because of the intricate and cadenced movements required by the dance, the horse must first build strong muscles, for the movements are not unlike those performed in *haute école*, particularly the *piaffe* and *pirouette*. Although Arab riders have never been exposed to dressage principles, they nevertheless have instinctively adopted its two main cornerstones: poise, which is based upon well-timed movement in a state of suppleness, and impulsion. Proper collection is expressed by vigorous and positive strides resulting from a lowered hindquarters and an elastic back, with the neck extended forward and upward. Listless dull gaits with lifeless haunches violate the spirit of the dance. Developing collection while the rider is dismounted and holding the reins has been found to be a useful exercise in the initial stages of schooling, and this also affords the trainer an opportunity to observe the horse overall and enables him to compare what he sees with what he feels when in the saddle.

The riders who have mastered this sport lay great stress on the presentation of their mounts, and most of them do not ride their dancing horses except for the express purpose of making them perform. The horses are kept fat and sleek, with long shining manes and tails, and a very special pride is taken in the grooming and spotless appearance of the animal. As in bygone days of pashas, sultans, and kings, the dancing horse is the prized possession of any man who can still afford to own one.

Today the General Federation of Rural Clubs manages the sport and provides money for holding exhibitions and competitions. Dancing horses perform at practically every celebration, festival, and village wedding, at national exhibitions such as Revolution Day at Abbasia Coliseum, at the circus, or at any place where entertainment is stressed. One of the most competitive performances is held annually in late winter at the Ferousiah Club on Gezira Island. The dancing horses are shipped from various parts of Egypt by train or truck and arrive a few days ahead of the scheduled competition day, which gives them a short rest from the trip and enables them to become familiar with new surroundings. Small picturesque tents are erected on the grounds and bleachers and chairs are provided for the many spectators, both foreign and Egyptian, who crowd in to see the performances. Barbecue pits are blazing with choice pieces of *sis kebap* sizzling on the grills, and refreshment stands provide ice-cold drinks which are usually welcome after one has sat for any length of time in the Egyptian sun, winter or summer.

Winter is delightful in Cairo, however; the skies are bright blue and shot with fleecy white clouds, the grass is Nile green, the palm trees weave lacily in the breeze, and the timeless river flows gently along the banks of Gezira. When the performance is ready to start one hears the lively folk songs being played by the musicians who are garbed in typical long flowing white or black *gallabias*. The tempos are spirited and cheerful, provided by the *rababah*, a stringed instrument once made in Ottoman Turkey; the *muzmar*, a flute; the *tablah*, drums; and the tambourine. The crowd loves the rhythmic beat of the music which sounds to foreign ears very much like Scottish bagpipes, and as the musicians raise the pitch and tempo, the spectators join in clapping to the rhythm of the tune.

Around the course one finds the dancing horses being groomed and made ready for the competition. Some of the horses are bred by private stables, others are from the E.A.O. which have been sold locally, while many are bred by the Tahawiya in Sharqiya, the "Eastern" horse province. Most of the animals are good looking by general standards and show the marks of Arab blood. Some display more coarseness than one might like in a "noble" Arabian, but nevertheless most of the basic Arab characteristics are present, even though the pedigrees might not be pure.

The competition is held in several divisions, for maiden horses as well as for champions. Professional dancing horse trainers, such as the well-known Abu Murrah or Kemal Azzam, are usually barred from competing as it is considered strictly an amateur sport. The amateur riders come from many walks of life. Hussein Mahgoub, who has trained the best dancing horses of recent times, is a baker; Zakariah Osman is a lumber salesman; Mohammed Ghoneim runs a riding stable; Ahmed Hegazi was a large landowner in previous times; and there are many more also worthy of note.

When competing, the rider is always dressed with utmost simplicity; a *gallabia* of grey, black, brown, blue, or white is typical. A small wool or cotton cap called a *takia* adorns the rider's head, and he wears regular walking shoes rather than boots. All the finery is for the horse, as the animal is the center of attention and nothing should detract the eye from its beauty and accouterments.

The saddles, breastplates, and bridles adorning the horses are embellished with the most elaborate Oriental designs. Costly gold thread is embroidered in Islamic motifs of crescents, flowers, and calligraphy, contrasting smartly against backgrounds of Nile green, bright fuchsia, royal blue, and gold. Equally striking are velvet black saddlecloths encrusted with silver. One is reminded of the prophecy about Egypt in

Zechariah: "There shall be upon the bells of the horses Holiness Unto The Lord." The Semitic peoples used both tassels and bells as amulets in ancient times, and the tradition has carried over to the present. The modern tassels on the breastplates match the color of the saddle; the top of each tassel is encased in a hand-hammered, bell-shaped piece of silver which touches its companions, producing the sound of tinkling bells when the horse moves to the rhythm of the music. Ornaments for the head and neck are solid silver chains from which are hung more crescents, actually detracting in some instances from the natural beauty of the Arabian head. The truly elaborate silver caparisons may cost upwards of £1000 or $2500, depending on the weight and amount of silver used. The saddles themselves are Arabian in style with high pommels and cantles which have been elaborately decorated. Stirrups are ornate in design and wide, with sharp edges which also serve as spurs.

Not every horse can dance, for as in *haute école*, only some are fitted for the advanced stages of performance. In addition to dancing ability, the most desired attributes are alertness and spirit, and particularly a beautiful head and high tail carriage, for the rider is focused between the two.

The judging of the dancing competition is based on definite rules and regulations which are worth noting due to the increasing popularity of the sport, and particularly for the many foreigners who enjoy watching it when they visit Egypt. A jury consisting of three persons appointed by the Federation Committee judges the contestants on the basis of 105 points distributed as follows: The first group of characteristics concern the beauty and type of the horse itself, taking into consideration shortness and alertness of ears, width of jaw, width of nostrils, shape of nose, high tail carriage in line with the croup, harmony of the body's parts with each other, shape of legs and soundness, complete harmony of the horse, and general appearance. These are worth 25 points.

Next are the riding accessories: the halter, its beauty and craftsmanship; the bit and its fit with the horse's mouth; the saddle and its approximation to correct Arabian structure and design, as well as its embellishments; the breastpiece and saddlecloth and the correctness of Arab design; the Arab stirrup of either copper or white metal, so fashioned as not to hurt the horse. These are worth 10 points. Next are the rider and his horsemanship ability—balance and overall appearance—which are worth another 10 points.

The scoring of the obligatory movements of the dance is based on seven sequences. As the band begins to play, the rider enters the rectangular arena, 60 meters long and 20 meters wide, his mount moving at the normal walk. The rider remains entirely passive, acting merely as living ballast that does not disturb the rhythmic timing but pliantly follows the movements of the horse. By easy contact with the mouth and with free swinging leg aids, the rider shows the horse what is asked of it and the horse's ears prick forward and backward, awaiting any whispered command as it prepares for the first step. The horse then approaches the jury and salutes smartly, first with the right leg, then with the left leg, as if shaking hands. The entrance and the salute are worth 5 points.

The Morabaa—*dancing in place to the rhythm of the music—is illustrated by Abu Murrah on Safi, a *Morafic son in Egypt.*

Next the horse gathers itself together, hindquarters balanced under it, and proceeds to the movement in the square, called the *morabaa*. Here the horse is collected in a movement similar to the *piaffe*. The horse now dances in place to the rhythm of the music, a maneuver requiring great coordination and strength. This is a phase sequence of the trot in which all thrust is converted into elasticity and carrying capacity is evenly distributed between both hind legs. If perfect responsiveness is achieved,

A stallion executing the morabaa *in hand.*

a lofty and sustained trotting action in place results. The bending of the hindquarters allows the forelegs to step loftily from the shoulder and to prolong their steps. Each hind leg can raise its hoof just somewhat above the pastern of the grounded hind foot, but it sustains this step in harmony with the motions of the diagonal foreleg once it reaches its maximum elevation. As in *haute école*, the lowering of the hindquarters, animated by impulsion, produces the correct action of the horse's back

Apollo sits and salutes the crowd.

and high neck carriage, which is raised with a supple poll. Proper balance and the rhythmic, springy advancing of the hind legs produce positive contact with the bit, giving the rider the feeling that the horse is always ready to shoot forward momentarily, passing into the *passage* of the trot. The stillness of the horse's body can be achieved only if the horse's feet do not hop. It is the rare dancing horse, however, that one sees doing a really smooth performance, the rising of the hind legs soft and gentle, their pushoff springy rather than abrupt. The rider's seat must be particularly steady and quiet for the correct *morabaa* can only be executed by the horse when its rider is able to adapt his seat and guidance to the rhythm of this gait, and if his legs abandon all tension. For proper execution of these movements 10 points are allowed.

The horse then proceeds into the figure eight at a collected gallop, the underlying principle of this exercise being the maintenance of liveliness, vigor, and cleanness of stride. The collected gallop should greatly improve the posture of the horse and the suppleness of its hindquarters. If the hindquarters fly upward when the hind legs leave the ground, the rider has to bend forward involuntarily with his upper body at every stride, which shows the hindquarters to be stiff in their principal joints. And of course the horse should smartly and easily change leads without losing collection as it executes the figure eight. This exercise is worth 10 points.

The horse then proceeds to the movement of the square again, in which the dance in place may be executed, or an additional movement such as the Charleston, in which the horse's front legs remain in place while the hind legs work sidewards. This is also worth 10 points.

Following this the horse moves out of the square and gallops away from the jury at a handgallop on the right lead, executing a flying change to the left lead as it heads towards the jury at full speed; then stopping abruptly, it executes the salute once again to the left and to the right. The gallop is worth 10 points, and the salutes, 5 points.

The rider then may elect to perform any optional movements which will show the steadiness and obedience of the horse. Some choose to perform the *mirmah*, afterwards galloping round the pole stuck in the ground while holding onto it; others have the horse bow on bended knee to the judges, or the horse actually may sit down on its haunches and execute a salute to them. Other tricks are performed such as doing a complicated step while standing on a table or placing the forelegs on a table while dancing with the hind legs on the ground. In a very difficult dance step, also an elective, the horse maintains balance on one foreleg while the other is lifted and the hind legs work rhythmically, in a manner similar to the *morabaa*. A particularly popular movement is the *piaffe* in hand, and the most adept animals may also execute a *levade* in hand. This final exercise is worth 10 points.

Whatever the jury's decision, there is no doubt in the minds of horse fanciers that they have watched a stimulating and colorful performance of horsemanship based on ancient Egyptian tradition. Nowhere else in the world can such a delightful exhibition be found.

Hussein Mahgoub, winner of countless competitions, gets ready to perform the mirmah, *a popular maneuver.*

CONCLUSION

〼᷸᷸〼

ARE CLASSIC Arabians exclusive to any one country, or has any one group of bloodlines contributed more than any other in maintaining classic type and purity? Can we improve the breed? What is the future of the classic Arabian horse in the world today? Arabian horse lovers everywhere are asking these questions.

Classic Arabians are not exclusive to any one country, or any one group of bloodlines. However, we owe the greatest debt of gratitude to Arabia and Egypt, for they have remained a pure source of supply since time immemorial. They are the rock upon which the Arabian horse world's foundation is built. Will the Western world carry on this heritage as Egypt and Arabia have done for hundreds of centuries? The opportunity is at hand.

This book has been written not to exclude or discredit bloodlines other than the Egyptian, but to record for the Arabian horse world the essential role which Egypt has played in Arabian horse history. The number of Arabians in the Western world not carrying Egyptian blood is infinitesimal.

It has been firmly established in breeding programs throughout the world that quality Egyptian Arabians provide the necessary elegance and refinement, the ancient look of the desert, which most closely approximates the standard or ideal. Egypt has long supplied the world with Arabian horses, but few countries have preserved records of breeding programs in the last 100 to 175 years except England, Germany, Hungary, Poland, and America. Germany obtained Egyptian horses in the mid-1800s and is again acquiring them in quantity. The Poles have obtained Egyptian blood through their Crabbet importations from England, through Khafifan from Prince Mohammed Ali in Egypt, and recently from the Russians through the Egyptian stallion Aswan, a gift to the U.S.S.R. from the Egyptian government. The Babolna stud in Hungary, once headed by General von Szandtner, has recently acquired a good nucleus of Egyptian horses. Austria has a small private studfarm of straight Egyptians. Holland, France, Australia, and South Africa have Egyptian breeding programs on a limited scale. The English have rediscovered Egyptian blood and the far-sighted breeders are re-infusing it into their herds bringing together the old Egyptian lines (through the Blunts' Crabbet stock) and the current Egyptian lines. They, like the Australians, have been purchasing their Egyptians from America.

Imports from Egypt to the U.S. since 1957 number about two hundred, with no cessation of interest despite increased costs and quarantine problems. Outstanding achievements in the show ring by the relatively few Egyptian imports shown to date and informative articles, as well as attractive magazine advertising by Egyptian Arabian owners, have served to focus the world's eyes once again on this exceptional bloodline within the breed. A group of breeders dedicated to preserving a nucleus of straight-Egyptian Arabians have formed the Pyramid Society, a fraternal organization (not a registry). Enthusiasm for the idea has drawn members to the society from all over the world.

Can we improve the breed? No. The standard was established thousands of years ago. Wilfrid Scawen Blunt summed it up perfectly in his memorandum of 1904 on the right policy in managing the Crabbet Arabian Stud—the leading Arabian stud of the Western world at that time: "Whoever would succeed in the breeding of Arab horses must divest himself of much English prejudice and accept as the basis of his policy the view of horse breeding held from time immemorial in Arabia. According to this the Kehailan (purebred Arabian) is the descendent of an original wild herd of the Peninsula, distinct from every other, the one noble horse of the world. He is also the one perfect horse which may indeed become degenerate by the violation of the traditional rules of breeding but which cannot be improved. It should therefore be a cardinal principle . . . that the object . . . is to preserve in its perfection, not to improve the breed."

Interest in Arabian horses has never been greater, nor the future brighter. Today by far the greatest number of Arabians are in America, as well as the Arabians of highest quality. Over one hundred thousand have been registered since 1908 when the Arabian Horse Registry of America was formed, and forty-five thousand of this total were registered in just the last four years! The growth rate has been phenomenal. Renewed enthusiasm for this original pure and naturally beautiful breed has been stimulated throughout the world. Arabian horse breeding countries are establishing new or stronger registries, and the World Arabian Horse Organization seeks to coordinate ideas and ideals among Arabian horse breeders around the globe.

Racing in the Middle East and Poland continues to enjoy great popularity and is growing in European countries and America. Trail rides, endurance rides, and horse shows are increasing at a rapid rate. They provide the perfect outlet for family recreation and togetherness, and young people gain a unique sense of sportsmanship, competitiveness, and comradeship with this breed of horse.

Arabian breeders work hard at upholding fair play in all phases of the industry. This breed is "special" and the people devoted to it intend to keep it that way. They have learned that Arabian horses provide the grand essentials to happiness in this life: something to do, something to love, and something to hope for.

BIBLIOGRAPHY

THE RESEARCH behind this work was exhaustive and a complete bibliography would be too lengthy. Therefore I have limited it to a selection which I consider would be most useful to students of the breed.

1580 B.C. TO 1800 A.D.

A New Commentary on Holy Scripture. Gore, Goudge, and Guillaume, eds. London, 1928.

Anati, Emmanuel. *Palestine before the Hebrews*. New York, 1963.

Ancient History. *The Cambridge Ancient History*. Cambridge, 1923 (vol. 1, Egypt and Babylonia to 1580 B.C.; vol. 2; The Egyptian and Hittite Empires to 100 B.C.).

Anderson, J. K. *Ancient Greek Horsemanship*. California, 1961.

Arberry, A. J. *The Koran Interpreted*. London, 1955.

Arnold, Rev. Dr. J. Muehleisen. *Ishmael*. London, 1859.

Badjirmi, Sheikh Fatouh el. *A Treatise Concerned with the Remarks on the Descriptions of the Praised Horses. . . .* Cairo, 1852. (In Arabic.)

Baikie, James. *Egyptian Antiquities in the Nile Valley*. London, 1932.

Baslan, Cheikh el-Hafez Siradje el-Din Omar Ibn. *Manuscript Arabe du XIIe siècle traitant des questions de sport Arabe*. Prince Mohammed Ali, trans. (Private printing, Cairo.)

Birdi, Abu-l-Mahasin Ibn Taghri. *History of Egypt: 1382–1469 A.D.*, translated from the Arabic by William Popper. California, 1954.

Boone, J. Allen. *Kinship with All Life*. New York, 1954.

Breasted, James Henry. *The Dawn of Conscience*. New York, 1933.

———. *Ancient Records of Egypt*. Chicago, 1906.

———. *A History of Egypt*. London, 1921.

Budge, Sir E. A. Wallis. *From Fetish to God in Ancient Egypt*. London, 1934.

———. *The Nile: Notes for Travelers in Egypt and in the Egyptian Sudan*. London, 1910.

———, trans. *The Book of the Cave of Treasures*. London, 1927.

Carter, Howard. *The Tomb of Tut-ankh-Amen*. London, 1927.

Cumberlage, Geoffrey. *The Life of Muhammad*, a translation of Ishaq's *Sirat Rasul Allah*. London, 1955.

Dickson, H. R. P. *The Arab of the Desert*. London, 1967.

Drummond, Rt. Hon. Sir W. *The Oedipus Judaicus*, London, 1811.

Dumas, E. *The Horses of the Sahara*. London, 1863.

Emery, Walter B. *Egypt in Nubia*. London, 1965.

———. *Archaic Egypt*. London, 1961.

Ettinghausen, Richard. *Arab Painting*. Treasures of Asia Series. Ohio, 1962.

Frazer, Sir James George. *The Golden Bough*. London, 1920.

Graves, Robert. *The White Goddess*. London, 1961.

Hartfield, George. *Horse Brasses*. London, 1965.

Hayes, Capt. M. Horace. *Training and Horse Management in India*. London, 1885.

Hitti, Phillip K. *History of the Arabs*. London, 1968.

Hogarth, David George. *Kings of the Hittites*. London, 1926.

Kalby, Ibn el. *Origin and Race of Horses during Pre Islamic and Islamic Eras: Investigated by Ahmed Zaki Pasha*. Egypt, 1946.

Keilland, Else. *Geometry in Egyptian Art*. London, 1955.

Keller, Warner. *The Bible as History*. London, 1956.

Laffont, Robert. *The Ancient Art of Warfare*. London, 1966.

Lane-Poole, Stanley. *A History of Egypt in the Middle Ages*. London, 1968.

Langdon, Stephen H. *The Mythology of All Races*. Vol. 5: *Semitic*. New York, 1959.

Lawrence, T. E. *Seven Pillars of Wisdom*. London, 1926.

Liebowitz, Harold A. "Horses in New Kingdom Art." *Journal of the American Research Center in Egypt*, vol. 6, 1967.

Malan, Rev. S. C., trans. *The Book of Adam and Eve*. London, 1882.

Maspero, G. *Life in Ancient Egypt and Assyria*. New York, 1892.

Montet, Pierre. *Eternal Egypt*. Trans. from French by Doreen Weightman. London, 1964.

Muir, Sir William. *The Mameluke or Slave Dynasty of Egypt*. London, 1896.

Murray, G. W. *Sons of Ishmael*. London, 1935.

Perron, M. *Le Naceri*. Paris, 1852.

Posener, Georges. *A Dictionary of Egyptian Civilization*. Paris, 1962.

Rawlinson, George. *History of Ancient Egypt*. New York, 1880.

Sadeque, Dr. Syedah Fatima. *Baybars I of Egypt*. London, 1956.

Sauvaget, J. *The Horse Poste in the Empire of the Mamluks*. Paris, 1941.

Schulman, Alan Richard. "Egyptian Representation of Horsemen and Riding in the New Kingdom." *Journal of Near Eastern Studies*, vol. 16, 1957.

———. "The Egyptian Chariotry: A Reexamination." *Journal of the American Research Center in Egypt*, vol. 2, 1963.

Scott, Sir Walter. *The Talisman*. Edinburgh, 1877.

Simpson, George Gaylord. *Horses*. New York, 1961.

Smith, W. Stephenson. *The Art and Architecture of Ancient Egypt*. Baltimore, 1958.

Springfield, Rollo. *The Horse and His Rider*. London, 1847.

Strabo. *The Geography of Strabo*. Trans. by Horace Leonard Jones. London.

Tietjens, Eunice. *Poetry of the Orient*. New York, 1928.

Te Velde, H. "The Egyptian God Seth as a Trickster." *Journal of the American Research Center in Egypt*, vol. 7, 1968.

Tesio, Federico. *Breeding the Race Horse*. London, 1958.

Vesey-Fitzgerald, Brian, ed. *The Book of the Horse*. London, 1947.

Vince, John. *Discovering Horse Brasses*. Tring, Herts., England, 1968.

Waterfield, Gordon. *Egypt*. London, 1967.

White, John Manchip. *Everyday Life in Ancient Egypt*. New York, 1963.

Wiedemann, Alfred. *Religion of the Ancient Egyptians*. London, 1897.

Wilkinson, Sir J. Gardner. *The Ancient Egyptians*. London, 1878.

Winlock, H. E. *The Rise and Fall of the Middle Kingdom in Thebes*. New York, 1947.

Wright, Edwin M. *The Horse in Middle Eastern Symbolism*. Princeton.

Wollaston, A. N. *Half Hours with Muhammad*. London, 1892.

1800 A.D. TO THE PRESENT

Alavi, Syed Muhammad Badruddin. *Arabian Poetry and Poets*. Cairo, 1924.

Ali, H. H. Prince Mohammed. *Breeding Purebred Arab Horses*. Vols. 1 and 2. Cairo, 1936.

Archer, Thomas. *The War in Egypt and the Soudan*. London, 1886.

Belgrave, James. *Welcome to Bahrain*. Bahreyn, 1968.

Blunt, Lady Anne. The Sheykh Obeyd Herdbook. Unpublished manuscript in the collection of Lady Anne Lytton. Cairo, 1870–1917.

——. *A Pilgrimage to Nejd*. London, 1881.

——. *Bedouin Tribes of the Euphrates*. New York, 1879.

——. *Crabbet Arabian Herdbook*. Private, Lytton collection.

——. *Diaries of Lady Anne Blunt*. Wentworth Bequest, British Museum.

Brown, W. R. *The Horse of the Desert*. New York, 1948.

Burckhardt, John Lewis. *Notes on the Bedouins and Wahabys*. London, 1831.

Burford, Robert. *Description of a View of the City of Cairo*. London, 1847.

Conn, George H. *The Arabian Horse in America*. Vermont, 1957.

Crabites, Pierre. *Ibrahim of Egypt*. New York, 1935.

De Forbin, Count. *Travels in Egypt*. London, 1818.

Description de L'Egypte au recueil des observations et des Recherches qui ont ete faites en Egypte. Vol. 18, Chapter 7. Paris, 1822.

Egyptian Studbooks: History of the Royal Agricultural Society's Stud of Authentic Arabian Horses. Compiled by Dr. Ashoub. Cairo, 1948.

Egyptian Agricultural Society Studbook. Vol. 2. Cairo, 1965.

The Inshass Herdbook. Compiled by Dr. Rashid. E.A.O. collection.

Hamza, Ahmed. *Hamdan Stables Studbook*. Cairo, 1969.

Forbis, Judith. "Henry B. Babson." *Arabian Horse World*, Springville, New York, 1965.

——. "Two Sheikhs and a Pasha." *Arabian Horse World*, Palo Alto, California, 1970.

————. "Nazeer." *Arabian Horse News*, Colorado, 1972.

————. "Pearls of Great Price." *Arabian Horse World*, California, 1971.

————. "Arabian Racing in the Moslem World." *Arabian Horse World*, New York, 1963.

Gisquet, M. *L'Egypt, Les Turks et les Arabes*. Paris.

Gouin, Edouard. *L'Egypte au xix Siècle*. Paris, 1847.

Hamont, P. N. *Egypte de puise la conquète des Arabes sous la domination de Mehemet Aly*. Paris, 1877.

Lamplough, A. D. *Cairo and Its Environs*. London, 1909.

Leigh, Thomas, Esq. *Narrative of a Journey in Egypt*. London, 1816.

Lytton, Earl of. *Wilfred Scawen Blunt*. London, 1961.

Lytton, Rt. Hon. Lord. *Zanoni*, 1845.

Madden, R. R. *Egypt and Mohammed Ali*. London, 1841.

Murray, Sir Charles Augustus. *A Short Memoir of Mohammed Ali*. London, 1898.

Palgrave, W. G. *Central and Eastern Arabia*. London, 1866.

Perrin, N. *Relation de la campagne d'Ibrahim Pacha contre les Wahabites*. Paris, 1833.

Raswan, Carl. *A Collection of Articles by Carl Raswan*. Chino, California, 1967.

————. *The Arab and His Horse*. Oakland, California, 1955.

————. *The Raswan Index*. México, D. F., 1957.

Roux. *Histoire de la nation Egyptienne*. Paris.

Seunig, Waldemar. *Horsemanship*. New York, 1956.

Shamashirgi, Ali Bey. The Abbas Pasha Manuscript. (In Arabic.) Unpublished manuscript trans. by Gulsun Sherif and Judith Forbis. Cairo, 1849.

St. John, James Augustus. *Egypt and Mohammed Ali*. London, 1834.

Twentieth Century Impressions of Egypt. Lloyd's Greater Britain Publishing Co., London, 1909.

Vertray, Capt. M. *Journal d'un officer de l'armee d'Egypte*. Trans. by Capt. G. L. B. Killick. London, 1899.

Vingtrinier, Marie F. A. *Soliman Pacha*. Paris, 1886.

von Pueckler-Muskau, H. L. H. *Egypt under Mehemet Ali*. Trans. by H. Evans Lloyd. London, 1845.

Vyse, R. W. H. *Operations Carried on at the Pyramids of Gizeh in 1837*. London, 1840.

Wentworth, Lady. *The Authentic Arabian Horse*. London, 1945.

————. *Thoroughbred Racing Stock*. London, 1938.

————. *The World's Best Horse*. London, 1958.

Winder, R. Bayly. *Saudi Arabia in the Nineteenth Century*. London, 1965.

Yates, William H. *The Modern History and Condition of Egypt*. London, 1843.

Zaher, Dr. Ameen. *Arabian Horse Breeding and the Arabians of America*. Cairo, 1950.

INDEX

THE AUTHOR

JUDITH FORBIS lived for fifteen years in the Arab world studying the Arabians bred by bedouins, royal families, and government stud farms. In the late 1950's she and her husband moved to the primitive sector of southeast Turkey, where she became the first woman jockey to ride and compete openly against the Arab and Turkish men. These unique experiences were chronicled in her book *Hoofbeats Along the Tigris*. She was contributing editor for *The Reference Handbook of Straight Egyptian Horses* and co-author of *The Royal Arabians of Egypt and the Stud of Henry Babson*. She contributed the sections on Egypt, Bahrain, and Turkey to *The Encyclopedia of the Horse* and has been writing regularly for Arabian and general horse journals since 1958. Many of her historical photographs appear in Arabian horse books around the world. Judith and her husband, Don, own the internationally famous Ansata Arabian Stud of Lufkin, Texas, which they established in 1959.

The author, with *Ansata Ibn Halima.

PHOTOGRAPH BY SPARAGOWSKI